L. F.

Gentrification and Distressed Cities

D0217175

Social Demography

Series Editors   Doris P. Slesinger
James A. Sweet
Karl E. Taeuber
Center for Demography and Ecology
University of Wisconsin-Madison

Gentrification and Distressed Cities

An Assessment of Trends in Intrametropolitan Migration

Kathryn P. Nelson

THE UNIVERSITY OF WISCONSIN PRESS

ALBRIGHT COLLEGE LIBRARY

Published 1988

The University of Wisconsin Press
114 North Murray Street
Madison, Wisconsin 53715

The University of Wisconsin Press, Ltd.
1 Gower Street
London WC1E 6HA, England

Copyright © 1988
The Board of Regents of the University of Wisconsin System
All rights reserved

First printing

Printed in the United States of America

For LC CIP information see the colophon

ISBN 0-299-11160-1

711.4
N 427g

214710

16.25

To all my parents,
with love and gratitude

Contents

Figures

Tables

Acknowledgments

Many people have helped greatly as I labored to finish this book. My family deserves the most credit and thanks for encouraging and aiding me in innumerable ways, from programming to typing to editing to cooking to listening! Without their support, this study never would have been completed.

My colleagues studying cities, migration, and gentrification have helped with data, comments, criticism, questions, and continued interest. I particularly thank Connie Casey, Judy May, and Duane McGough for reading the entire manuscript. Among the many colleagues I thank for assistance and encouragement are Paul Burke, Celia Boertlein, Harold Bunce, Don Dahmann, Bob Ebel, Dick Forstall, Dennis Gale, Harold Goldsmith, Jack Goodman, Stella Hall, Kristin Hansen, Ray Kahn, Jack Kasarda, Cliff Kern, Greg Lipton, Larry Long, Katharine Lyall, Ann Markusen, Phyllis Myers, Betsy Roistacher, Daphne Spain, and Howard Sumka. Their help and questions have greatly improved the analysis, while I am responsible for its remaining weaknesses.

As chairman of my dissertation committee, Thomas Vietorisz was a patient critic and helpful sounding board, and I also thank David Gordon and Robert Heilbroner for their advice and useful comments. Last, temporally, but far from least, Carolyn Moser's guidance has been invaluable in pruning and strengthening the prose, and Chris Johnson and Lisa Blanc of the University of Maryland's Cartographic Services have transformed computer hieroglyphics into recognizable maps. I hope that the content in some measure rewards these efforts, and that its results contribute to ongoing efforts to make cities and their people flourish.

Gentrification and Distressed Cities

Introduction

Gentrification and Urban Revival

Reviving deteriorating cities has been a continuing aim of urban policy in the United States over the past four decades. Programs ranging from urban renewal to urban enterprise zones have attempted to attract and retain residents, employment, and tax bases in cities. But distress has intensified and spread despite such efforts, while ideas and public resources for helping cities have dwindled. Partly because higher outmigration of upper-income groups seemed self-reinforcing, urban decline was feared to be cumulative.[1] Therefore, evidence that decaying inner-city areas were newly attracting middle-class white movers during the 1970s was greeted with enthusiasm and relief. For a heady time, some thought that private-sector activity would revitalize distressed cities.[2] Indeed, inner-city revival seemed so assured that others worried that excessive revitalization might displace as many poor residents as urban renewal had.[3]

---

1. Burchell, Listokin, Sternlieb, Hughes, and Casey (1981) summarize efforts to measure distress in cities and the evidence that different measures and indices used—population loss, employment losses, fiscal problems, concentrations of poverty, old housing, etc., in different combinations—tend to rank the same cities as most distressed. Nathan and Fossett (1978) conclude that through the mid-1970s distressed cities were becoming more rather than less distressed: "The most severely distressed cities do not show signs of improvement [between 1960 and 1975]; quite to the contrary, their problems appear to have deepened and worsened" (1978, 17), ACIR (1980b) presents detailed data on central-city–suburban disparities and city distress through 1977.

Hypotheses and evidence that outmovement by upper-income residents is self-reinforcing are presented in Albin (1971), ACIR (1965, 1980b), Birch (1970), Bradford and Kelejian (1973), and Frey (1980). Bradbury, Downs, and Small (1980, 1982) discuss the self-reinforcing nature of urban decline in detail.

2. Two of the most optimistic assessments of the implications of "back-to-the-city" movement in the late 1970s were made by Allman (1978) and Fleetwood (1979). See also Pierce (1977) and *Newsweek* (1979).

3. Early reports on the extent of displacement are given in Dolbeare (1978), Embry (1977), and Grier and Grier (1978). The exchange between Hartman (1979a, 1979b) and Sumka (1979) exemplifies disagreements about the need for policies to reduce displacement. According to a *Newsweek* article quoted in Palen and London (1984, 257), in 1983 gentrifica-

As publicity about such "gentrification"[4] intensified during the 1970s, policy-makers received contradictory advice. City residents and urban experts disagreed about the extent of gentrification, about its causes and future implications, and about appropriate policy responses. Many observers welcomed the prospects of renovated, vibrant neighborhoods and stronger city tax bases. In view of the past persistence of urban decline and distress, they hesitated to discourage any possible source of renewal.[5] But others, fearing displacement and sharp reductions in low-cost housing opportunities, advocated strong controls on gentrification.[6] To the extent that reinvestment and upgrading in cities occur at the expense of poor residents, they thus present a continuing dilemma for those seeking to aid both distressed cities and their residents.

Despite policy differences, in the late 1970s both opponents and proponents predicted that gentrification would continue and spread. Real estate investors touted potential gains from investments in inner-city properties; activists argued the necessity of anti-gentrification policies such as controls on rents and condo conversions; fiscal conservatives foresaw less

---

tion was still popularly perceived as causing excessive displacement: "We are driving out the poor and middle class, making cities the exclusive domain of the young and affluent" (*Newsweek*, 3 January 1983).

4. "Gentrification" is a term borrowed from the British (Hamnett and Williams 1980). The U.S. Department of Housing and Urban Development (1979, 4) defines it as "the process by which a neighborhood occupied by lower-income households undergoes revitalization or reinvestment through the arrival of upper-income households." Yet as both Laska and Spain (1980) and London and Palen (1984) discuss, connotations that the upper-class "gentry" are moving into "gentrifying" neighborhoods are often inappropriate for describing the actual neighborhood changes occurring in the United States. Clay's (1979) study of neighborhood renewal showed that in many instances neighborhoods were being upgraded by previous residents ("incumbent upgrading") rather than by in-movers. Laska and Spain discuss in more detail the differences among the various terms that have been used—"reinvasion," "resettlement," and "urban pioneering."

5. See Kasarda (1982) and Sumka (1980). Reports from the U.S. Department of Housing and Urban Development (1979, 1980a) reflect explicit assessments of the extent of revitalization and the conclusion of the Carter administration that more urban aid was needed to stem continuing decline.

"Decline" is used in many ways by different authors, usually to refer to drops in population, employment, or income. According to Bradbury, Downs, and Small (1982), the several dimensions of urban decline are closely linked. As they use the terms, "descriptive decline is any loss of population or jobs in an urban area. Functional decline denotes changes that are undesirable because they reduce the ability of a city to perform its social functions effectively" (1982, 4). To measure decline and distress they use as indicators crime rates, unemployment rates, real income per capita, tax rates and city-SMSA tax disparities, percentage of population in poverty, and percentage of older housing, with changes in per capita income considered the best measure of functional distress. Kain (1979) argues strongly that population decline is a symptom rather than a cause of distress. He judges concentrations of poor and minority populations to be the main cause and indicator of distress.

6. The articles by Levy, Sumka, and Houston and O'Connor in Laska and Spain (1980) describe some of the controls advocated.

need for public aid to cities benefitting from private investment. Influenced both by the persistence of past decline and by theoretical models which imply continued decentralization of upper-status groups, urban experts were more cautious. But they acknowledged that gentrification might indeed signal a reversal in prevailing trends toward selectively greater outmigration from cities by higher-status movers, and advanced a host of possible explanations.[7]

After 1980, depressed housing markets and recessionary conditions muted speculation, both verbal and financial, about future gentrification. Surveys showed that most movers to gentrifying neighborhoods originated elsewhere in the city, discrediting claims of "back-to-the-city" movement. Analysis of 1980 census data also deflated hopes that distressed cities were revitalizing during the 1970s. Over the decade, population losses from central cities accelerated, relative income fell, and in general cities which were distressed became more distressed.[8]

Yet as interest rates drop and housing investment recovers, opinions still differ greatly about prospects for distressed cities and optimal policies for aiding them and their poorer residents. Observers still cite instances of recent gentrification and reinvestment in cities as opportunities for investment, as evidence of future urban renaissance, and as proof that foresighted decision-makers can revitalize cities if they anticipate trends correctly and capitalize on each city's comparative advantages.[9] Although the

7. See, for example, the articles in Bryce (1979) and Solomon (1980b). According to Long (1980b, 19), "researchers concluded that [the back-to-the-city trend was] bound to occur sooner or later for several reasons: commuting from the outer fringes of suburbia was becoming too expensive, too much of a hassle, and too time-consuming, especially for the increasingly prevalent two-earner households; childless couples were on the increase, and they probably preferred city life to suburbia; and young couples, reacting to the soaring prices of suburban housing, were investing 'sweat equity' in refurbishing inner-city townhouses."

8. Bunce and Neal (1983, 1) conclude from an assessment of changes in distress between 1970 and 1980 among all cities and urban counties eligible for Community Development Block Grant (CDBG) funding that "the more distressed cities did experience the greatest increases in problems such as poverty, unemployment and crime during the 1970s and, as a result, became even worse off relative to the less distressed cities." Their results, however, make it clear that not all central cities are distressed. Distress tends to be correlated with size and age, but even some of the largest cities are relatively undistressed. For example, ACIR (1980b, 30) observes that "the bleak picture of the beleaguered, poverty-ridden central city surrounded by rich white suburbs does not describe current reality in most Southern and Western and even some Midwestern metropolitan areas. In these regions most central cities appear to be viable units, often because they have been able to use annexation or consolidation to capture a considerable amount of what would otherwise be suburban growth."

9. Articles such as those by Pierce (1983) reflect this attitude in the press, while the Reagan administration's urban policy reports also appear to be based on this assumption. See Savas (1983) for an explicit statement of his thoughts about urban policy as a spokesman for the Reagan administration, and Ahlbrandt (1984) for a discussion of how such ideology influenced the preparation of the 1982 Urban Policy Report (HUD 1982a).

Reagan administration acknowledges some responsibility to help lagging cities adjust to structural economic changes, it considers economic growth to be the best federal urban policy, and many experts agree that evolution to an advanced (service-based) economy offers hope of revitalization for central cities.[10] But others question whether such restructuring can aid the most distressed cities. Instead, concentrations of poor and minorities in distressed cities and the self-reinforcing nature of urban decline imply a "dismal" future and the need and responsibility for federal and state aid in combatting poverty and aiding cities.[11]

The current policy context makes a thorough assessment of the extent and implications of past gentrification particularly important. Fiscal pressures and reexamination of federal responsibilities will continue to inspire debates over urban policies and the proper types and amounts of state and federal aid to be given cities and their residents.[12] Symptoms of gentrification and private reinvestment in city neighborhoods will undoubtedly be cited as evidence of urban well-being in these debates. But much past evidence of gentrification is anecdotal or fragmentary, providing little guidance to policy-makers about the extent, causes, and effects of gentrification or about the likelihood that private-market action will substantially help either distressed cities or their poorer residents.[13] Future efforts to measure the extent of gentrification will suffer from similar defects, making it difficult to assess whether particular policies will promote revitalization, displacement, or both.

The Significance of Migration to Revitalization

As Ley (1983, 238) observes, "The rapid transformation of American cities and the plight of their dwindling fiscal base was caused in part by the massive migration of the middle class to the suburbs." Therefore, distressed

10. U.S. HUD 1982a, 1984. As discussed at more length below, Kasarda (1982), Noyelle and Stanback (1983), and Hanson (1983) are among those stressing the importance of advanced services to the U.S. economy and particularly to cities.

11. See Lowry (1980); Bradbury, Downs, and Small (1982); Fainstein and Fainstein (1983); and National Urban Policy Advisory Committee (1984).

12. The impacts of reduced federal expenditures and programs on cities are discussed, inter alia, in Hanson (1982), Glickman (1984), Ebel (1984), and Burchell, Carr, Florida, and Nemeth (1984).

13. As discussed in detail below, lags in the availability of census data on small areas, combined with the unavailability between censuses of data on changes in population and their characteristics within cities or smaller areas, mean that it is hard to determine *what* is happening, let alone why. Between censuses, the most current data available on trends for cities and suburbs come from the Current Population Survey, but the sample size of this survey gives very little reliable detail about what is occurring in individual cities. Fossett and Nathan (1981) discuss in some detail the problems of monitoring changes in cities with present data.

central cities are unlikely to revive[14] unless past patterns of selectively higher net outmigration by higher-status and upper-income movers from those cities slow drastically or reverse.[15] This premise is supported by expert opinion: many current assessments of the likelihood of recovery hinge on the residential decisions of higher-income groups. Therefore, a comprehensive way to evaluate whether chances of revitalization are improving is to determine whether migration trends have become more favorable to distressed cities in recent years, so that cities are indeed attracting more higher-status residents than previously. Because migration is a major component of population change, trends in migration to and from cities over time provide a sensitive leading indicator of future changes in city population composition by income. Studying trends in migration can also provide a way of monitoring the attractiveness of cities, since intercensal data are available for sixty large Standard Metropolitan Statistical Areas (SMSAs).[16]

14. "Revitalization," "recovery," and "revival," like "gentrification," have been used imprecisely in relation to the back-to-the-city movement. Like Bryce (1979), I use "revitalization" to denote improvement in the economic and social conditions of a city (not merely selected neighborhoods therein) but not necessarily population growth. According to Bryce (1979, xii), revitalization "requires 1) greater employment opportunities, 2) a reduction in the exodus of middle and upper-income residents, 3) a reduction in the plight of the poor and disadvantaged, and 4) improvement in the quality and distribution of services." Because this study focuses on "the exodus of middle and upper-income residents," I do not explicitly deal with employment opportunities, despite their importance to revitalization. But I argue that a reduction in this net exodus should contribute to "revival," defined most narrowly as increases in per capita income in a city. (As noted in n. 5 above, Bradbury, Downs, and Small [1982] use per capita income as their best measure of functional decline.)

For purposes of this study, I also assume that increases in per capita income should increase the tax base and thus both improve services and reduce the plight of the poor (although as discussed in n. 19 to Ch. 1 and in Ch. 5 below, this may not be the case). Rothenberg (1972) discusses in some detail why attracting middle-income families to central cities was considered a goal of the urban renewal program and why this goal could have general social benefits. My concern with revival and revitalization implies particular interest in developments in distressed cities.

15. "Selective" net outmigration refers to higher rates of outmovement by higher-status groups. Although comprehensive information on total migration to and from cities by indicators of status has never been available, studies of flows between cities and suburbs show clearly that suburbanization has been selective in income, education, and occupation (Taeuber and Taeuber 1964; Schnore 1972). Since I am focusing on population decentralization, I do not study decentralization of employment despite the evidence that they are closely intertwined (Mills 1972; Greenwood 1980).

16. The Annual Housing Survey has provided data on migration to cities and within metropolitan areas for sixty large SMSAs on a rotating basis since 1974. Although the number of SMSAs surveyed is being reduced, equivalent data will continue to be collected once every four years for 44 of the largest SMSAs. Like the Annual Housing Survey, I define "migration" to include movement across a city boundary as well as across county boundaries (the usual definition). "Movement" denotes changing residence no matter what the distance of the move.

To provide a firm basis both for evaluating the extent and implications of gentrification to date and for monitoring progress toward revitalization in the future, this study examines changes in movement to and from cities and within metropolitan areas in as much detail as available time-series data allow. This approach reflects the judgment of Laska and Spain that gentrification's potential significance derives in large part from its implication that cities have recently been attracting more "Americans wealthy enough to choose their places of residence" (1980, xii). But I argue, in addition, that distressed cities can "revive"—defined narrowly as relative gains in per capita income—only if migration to and from cities markedly changes from past net outmigration in level or in migrant characteristics. Much of the early publicity about gentrification and back-to-the-city movement (Pierce 1977; Allman 1978) implied that migration levels and patterns were dramatically changing, as would be necessary to reverse past patterns of net outmigration by whites, with selectively greater outmigration among higher-status groups. Any level of net migration, however, is only the difference between larger gross flows in and out. Although white outmigration from older, larger central cities has exceeded inmigration to these cities over the last several decades, these cities have continued to attract some inmigrants. Movers to and within cities during the 1970s thus could have quite visibly upgraded particular neighborhoods without markedly altering past patterns of selective net outmigration. Rather than representing a net improvement in the ability of cities to attract and retain upper-income residents, gentrification could imply only that some neighborhoods are gaining while total outmigration from the city continues unabated. As New York's Greenwich Village and Washington's Georgetown demonstrate, reinvestment has shifted within cities before without changing prevailing trends toward urban decline. The real implications of recent movement to, within, and from cities can best be evaluated by examining it in historic perspective.[17] Only thus can we see whether migration levels and differentials are changing sufficiently and determine the number and kinds of cities affected.

Overview of This Study

After reviewing the literature on migration, distressed cities, and revitalization to demonstrate the relevance of studying trends in migration, this study analyzes available data on migration in the United States to see

17. Marshall and Lewis (1982) discuss the advantages of studying trends rather than cross-sectional differences. Discussing the proper interpretation of findings that show only a relatively small proportion of "gentrifiers" moving into cities from suburbs, Cybriwsky (1980) also argues that examining changes over time is important: "While only a small percentage of newcomers may have moved directly from suburbs, this figure might be growing. Several years ago, . . . the number of suburbs-to-inner-city movers may have been virtually nil. It

whether they support the popular perception that cities became more attractive to migrants during the 1970s. Because of current and past constraints on residential mobility by blacks, whether *white* migration increased is particularly relevant to the question of attractiveness.[18] Because of the fiscal problems and imbalanced needs and revenues resulting from selective outmigration (ACIR 1965; Wasylenko 1984), whether distressed cities are attracting more *upper-income* migrants is the other key question. Available migration data are far from perfect for these purposes, but they allow an overview of changes since 1970 in total migration to and from all central cities in the United States, as well as a more detailed examination of changes in migration to and within forty of the largest metropolitan areas over the last two decades.

The first two chapters set the stage. To show why accurate assessments of gentrification are important, Chapter 1 reviews the recent history of urban decline and the seemingly futile attempts to combat it that made gentrification appear so welcome. Since both wishful thinking and private interests encourage overstatements of gentrification, past efforts to assess its extent and implications are then summarized. Current opinions about the likelihood of reviving distressed cities are mixed, but most experts agree that attracting more upper-status residents is crucial to future revival. Fueling past controversies about displacement, however, the absence of lower-income residents is often considered a prerequisite for revival. If this is the case, it raises serious issues about the propriety of public policies that use programs intended to aid poor residents to support revitalization of places.

Because the local decisions of higher-status residents are crucial for city revival, Chapter 2 reviews what is known about selective outmigration and the important factors influencing residential choices within metropolitan areas. Since selective outmigration of upper-income movers from distressed cities interacts with changes in taxes, services, and employment bases in a self-reinforcing cycle that tends to make decline cumulative, some experts expect further decline in distressed cities. However, at least four major reasons for increased selection of city residence in the 1970s have been identified—greater preferences for cities, advanced services employment, demographic changes, and cost constraints. Since each has rather different implications for future revitalization, distinguishing their relative roles in past changes is important to help assess the likelihood of future revival in different cities and circumstances. Therefore, I attempt to ascertain both whether and *why* migration to cities is increasing.

could well be that the [present percentage] should be interpreted as impressive gains for central cities over a short period, rather than simply as a small percent" (28).

18. Equivalent analysis of trends in mobility between cities and suburbs by blacks is reported in Nelson (1980).

Chapter 3 begins answering these questions with national and regional data on all migration to and from central cities of metropolitan areas since the 1960s. National sample data are used to examine changes during the 1970s in total movement between cities and suburbs of metropolitan areas by migrant characteristics, such as age, race, household type, occupation, education, and income. This national overview provides a basis for determining whether increased migration to cities was widespread or only localized. It apparently was *not* widespread: although some changes favorable to cities occurred, the improvement during the 1970s was so slight at the national level that few if any cities could expect to be revived by major shifts in migration. Whether any distressed cities were so aided is the question of Chapter 4.

Chapter 4 examines trends for forty individual large metropolitan areas (SMSAs) over a longer time frame, using data from three periods between 1955–60 and 1978–81. Comparing survey data from the years around 1980 with trends observed between 1960 and 1970 supports the perception that past outmigration is slowing. The proportion of movers choosing cities, after dropping markedly in nearly all major SMSAs between the late 1950s and the late 1960s, did increase in some metropolitan areas during the 1970s. Annual changes since 1973 in the proportion of migrants selecting residences in cities rather than their suburbs show cities in the more distressed Northeast and North Central regions sharing such improvements. However, increases in city selection were much less common among the upper-income groups important to future revival.

These results suggest that through 1981, migration to cities had not increased sufficiently to revive many, if any, distressed cities. It is thus unlikely that many cities gained financial resources from higher-income households to ease fiscal strains or improve city services. But Chapter 5 confirms that migration increases *were* related to neighborhood gentrification within cities. To evaluate some of the impacts of gentrification on city residents, it focuses more closely on changes in income and population during the 1970s at the census tract level in ten of the distressed cities that had relatively favorable changes in migration then. In view of past controversy and concerns about displacement, identifying the location of gentrifying areas and the effects of gentrification on the relocation of the poor population is of particular interest.

Chapter 6 concludes by summarizing the evidence of the previous chapters about tendencies toward recovery or further decline in both distressed and less distressed cities. After discussing the relative importance of factors influencing actual changes in migration, it briefly reviews probable developments in these factors to assess the likelihood of future revival or decline in America's cities and their implications for urban residents.

1. The Ongoing Need to Assess Gentrification

The controversy and publicity surrounding gentrification reflect its importance to almost all those who are concerned about the future of older, distressed central cities and their poorer residents. In the late 1970s, gentrification was hailed as leading to a "comeback" for cities, "urban revival," and "urban renaissance" (Pierce 1977; *Newsweek* 1979; Fleetwood 1979). In 1982, it was still being characterized as "the one process that is providing hope that our cities can demographically and economically revitalize" (Kasarda 1982, 174). Such descriptions reflect prevailing opinions that, absent gentrification, the trend toward continued urban decline may well be inevitable.

This chapter begins by portraying the context of urban decline in which gentrification was "discovered" and lionized. As urban decline continued and deepened into distress over the past half-century, despite policies and programs to renew cities, decline came to be considered irreversible. Thus, the possibility that private preferences and market forces might renew cities first seemed almost providential, particularly during the 1970s, when both public financial resources and new ideas about ways to aid cities were in short supply.

But as gentrification created losers as well as winners, controversy mounted about whether to promote or curtail it. Understanding where and when further gentrification is likely is essential to crafting appropriate policies for urban areas: nurturing gentrification may be desirable where urban decline is well entrenched, whereas controls are warranted when private demand is strong. Yet attempts to assess the strength of gentrification tendencies objectively are hampered by the conflicting claims of major actors and interest groups, and by empirical difficulties in measuring the extent and impacts of revitalization. The chapter demonstrates the ongoing importance of thorough evaluation of the extent and causes of past gentrification by reviewing past efforts at assessment, current opinions about the possibilities of urban revival, and continuing differences about appropriate policies for urban areas.

An Irreversible Trend toward Urban Decline?

The problem of deteriorating urban neighborhoods has been recognized for decades: social reformers were exposing slum conditions at the turn of the century (Glaab and Brown 1967). Renewed attention was paid to "slums" and "blighted areas" in the 1930s, but the Depression and World War II delayed concerted response until the Urban Renewal program was passed in 1949. Authorized by an uneasy coalition of mayors, developers, housing experts, and reformers, urban renewal was designed to remove slums and blighted conditions by demolishing old buildings and redeveloping in their stead. As the human, social, and economic costs of clearance were slowly recognized, program funds gradually shifted to support rehabilitation more than demolition and new construction.[1]

The 1960s brought gradual acknowledgment that improving urban conditions required more than physical renewal. The panoply of subsidies to new construction, rehabilitation, public infrastructure, and other physical improvements expanded, and the War on Poverty and the Model Cities program were initiated to reduce socioeconomic distress and thus "contribute to the sound development of the entire city."[2]

Recognition that spreading suburbanization might exacerbate city problems also grew in the 1960s, along with concern that federal programs, such as FHA insurance and highway construction, might hurt cities more than explicit efforts at aid could help (ACIR 1965). However, evidence suggests that both employment and population had been decentralizing since at least the turn of the century (Bogue 1953; Mills 1972a; Taeuber 1972) and that as cities developed, upper-class residents were more likely to move to or beyond the fringes of the central city (Schnore 1972). Such findings imply that suburbanization stemmed from basic long-run changes such as rising income and improvements in production and transportation technology; they thus reinforce conclusions that changing deep-seated trends through public policy would be difficult, particularly in older cities (Kasarda 1982).

---

1. Policies and programs aimed at renewing and revitalizing central cities are summarized in Hanson (1982) and their contradictory rationales and aims critically reviewed by Fainstein et al. (1983).

Frieden and Kaplan (1975) provide a detailed analysis of the hopes and intentions behind the Model Cities program, and of the lack of political consensus and priority that led to its demise. Extensive criticism of the human costs of redevelopment was necessary to shift emphasis to rehabilitation, and rehabilitation also has been shown to have severe negative effects on neighborhoods and their residents.

2. Comprehensive City Demonstration Program, Public Law 89-754, sec. 103(2). But see Frieden and Kaplan (1975) for a thorough examination of the extent to which the Model Cities program was underfunded and neglected, and of the political reasons underlying this neglect.

Perceptions that decline in older cities was inevitable despite federal and local programs were reinforced by spreading population losses and increasing concentrations of poor and minority populations in central cities. Most devastating, however, were hypotheses and supporting evidence that decline was cumulative and self-reinforcing. Fiscal disparities between cities and suburbs and concentrations of poverty and minorities in cities, each the outcome of past selective suburbanization, would accelerate selective outmovement of both population and employment; and this process would further concentrate populations with high service needs in cities while reducing the cities' economic and fiscal base (Bradford and Kelejian 1973). Thus, as policy disagreements about dispersal versus "gilding the ghetto" illustrate, concern about whether aiding poor people in poor places is actually detrimental to their welfare was added to recurring issues about whether aid should be directed to people or places (Harrison 1974; Kain 1975; Edel 1972a).

Recognition of increasing distress in large old central cities led to efforts to measure distress, identify its causes, and target scarce federal aid more precisely to those cities most needing help.[3] A variety of attempts were made to identify the most distressed cities and determine their characteristics. To target and evaluate federal programs, cities were ranked in terms of fiscal distress, poverty, old housing, population decline, and a variety of other measures. A review of these different efforts concluded that alternate measures rank distressed cities quite similarly, and that different elements of distress were highly correlated (Burchell et al. 1981). Distress was most likely in older cities with an industrial economic base and was more common among larger cities of the Northeast and North Central regions than in the (generally newer) cities of the South and West (Burchell et al. 1981; Nathan and Adams 1976; Bunce and Goldberg 1979). Between 1960 and 1975 relative distress rankings of cities stayed quite constant, but the more distressed cities apparently became relatively worse off (Nathan and Fossett 1978).

In the early 1970s, fears that urban decline might be inevitable were exacerbated by perceptions that public programs to aid distressed cities had generally failed.[4] Not only had a wide variety of programs, from re-

3. There are, however, many problems, both political and technical, associated with targeting aid to more distressed cities or to poorer residents within cities. See, for example, Markusen, Saxenian and Weiss 1981; Fainstein et al. 1983.

4. Lowry (1980) cites as a common opinion: "Federal programs have tested a variety of remedies and spent many billions, all to little avail." And according to Frieden and Kaplan (1975, 243), "During the 1960s, problems of the urban poor and minority groups had high visibility. Since then, the public and the communications media have revealed a short attention span for any problems that cannot be solved in a few years. As a mood of disenchantment settled over the unmet promises of the Great Society, many people began to question not only the effectiveness of federal programs but also the worthiness of their objectives."

development to social services, failed to stem declines in central-city population, employment, and revenue, but they had spawned a maze of conflicting and highly confusing requirements, definitions, and local agencies. Revenue sharing and the Community Development Block Grant (CDBG) program were instituted in large part because of dissatisfaction with past programs and a growing sentiment that nationally conceived and directed programs could not help cities in very diverse circumstances.[5]

Although revenue sharing and CDBG funds had provisions to maintain levels of funding for several years, their ultimate effect was to reduce federal funding for individual cities (Peterson 1976). Yet, partly because of needs/revenue imbalances resulting from growing concentrations of poor, cities were becoming more dependent on federal funds (Burchell and Listokin 1981). The recession in 1975 brought several cities—most notably New York City and Cleveland—to the brink of bankruptcy.[6]

Meanwhile, pressures were mounting at both state and national levels to reduce governmental taxation, spending, and programs (Hanson 1982). Although the Carter administration tried to target funds more specifically to distressed cities and neighborhoods than had the previous administration, it also tried to reduce both spending and the size and intrusiveness of federal government (Glickman 1984).

The Promises and Perils of Gentrification

The diminishing likelihood of further public support and program initiatives for distressed cities reinforced the conclusion that decline was inevitable. Private gentrification thus appeared essential if distressed cities were to be rescued. "Gentrification" is an awkward term for a controversial—and arguably atypical—process. Coined in England to describe the return of "landed gentry" to inner-London slums (Hamnett and Williams 1980), in the United States "gentrification" has been variously applied to middle-class movement into deteriorating city areas, to housing rehabilitation or commercial improvements there, and to residential succession of blacks by whites. The common theme in these different usages is reversal in dominant trends toward decline and downward filtering of areas and housing stock. Rather than continuing to decline, poorer areas attract more investment and higher-income residents than previously. Gentrifi-

5. See Hanson (1982) on the compromises underlying the passage of the CDBG program, and Markusen, Saxenian, and Weiss (1981) on the political difficulties of adopting an alternate formula to target aid to distressed cities.

6. The reasons for New York's near-bankruptcy are of course much more complicated than simply changes in federal aid or selective outmigration. Alcaly and Mermelstein (1976) present a comprehensive discussion.

cation further connotes that upgrading is due to private market forces rather than to public investment or programs.[7]

Against the context of urban decline, first reactions to reports of gentrification were almost invariably positive. Private rehabilitation of housing by young professionals showed that deteriorating, poorer neighborhoods could be considered for residence; evidence that housing could "filter up" rather than almost inevitably "down" raised hopes that trends toward cumulative decline in distressed cities could also reverse. Hampered by fiscal stringency and discouraged by the failure of public programs to halt urban decline, public officials were particularly encouraged by evidence that private investors and private money were finally improving central-city neighborhoods.

Gentrification was touted as much for its promise of private profits as for signaling urban revitalization (Downs 1976). Both consumers and real estate investors saw possibilities of private gain and/or cheaper housing at a time in which escalating housing prices made home ownership appear the best investment for the middle class. Media coverage of young professionals buying and renovating deteriorated central-city housing responded to concerns about affordability and home ownership. The conjunction of tax incentives for homeownership, low interest rates on mortgages, and inflation kept the real after-tax cost of ownership artificially low until around 1979 (Daugherty and Van Order 1982). Spurred by demand for housing from the baby-boom cohort, housing prices rose more quickly than inflation, so that home ownership and investing in real estate appeared a promising way of accumulating wealth. Older central-city housing was especially attractive to young adults willing to invest time and "sweat equity" in rehabilitation; its attractions were enhanced by growing interest in—and tax incentives for—historic preservation.

Thus, gentrification was welcomed both by those seeking entree to home ownership and by those hoping for speculative gains from urban real estate. Publicity about gentrification and central-city revitalization strengthened local real estate markets and also heartened officials and policy-makers seeking to attract or retain "upscale" residents and employment opportunities in the central city. Some praised its potential for bringing economically integrated neighborhoods as well as greater fiscal resources for distressed cities.

7. Grigsby (1963) describes the "well-recognized phenomenon" of filtering, in which housing that had been occupied by one income group becomes available to the next lower income group as a result of declines in the market price. Palen and London (1984) discuss the connotations of the term "gentrification" and argue that its implication that the "gentry" are returning to inner-city neighborhoods makes it an inappropriate description of the private upgrading occurring in cities in the United States. See also Black (1975), Long and Spain (1978), and Laska and Spain (1980).

Many lower-income residents of gentrifying neighborhoods first welcomed the greater investment and interest in their neighborhoods, but then reconsidered, seeing themselves as definite losers in a struggle for turf. Rents increased, buildings changed ownership, rental apartments were converted to cooperatives or condominiums, shopping opportunities (and prices) changed, and low-cost housing vanished. Slowly, residents mobilized to restrict gentrification and protect themselves against displacement. They urged cities to control rents, restrict condominium conversions, and subsidize continued residence by the poor and elderly in gentrifying neighborhoods (Dolbeare 1978; Levy 1980). Arguing that gentrification would bring a level of displacement approaching that caused by urban renewal, advocates also claimed that federal intervention was needed.[8] Such efforts to enlist public support for antidisplacement policies further contributed to the public's conception that gentrification was widespread. Ironically, therefore, these attempts to curtail displacement may have contributed to further displacement by fueling speculative demand.

In sum, many actors—city officials, developers, homebuyers, real estate investors and sellers, and city residents—wished to influence public perceptions about the extent of gentrification. Unfortunately, almost all had reasons for overstating its extent and possibilities, and for seeking publicity to influence public opinions and public decisions about zoning, redevelopment, and controls on condominium conversions. These efforts and motivations increased public recognition of gentrification but made accurate assessment difficult. Such a variety of concerns will continue to draw attention to ongoing urban changes, maintaining the need for accurate current evaluation.

Past Assessments of Urban Gentrification

As scholars and public officials tried to assess the extent and implications of gentrification, initial claims and hopes that gentrification was widespread and "snowballing" have been deflated. But attempts at comprehensive assessment have been hampered by difficulties in measuring gentrification through various proxies and by the general scarcity of timely, relevant, and geographically detailed data (Fossett and Nathan 1981). Because of the difficulties of tracking outmovers, determining the extent of

8. See Embry (1977), Kotler (1977), and Schur (1977) testifying before the U.S. Senate in the Senate hearings on displacement. Sumka (1980, 269) summarized: "From cities across the country, there are reports of lower-income families being forced out of their neighborhoods as a result of extensive revitalization activity stimulated by increasing demand among middle-income families. These reports have led, in turn, to increasing calls for ameliorative or preventive action by the federal government."

displacement caused by private reinvestment has been, if anything, even harder. Until 1980 census data started emerging in 1982, estimates of the extent of gentrification were based on journalistic accounts, special surveys and case studies, and inferences from national sample data.

The first reports of gentrification emerged from newspaper accounts and city-specific case studies of young professionals renovating deteriorated housing (Goodman 1980).[9] As city after city displayed similar symptoms, the media began to speculate about a back-to-the-city movement and its possibilities for rescuing distressed cities (Pierce 1976; *Newsweek* 1979). Comparisons among cities were then commissioned to evaluate the extent and scope of gentrification. Surveys by the Urban Land Institute in 1975 and by Clay in 1978 provided evidence that private investment and housing renovation were under way in many central cities. ULI's informants reported renovation activity in 48 percent of large cities.[10] Clay's study of 105 neighborhoods in thirty cities showed that incumbents as well as new residents were upgrading their housing, although he estimated that fewer than 5 percent of the neighborhoods were being upgraded within the cities he studied. But the results of such surveys of local informants have been criticized as "a mixture of data, opinions and judgments" (Gale 1980, 928). Furthermore, since case studies typically report only on inmovers and continuing residents, they omit information on the destinations, characteristics, and motivations of outmovers (Sumka 1980, 273). Case studies have helped identify the characteristics of gentrifiers and gentrifying neighborhoods, and they often provide more current and detailed descriptions of ongoing events than official data. They are, however, unable to evaluate the net impacts of gentrification in particular neighborhoods or on the entire city, and follow-up studies suggest that they tend to overestimate the extent of change that is occurring.[11]

9. Laska and Spain (1980), Stegman (1979), and Palen and London (1984) each contain examples of case studies of particular cities and neighborhoods.

10. Black (1980, 7) summarizes the ULI survey: "Based on the survey results, it is estimated that 124 (or 48 percent of 260) central cities with a population of over 50,000 are experiencing some degree of private-market, nonsubsidized housing renovation in older, deteriorated areas. The incidence of renovation activity varies considerably by city size. . . . 73 percent, or 19 of 26, of the central cities in the 500,000-and-over population group are reported to be experiencing this type of renovation activity. This percentage drops, with the size class, down to 63 percent of the 250,000 class. . . . There is also considerable variation in the incidence of renovation activity by region. . . . Central-city housing renovation is most extensive in the South. . . . (and next most extensive in the Northeast)."

11. Gale (1984), Spain (1982), and Chall (1983–84) have done follow-up studies of neighborhoods identified as gentrifying during the 1970s. Their results show some changes in income and population that are consistent with claims made for gentrification, but generally reveal less dramatic change (at least at the tract level) than they had expected to find. Reporting on his examination of possible gentrification in New York City, for example, Baldassare (1984, 95) notes that the general evidence of decline was so great that the bulk of his study had to be done in terms of "relative [rather than absolute] improvements."

Attempts to evaluate the extent of displacement and its consequences for lower-income residents have faced even worse data problems (Grier and Grier 1980; Sumka 1980). High mobility levels among lower-income residents and the difficulty of tracing outmovers impede local attempts at measurement, while national estimates are flawed by the difficulty of distinguishing displacement resulting from reinvestment and renovation from that caused by abandonment or other market processes, including eviction for cause. The 1981 HUD report on displacement estimated that nationally, 4 to 6 percent of all movers were displaced by private action in 1979, but that displacement could be many times higher among movers from gentrifying neighborhoods. It judged nevertheless that housing abandonment caused more displacement than reinvestment did. It also concluded from national longitudinal data covering the early 1970s that displaced households experienced significant increases in crowding and housing cost burden. A specific attempt to track all movers from a gentrifying San Francisco neighborhood, however, found that displaced households "have not experienced severe negative changes in housing conditions either absolutely or in comparison with other groups" (HUD 1981, 47–50). But sceptics were not convinced: Smith and Le Faivre (1984, 55), for example, argue that "the HUD report and related publications underestimate the extent of displacement as part of a deliberate attempt to encourage gentrification."

In another approach to evaluating the extent of gentrification, scholars examined intercensal sample data to ascertain whether major changes in past trends occurred during the 1970s. Several careful analyses of changes between 1960 and 1970 had documented improvements in some neighborhoods within cities despite predominant declines in population, employment, and per capita income. Lipton's (1977) analysis of census-tract-level changes in higher income and education in twenty large cities had shown some "revival" near central business districts, and White's (1980) detailed study of the impacts of urban renewal in four large cities also found upper-income population and higher-status occupations increasing by 1970 in renewed areas.[12] Findings about changes during the 1970s supported the impression that past patterns were indeed altering. During

12. More recently, Marshall and Lewis (1982) reported on a comparison of changes in migration to large central cities between 1955–60 and 1965–70 that examined "the ability of central cities within 61 large metropolitan areas to attract high-status inmigrants and those in their most economically productive years" (1982, 19). Based on increases in the number of "high-status" men (professional, managerial, and sales occupations), especially in large northeastern and midwestern cities, they find support for the hypothesis "that the worst may indeed be over for northern central cities." However, their study does not control for annexations, suburban population growth, or—most important—changes in occupational composition over the decade; and even the "improved" 1970 situation shows high-status city-to-suburb movers far outnumbering the opposite flow.

the mid-1970s, expenditures on existing housing increased (James 1977a), as did black-to-white successions in city housing and successions in which inmovers were of higher socioeconomic status (Spain 1980).[13] Some large cities also attracted higher proportions of young and better-educated movers (Nelson 1981).

However, the net effects of such shifts were apparently small during the 1970s. Instead, cities became more distressed (Nathan and Fossett 1976), outmigration from cities continued (Goodman 1980) and income gaps between cities and their suburbs further widened in most SMSAs (Long and Dahmann 1980). Because only sample data were available, however, few cities could be studied specifically. Therefore the 1980 census was awaited with interest. As Long noted, its small-area capabilities could be used to assess "the degree to which a return to city living has spread to cities of intermediate size which have not been the subject of case studies, [and] . . . whether changes in individual city neighborhoods have been great enough to alter the character of city populations" (1980b, 20).

As 1980 census data have become available, studies have begun to analyze the effects of changes over the decade for both specific neighborhoods and city populations overall. Despite indications that expected changes in population composition, household size, and the like have occurred in some neighborhoods, the overall results suggest further compounding of distress rather than general revitalization. Population losses from central cities continued, and even many SMSAs lost population, especially in the northern regions (Long 1981). In most large distressed cities, per capita income grew more slowly than the national average.[14] Confirming Nathan and Fossett's inference from intercensal estimates, Bunce and Neal (1983) concluded from careful examination of changes between 1970 and 1980 that distressed cities had become more distressed.

Within cities, analysis of change in census tracts thought to be gentrifying confirms that some of the expected changes in population and to a lesser extent in socioeconomic status did take place (Spain 1982; Chall 1983–84; Gale 1984). But Lipton's follow-up to his earlier study (1984), which examines tract-level changes in income and race in twenty-two large cities, suggests that though upgrading occurred in some tracts within cities, many more tracts experienced increases in poverty or racial concentration.[15]

---

13. Spain's 1980 study explicitly attempts to update findings on black-to-white successions reported in Long and Spain (1978). This research is one of the earliest to compare equivalent data for different time periods to assess the extent to which behavior was actually changing.

14. Washington, D.C., in which per capita income growth was 1% above the national average rate of growth, is one of the few exceptions.

15. Lipton (1984) examined changes in the distribution of tracts with respect to income, racial concentration, and tenure. He found many more tracts in the "lower" categories of

Data from the 1980 census on conditions and changes in all cities and in particular neighborhoods offer opportunities to evaluate gentrification during the 1970s more thoroughly. Such analysis is essential to provide a comprehensive overview that places gentrification in context and determines its net effect on different cities. But as 1980 recedes, even such detailed analyses will soon be outdated, while the need for measuring and evaluating current trends will remain.

Is Revival Possible?

As Chapter 3 shows, conditions were more favorable for central-city revitalization in the late 1970s than earlier in the postwar period. Experts nevertheless disagree about the likelihood that past decline in distressed cities will reverse or slow. No one argues that revival is assured, but some are more sanguine than others. There is even wider disagreement about preferred policies for aiding cities and their poorer residents, and about the responsibilities of different levels of government. Recommendations for policies tend to vary with assessments of the strength of gentrification trends and of their probable impacts on the poor.[16]

Despite improved prospects for revitalization, at least two noted experts have recently concluded that the situation of distressed cities will further deteriorate. Both judge that mutually reinforcing negative trends far outweigh the few positive developments. Because the "emerging economic problems of large cities interact with the inherited social problems of race relations in ways that worsen both," Lowry foresees a "dismal future," with spreading and accelerating deterioration and further evolution toward the two separate but unequal societies predicted by the Kerner Commission (Lowry 1980, 163). A thorough study of trends from 1960 to 1975 by Bradbury, Downs, and Small (1982) similarly concludes that further losses of population and employment are unavoidable in the most severely declining cities, despite "expanding revitalization in many older neighborhoods." Decline will be most likely in cities with high concentrations of poor and will impose the greatest burdens on those poor. Because many problems related to decline are caused by externalities that are not

---

such distributions in 1980 than in 1970 in all of the twenty-two large cities that he studied, along with some indication that lower-income tracts were also becoming more common in suburbs. The meaning of his results, however, is made less clear by the procedures he used. The results are based only on counts of tracts, without accounting for differences resulting from splits or other changes in tract boundaries, annexation, and newly tracted areas at the urban fringe. Furthermore, since population per tract does vary greatly from the intended 4,000 persons per tract, weighting his results by tract population would be desirable.

16. The *Urban Affairs Quarterly* symposium on the future of cities (Gans, Kasarda, and Molotch 1982) provides a good example of different perspectives and policy recommendations.

amenable to market solutions, Bradbury and her colleagues recommend that federal and state governments support a variety of policies to combat poverty, aid city residents, and help cities adapt to decline.[17]

Less pessimistically, other experts perceive possibilities of revitalization in "a select number of nonsmokestack cities." Observing "visible stirrings . . . of urban resurgence" in offices, hotels, rehabbed brownstones, and other residences for the elite, Sternlieb and Hughes (1983) foresee the promise of a "critical mass of appeal . . . that in turn fosters a greater pulling power of the central city as an alternative lifestyle." If the poor recognize that they need the resources of the rich to support city services and do not retard such developments by conflict and confrontation, such cities have "potentials for positive rebirth."[18]

In a similar vein, Fainstein and Fainstein (1982) argue that some—but hardly all—older American cities are "restructuring" toward the (idealized) model of European metropolises, which display "a preserved historic center serving expensive consumption, surrounded by high-rise commercial and residential development." This is occurring because worldwide economic transformations mean that "urban locations are resuming the classic [commercial and headquarters] economic functions of the preindustrial town." Nevertheless, only some older cities will be helped: the increasing private investment essential for restructuring will occur only "where the interaction of a number of variables, some fortuitous, have produced the opportunity for large speculative gains," one "prerequisite" being "the absence whether preexisting or forced of low-income inhabitants." Thus the Fainsteins do not expect the poor to share the benefits of restructuring unless they can and do exert strong political pressure.[19]

17. The policies Bradbury, Downs, and Small (1982, 15–17) recommend are as follows: (1) removing anti-city biases from federal policies; (2) helping cities adapt to smaller populations and fewer jobs; (3) establishing effective ways of providing federal aid to cities (which would include more of a "menu approach" so that local governments can choose programs best for their situation); (4) coping with fragmented urban governments, preferably by tax-base sharing; and (5) empowering individuals and households injured by decline. They characterize these recommendations as "relatively marginal changes in existing institutions and policies" and recommend them because there are not "any major sources of political support" for the more radical changes that would be necessary to "solve" urban problems.

18. This is a more optimistic conclusion than that by the same authors two years earlier (Sternlieb and Hughes 1981). Then they concluded an assessment of the urban crisis by stating: "A thin facade of office structures, of new swinging single groups, distracts the eye from the functional reality [of continued crisis]" (75).

19. The Fainsteins claim that the typical conversion process hurts the poor in at least two ways. First, the new prosperity is not accompanied by improvement in the material condition of the lower classes, who experience revitalization in higher transportation costs and loss of such strategic advantages as derived previously from concentration on prime real estate" (1982, 165). Furthermore, as lower classes are displaced by the "private" market

The most sanguine assessment of possible revival is that by Kasarda (1983). Although revival is not assured, he argues that the transformation of older cities from production centers to centers of information exchange and higher-order service provision offers city decision-makers possibilities for effective economic revitalization policies. Such policies should help cities exploit their emerging competitive strengths "in the administrative, office, financial, professional and business service sectors, and in cultural, recreational, and tourist industries"; and policy-makers should definitely encourage gentrification. They should also plan for demographic shrinkage, since job opportunities for low-income, unskilled workers are rapidly decreasing in cities. In this regard he recommends that the most humane policy would assist the disadvantaged to move "to places where jobs appropriate to their skills are still expanding."[20]

Policy Differences

Different assessments of the likelihood of revival and its causes underlie current differences about urban policy at all levels of government. Although the range of suggested policies and programs associated with various perspectives is too great to detail here, it is clear that opinions about the extent and meaning of past gentrification and about the possibility of future revitalization in distressed cities will continue to influence debates at the city, state, and federal levels about appropriate amounts, types, and targeting of urban aid.

Contrasts between the 1980 (Carter) and 1984 (Reagan) Urban Policy Reports (HUD 1980a, 1984) exemplify some of these differences. As budget constraints and publicity about gentrification both increased, the Carter administration was pressured in two directions—to reduce urban aid because gentrification meant that cities would be revitalized through private action, or to develop programs to fight displacement. The administration judged, however, that neither gentrification nor displacement was great enough to justify diverting "the resources available for assisting cities . . . from their broad purpose of encouraging reinvestment" (Sumka

---

forces, "lower-class areas of converting old cities may experience further 'decline' and devalorization as they absorb this [displaced] population" (167).

20. Like Kasarda, Carter's Commission for a National Agenda for the Eighties argued that "the main thrust of policy should be to aid people directly by helping them move or by supporting job-retraining programs" (Hanson 1982, 57). James (1984) summarizes the (scanty) evidence on the results of migration by lower-income workers and advocates policies reducing barriers to migration. The National Research Council (1982) also identifies mobility of people and jobs as one of the critical issues for urban policy. Although Bluestone and Harrison (1982) have thoroughly discussed the implications for communities of capital disinvestment, to my knowledge no one has attempted to ascertain "where jobs appropriate to the skills [of the disadvantaged] are still expanding."

1980, 274). Therefore, the 1980 Urban Policy Report reaffirmed continued targeting of resources to troubled, older, large central cities and suburbs rather than taking a "wait for market equilibrium" approach. Hanson (1982, 52) notes that this commitment "was balanced by recommending continued and sustained efforts to improve opportunities for increasing numbers of poor and minorities located in urban areas."[21]

The Reagan administration, by contrast, has both made and welcomed claims that cities are reviving.[22] Both the 1982 and the 1984 reports make the Economic Recovery program "the foundation for President Reagan's Urban Policy" (HUD 1984, 4). They argue that economic growth requires less government spending overall, devolution of decision-making to state and local governments, and greater reliance on market forces. The 1984 report acknowledges that general economic recovery will not be sufficient to help cities with long-term structural problems, but argues that removing "regulatory burdens created by too many years of centralized planning" (12), together with Enterprise Zones and other programs such as Community Development Block Grants (CDBG) and Urban Development Action Grants (UDAG), will provide the flexible support necessary for transition.[23]

Critics of Reagan's policies, while agreeing that economic growth is important, do not think that a hands-off policy is the "appropriate role of the Federal government in fostering the economic and social vitality of America's cities" (National Urban Policy Advisory Committee 1984, 1). Assessing Reagan's *real* urban policy, (i.e., the effects of budgetary priorities and tax policies in addition to explicit urban policies), Glickman concludes that "growing Sunbelt cities benefit most . . . at the expense of distressed central and northern cities" (1984, 471). Furthermore, because of the negative effects of transfer burdens and progressive tax systems on migration, the "New Federalism" could further widen interstate income differ-

21. Carter's approach, however, has been criticized as also being biased in favor in redevelopment by Smith (1984).

22. The Congressional Research Service's "critique" of the Urban Policy Report, for example, concludes by noting that "the 1984 Report presents a glowing picture of the economic health of the nation and the cities resulting from the Administration's policies" (1984, 6). HUD Secretary Pierce's transmittal letter, for example, had claimed that "the outlook for our urban areas today is much better than it has been since the Urban Policy Reports were initiated" (the first was in 1972). In the report, Baltimore is cited with other cities as examples of revival, but Baker (1984) documents some of the problems with unemployment, poverty, and poor housing that persist outside of Harborplace.

23. This claim preceded the proposed FY1986 budget, which calls for eliminating the UDAG program and cutting CDBG funding by 10%. Glickman (1984) discusses some of the other ways in which aid to cities has been reduced under the Reagan administration; Ahlbrandt (1984) describes how the ideology of private enterprise influenced the preparation of the 1982 Urban Policy Report.

ALBRIGHT COLLEGE LIBRARY   214710

entials (Althaus and Schachter 1984), thus reducing the capabilities of states to aid their cities. In such a context, critics argue, cuts in federal programs, aid, and responsibilities will only exacerbate the widening gap between the growing needs of distressed cities and their lagging ability to respond to them. The National Urban Policy Advisory Committee (1984, 2) categorizes the "most important" difference between Reagan's policies and its "alternative vision" as "acknowledg[ing] the need for federal assistance to aid cities ameliorate the hardship experienced by the poor or near-poor." Economic recovery alone, they argue, has stimulated few improvements "for many areas and their residents, particularly their minority and less affluent residents."

Summary

To date, then, comprehensive assessments of the implications of gentrification for the revitalization of distressed cities have been seriously hampered by shortages of relevant, current, geographically focused data about what is happening where. Despite early hopes and despite improvements in some neighborhoods in some cities, 1980 census data suggest that the relative position of distressed cities generally worsened over the decade. Thus, gentrification appears to have reflected shifts in investment within or among cities in the context of ongoing decline, *not* a major break away from past trends toward city decline.

But in today's political climate, pressures for wishful thinking persist. Faced with severe budget constraints, policy-makers at all levels of government would like to believe that city conditions are improving. At the federal level, reports of improvements could be used to justify further reductions in domestic programs. Within cities, persons arguing about issues such as allocation of public investment between core and peripheral areas or between capital accumulation or social consumption (Fainstein and Fainstein 1984, ch. 7) also will cite different assessments of gentrification, revival, and displacement. In each case, those making policy decisions are dependent for current information on impressionistic partial accounts, which may well be biased because of the interests of the major actors involved.

This study therefore aims to evaluate whether distressed cities can be revived by determining whether past trends in selective outmigration have recently changed in ways favorable to distressed cities. In particular, I ask whether and where prevalent patterns of selectively higher net outmigration of higher-status groups have slowed or reversed since 1970. In addition to documenting comprehensively what has occurred in the most important demographic process determining population change and composition, the results of this study should improve our capabilities for monitoring and interpreting intercensal data on mobility. The information on differentials, levels, and trends in migration for major cities and the nation should provide a baseline against which current data can be compared to better evaluate and direct demand for housing and central location in each city.

2. The Prospects for Reversing Selective Outmigration: A Literature Review

Major theories of intrametropolitan location and the literature on suburbanization both imply that reviving distressed cities will be difficult if this requires attracting more upper-income movers. Suburbanization is a trend of long standing in the United States and most other industrialized nations (Mills 1972; Renaud 1984). All common models of intrametropolitan location and evolution show net movement toward city peripheries: inner neighborhoods and housing are expected to decline and "filter" down the socioeconomic scale unless they are rebuilt at higher density or redeveloped with government subsidies (Johnston 1971; Grigsby 1963). Both economic models of residential location and sociological theories derived from Burgess expect higher-income residents to live farther from the city center, with status directly related to distance.

Data on migration are consistent with such theories. On net, higher-status people have been more likely to move away from large central cities. Although counterstreams always occur, studies of migration by education and income show greater net outmovement from cities by higher-status people over the past four decades (Taeuber and Taeuber 1964; Pinkerton 1968). Frey (1980) documents the extent of selectivity in suburbanization by education in the late 1960s and shows that outmovement was more selective for distressed cities such as Detroit. Exacerbating local decentralization, regional shifts over the past two decades have been differentially drawing better-educated migrants away from the Northeast and North Central regions, where many of the most distressed cities are located (Long 1981; Nelson 1984).

Many recent trends in major determinants of intrametropolitan location point to further suburbanization or decentralization into nonmetropolitan areas, especially from distressed cities. New housing and job decentralization appear to be the major causes of past population decentralization (Greenwood 1981); and during the 1970s most housing was constructed in the less-dense fringes of SMSAs, and employment consistently decentralized both within and among regions (Nelson 1984; Sternlieb, Hughes, and Hughes 1982). Central city concentrations of poor and

minority populations, associated in many studies with accelerated outmigration from cities, are increasing, especially in the most distressed
cities (Bunce and Neal 1983). Intrametropolitan differences in services
and taxes, which strongly influence the location decisions of higher-status
movers, continue to widen as intergovernmental revenue transfers shrink
(Burchell et al. 1984).

Even more damning for the future of cities is the evidence that these
factors interact in self-reinforcing ways. Bradbury, Downs, and Small
(1980, 1982) identify both self-reinforcing and self-limiting influences on
urban decline, but conclude that at present the "self-limiting elements
are weaker than self-reinforcing ones" in declining cities (1982, 211). As
self-reinforcing elements they cite differential outmigration of persons by
race and income, changes in local taxes and government services as tax
bases erode, loss of agglomeration economies among firms and other critical mass activities as employment decentralizes, the decreasing political
power of cities, and poorer maintenance of residential property. They see
falling housing and land prices as the only self-limiting factor that might
reverse urban decline: "Eventually, vacant areas created by building
abandonment will become sufficiently inexpensive and isolated from surrounding blight to entice developers to build new, lower-density structures on them" (1982, 215).

Yet the evidence supporting conventional wisdom about where different socioeconomic classes locate in metropolitan areas, and why, is hardly
monolithic. Many cities and neighborhoods are exceptions to simple
models and expectations. Even aggregate city-suburbs comparisons do
not always show cities poorer than their suburbs, and some higher-status
neighborhoods have persisted within cities (Johnston 1971). Furthermore, cities are dynamic rather than static. Scholars question whether
theoretical models of location patterns apply to dynamic situations, with
particular questions about which ways cities will evolve and whether past
trends will alter. Most empirical tests of present theories are based on
relatively recent cross-sectional data—often on population location, which
represents the accumulated results of past decisions, rather than on current migration. Thus, generalizing from their conclusions to dynamic
situations may well be inappropriate.[1] Yet many arguments that cities
might revitalize explicitly or implicitly claim that basic forces are changing

1. As Bradbury, Downs, and Small (1982, 132) caution, analysis of cross-sectional differences "can examine variations among areas in growth rates, but not overall urbanization and
suburbanization trends. Birth rates, flows from farms, wars, and technological changes affect
city growth in ways [such] analysis does not explain, since all the cities . . . are similarly
affected." In particular, examining cross-sectional differences cannot explain the reasons for
the overall slowing in rate of suburbanization that they observe between the 1960s and the
early 1970s.

in ways that supersede conclusions based on the experience of the last few decades. This is particularly true of explanations advanced from a Marxist perspective, which argue that the spatial form of cities and their evolution are heavily influenced by conflicting and evolving economic and political forces.[2]

Therefore, this chapter summarizes current knowledge about questions crucial for evaluating whether or where distressed cities might revive, and whether inmigration and retention of higher-status groups might be more likely now than in previous decades. It reviews theoretical and empirical information about influences on the intrametropolitan location of U.S. population, especially upper-income movers; about fears that urban decline may be self-reinforcing in distressed cities; and about developments that might instead promote revival. Because most studies and models of intrametropolitan location have focused on suburbanization rather than on city revitalization, the first section briefly reviews theories and facts about suburbanization and selective migration in the past; the second summarizes statistical evidence on the most important determinants of intrametropolitan location. The third section develops alternate interpretations of this evidence, widening the historical perspective to question whether conventional wisdom is based on special circumstances that are changing. Recent trends in the major determinants of intrametropolitan location are then considered to isolate major hypotheses about cumulative decline or revival. The chapter concludes by distinguishing among four major hypotheses about why migration to cities might increase and by examining their rather different implications for the futures of cities.

Selective Suburbanization and Cumulative Decline

Decentralization of population and employment has been under way for many years, since at least the turn of the century. This is commonly thought to have occurred because of "powerful, long-established forces such as rising real incomes, expanding use of automotive vehicles, widespread preferences for low-density living, and technological advances in communications and industrial processes" (Bradbury, Downs, and Small 1982, 211). However, political considerations also influenced the decisions about annexations and jurisdictional boundaries that determined how far central cities spread (Norton 1979; Gordon 1977b; Ashton 1978).

2. As discussed further below, Marxist analyses of suburbanization and urban redevelopment stress the need to consider the historical context of urban growth and form, in particular the influences of the slowly changing modes of production, of capital, and of political conflict between the interests of labor and capital (Edel 1981; Walker 1981; Gottdiener 1983).

Although wealthier, more influential groups lived in city centers in pre-industrial cities (Ley 1983), even in colonial America those who could afford horse or railroad transportation and new housing were likely to move to housing built at the urban fringe. Industrialization during the 1800s gave wealthier groups additional reasons to avoid the dirt and noise of industry centrally located near wharves and railroad terminals, but poorer residents remained for access to centrally located jobs (Walker 1982). Warner's study of Boston, for example, shows that although the poorest class remained in downtown Boston, the streetcar suburbs attracted people from all other classes. Pinkerton (1968) and Johnston (1971) summarize similar findings about selective suburbanization in other cities.

Observing such changes in Chicago, Burgess formulated the "concentric-ring" theory of urban growth: as poor inmigrants to the city occupy cheaper, older, more central housing, higher-income residents move to newer homes built on vacant land at the fringe (Johnston 1971). Studying the location of rich and poor in many cities during the 1930s, however, Hoyt (1939) observed that some "pie-shaped" sectors seemed to remain more attractive to the rich than others, so that the concentric-ring theory was too simple. Yet he agreed that within sectors, richer groups did tend to live farther from the center in newer housing, while inner neighborhoods tended to decay.[3] White's detailed estimation of income and status gradients in four major American cities (1980) found elements of both concentric and sectoral patterns of location within a variegated mosaic as population density declined between 1940 and 1970.

Economic models of residential land use (Alonso 1964; Alonso 1972; Muth 1969) are derived from assumptions that households trade off land against access to the city center within a budget constraint, but in most formulations they also show richer people living farther from the city center. Higher-income households are assumed to value space more than the cost of their commuting time, and thus consume more low-cost fringe land, while poorer households are constrained to higher densities on more central, more expensive land.[4] In most models all employment is

3. The abundant sociological-ecological literature on neighborhood change and the invasion-succession process that has developed from these theories is discussed at length in Johnston (1971). Interestingly, Ley (1983, 22) notes that both the ecological and the economic model are originally based on changes observed in Chicago in the decades prior to 1920.

4. However, there is abundant literature (e.g., Wheaton 1979; Follain and Blackley 1984) suggesting that these assumptions do not hold. Edel and Rothenberg (1972, 2–3) comment:

> Although such models do not themselves strictly imply a particular spatial pattern in terms of household income level . . . if some allegedly "reasonable" assumptions are added, the models generate a pattern of monotonically decreasing use density and rising income level with distance from the city center. The poor therefore occupy the most cen-

located at the city's center, and the costs of commuting—in both time and money—form part of the budget constraint within which a household acts on its preferences.[5]

Although it has proved difficult to incorporate the fact of job decentralization into such models, the idea that constraints of cost and current technology restrict employed persons to the vicinity of their place of employment is basic to most economic explanations of intrametropolitan location and evolution.[6] In this view, suburbanization resulted as technological change and income growth allowed more people to act on preferences for lower-density living within their budget constraints. As changes in production technology freed manufacturing from central city locations near wharves and railroads, jobs decentralized; improvements in transportation allowed workers to commute longer distances; and rising incomes in-

---

tral, most expensive, and smallest parcels of land, whereas the rich occupy the most distant, least expensive, and largest parcels.

The anomaly of poor people on highly expensive land is, however, only quite tenuously derivable from models such as these. . . . the observed [patterns] are more easily explainable by taking account of some of the other . . . characteristics of land that are omitted from these models. In particular, the type of structures, the cost of demolishing old units and building new ones of different types, the neighborhood characteristics, and the multiplicity of desirable destinations are important. In the United States, where housing for the poor is provided predominantly not by new construction, but by the filtering down in quality of existing units. . . , it is the geographical distribution of such older filtered units and their clustering in relatively homogeneous neighborhoods that go far to explain the location of the poor.

5. Richardson (1977) and Wheaton (1979) thoroughly discuss the utility and major shortcomings of these models and the "new urban economics" derived from them. Wheaton summarizes (124):

Taken as a group, monocentric city models have three characteristics in common: they assume that all employment is centrally located; they assume that locational choice depends only on commuting cost and space consumption; and they assume that all housing capital is fluid and mobile.

These assumptions illustrate an important problem in any scientific research: models that are simple enough to yield general, deductive conclusions frequently require overly restrictive assumptions. The monocentric city models are an excellent case in point. On the one hand, the assumptions are essential for mathematical tractability; without them, solutions to the models become less general in character, and noticeably more difficult to obtain. On the other hand, the assumptions are sufficiently unrealistic that doubts are raised about their usefulness. Each assumption eliminates an important and essential feature of urban structure. These features are often the core of many current urban policy issues.

Follain and Blackley (1984) provide evidence that these models and their assumptions imply outcomes greatly at variance with actual urban form and commuting distances.

6. Access and journey-to-work constraints are also crucial to the more empirically oriented transportation and simulation models of urban location. Ingram (1979) provides a summary of progress and problems in estimating such models.

creased effective demand for new housing production and purchase on accessible fringe land.[7]

Such interpretations emphasize the primary role of market forces and personal preferences in influencing the evolution of intrametropolitan and interregional location. But because of the fixed, long-lasting nature of residential and industrial construction, large urban areas and specific activities within them are also heavily influenced by their industrial structure, the capital infrastructure, and the technology at the time of their major growth. As technological requirements for industry and preferences for residences have changed, older cities are considered less attractive because of their aging stock and denser development. Growth shifts to less developed areas, either in suburbs or different regions. As this process continues, suburban areas develop the critical mass needed to support production and distribution facilities, along with more of the facilities and amenities that once attracted growth to central cities. Yet decline is not purely a function of age; early leaders in the hierarchy of cities retain many advantages.[8]

In both sociological and economic models, richer households are presumed to decentralize more rapidly than others because their higher income allows them to act more freely on preferences for newer housing and other amenities. Therefore, much attention has been paid to identifying the amenities that attract and the problems that repel upper-income movers. Preferences for suburbs have been attributed to newer housing, lower-density living, better schools, a more attractive natural environment, better shopping opportunities, lower crime rates, better services, and lower taxes (or a more desired mix of services per tax dollar).[9] Con-

7. This is the conventional view of the factors contributing to suburbanization used in most economics texts (see, e.g., Mills 1972a); it also underlies the discussion of suburbanization and urban change in the 1982 National Urban Policy Report (HUD 1982a). Gottdiener (1983), however, criticizes it as "technological determinism" and argues that the Marxist paradigm is superior in explaining why such changes are occurring.

8. Watkins (1980) assesses interregional shifts in economic development and the influence of the age of city development on growth, and he also summarizes the work of Pred and others on the role of the hierarchy of cities. Watkins and Perry (1977) discuss the effects of interregional shifts on the urban hierarchy. As Stephens and Holly (1980, 179) note in discussing the impact of corporate headquarters locations on urban growth, "Both the urban hierarchy and the distribution of corporate influence [among cities] have a tendency toward long-term stability, probably because of the specialized information advantages noted by Pred: (1) greater inter-organization face-to-face contacts, (2) availability of specialized business services, and (3) high levels of intermetropolitan accessibility, advantages which seem to be self-reinforcing."

9. The Tiebout model of residential choice suggests that in metropolitan areas with several communities, people freely shop among communities seeking a "market bundle" of local government services that best fit their preferences. Although some therefore argue that having a variety of communities is beneficial in increasing the range of choice for mov-

versely, older housing, industrial facilities, congestion, air and noise pollution, high crime rates, poor schools, and concentrations of poor or minority populations are considered problems that repel movers, especially higher-status movers. Poorer city services and higher city tax burdens induce selective outmigration and thus cumulative urban decline, especially when there are wide fiscal disparities between cities and suburbs in the same metropolitan area.[10]

Conventional models do acknowledge that some types of households may prefer living in cities rather than in suburbs, although this is not stressed. Sociological theories consider life-cycle stage an important determinant of preferences. In part because of differentials observed in 1950, they expect both younger and older adults without children to find cities more attractive than do other households, while households in the child-raising stage are most attracted to suburbs. Alternate preferences are less integrated into economic models, but Kern (1981) has shown that the standard urban economics model locates young and single households nearer city centers when different preferences are assumed for different demographic groups.[11] Edel (1972b) demonstrated that the rich might well outbid the poor for central land within the standard model if the income elasticity of demand for proximity exceeds that for space. He argues that such preferences for proximity to the urban core do exist among the wealthy, and that their desire for urban residence is one of the reasons for the urban renewal program, since conversion of land to upper-income residences is difficult through normal market mechanisms.

In an intriguing geographical reformulation of the relationship between preferences and distance from the city center, Ley (1983) has argued that desires for location depend on the interaction of status, stimula-

---

ers, others note that different communities increase the incentives for excluding the poor from the local property tax base and services of wealthier communities. Examining such issues with 1970 data, Schneider and Logan (1982, 91) find that "in contrast to low-income families, high-income families cluster in suburban communities with higher fiscal resources, giving them greater policy options in choosing service levels and tax rates." See also Markusen, Saxenian, and Weiss 1981.

10. Bradbury, Downs, and Small (1982, 78–82) discuss the various "disamenity avoidance" theories that have been advanced. The role of fiscal disparities in promoting suburbanization has been documented and discussed thoroughly by ACIR (1967, 1973, and 1980). Bradbury, Downs, and Small (1982, 108) conclude from their study of 131 SMSAs that "SMSA disparities in taxes . . . increased suburbanization." Oakland (1979) reviews the sources and consequences of fiscal disparities and recommends policies to "neutralize adverse fiscal incentives."

11. Kern (1981) explicitly included centrally supplied activities and commodities in the formal "standard" model of residential choice and introduced differences in behavior by assuming different preferences for demographically different consumers. He differentiated childless households and unmarried adults, and also differentiated by education.

tion, and safety. He theorizes that psychic stimulation is greatest at the city center and declines monotonically with distance, that status is greater at the center and periphery than in the middle, and that safety increases with distance from the center. Among the urban amenities that have been shown to command higher rents are cultural activities, specialized retail shopping, historic neighborhoods, and distinctive architecture (Diamond 1980a; Ellickson 1981).

Such perceptions of the main determinants of intrametropolitan location underlie many of the policies aimed at renewing cities and their decaying downtowns. Urban renewal was specifically intended to fight blight: reducing slums, congestion, and obsolete buildings would, it was hoped, reinstate the downtown's role as shopping center for the metropolitan area while also attracting middle-income residents and new employment.[12] The variety of urban programs that followed urban renewal included provisions for housing rehabilitation, parks and recreational facilities, and other sprucing-up activities; Community Development Block Grants have "fighting slums and blight" as one of their two major goals. Much urban renewal funding supported institutional and office development to retain employment, as do the current Urban Development Action Grants.

The failure of such programs to stem urban decline has often been interpreted as implying that the economic and social forces underlying decentralization are too powerful to change. In particular, urban decline is thought to persist because it feeds on itself (Albin 1971; Heilbrun 1972). The hypothesis that "the problem of U.S. cities is the self-feeding flight of the middle classes to the suburbs," as Bradford and Kelejian (1973) put it, has been supported by both their findings and those of others. They argue that their results "clearly support the view that central cities are caught in a vicious circle, whereby the more rapidly the middle-class families move to the suburbs, the greater is the incentive for the exodus of those remaining. This feedback relationship is both direct—the location of the middle class depends directly on the fraction of the population in the central city that is poor—and indirect, through the fiscal system—the fewer the middle-class families in the city, the heavier the tax burden on all remaining families, especially the remaining middle-class families" (567).

---

12. Rothenberg (1972, 216) concludes: "Redevelopment has had a variety of explicit and implicit aims. The more significant ones seem to be:

1. The elimination of blight and slums.
2. The mitigation of poverty.
3. Provision of decent, safe, and sanitary housing in a suitable environment.
4. Revival of downtown areas of the central city.
5. Attraction of middle-income families from suburbs back to the central city.
6. Attraction of additional 'clean' industry into the central city.
7. Enhancement of the budget balance of the central city."

Which Factors Most Influence Intrametropolitan Location?

As even this truncated history suggests, it is generally agreed that individual decisions about intrametropolitan location, and the resulting residential patterns, depend on the interaction of personal preferences and economic forces. There is less agreement about the influence of public policies on suburbanization. Some argue that public policies played only minor roles compared to market forces; others stress that public decisions facilitated and accelerated suburbanization and still form the context in which decisions are made (Vaughn 1980; HUD 1980a). Many statistical efforts to determine the relative importance of "causal" factors aim to identify policies that can help stem urban decline. They seek to evaluate the relative efficacy of such policies as providing new housing, fighting crime, improving schools, reducing disparities in taxes and services, or subsidizing job creation or tourist developments.

Yet most of the econometric evidence developed over the past three decades has been interpreted to support the view that decentralization and suburbanization result mainly from economic evolution. Studies have found close ties between population decentralization and the spread of housing and jobs into the suburbs (Greenwood 1980; Bradbury et al. 1982). Although Kain (1975) hypothesized that the decentralization of employment preceded and induced that of population, results of simultaneous equation models of housing, employment, and population relocation since 1950 suggest that new housing has been more important than jobs in attracting population to the suburbs. In both the 1950s and the 1960s, population followed new housing and retail employment followed population to the suburbs, but the decentralization of manufacturing employment showed little relation to that of population (Greenwood 1980). Indeed, results by Steinnes (1977) suggest that manufacturing employment in cities induces outmigration.[13] Marshall (1979) also concluded that the location of new housing and the availability of space for residential development in cities were important in explaining suburbanization, but that the location of new housing did not respond to that of jobs.

The relative importance of city problems as "push" factors or of suburban amenities as "pulls" has been harder to evaluate.[14] Many studies have found that the presence of older housing in cities does deter popula-

---

13. Greenwood (1981) studies migration flows by the labor force from cities to suburbs and from suburbs to cities separately. He finds that central-city manufacturing, rather than increasing outmovement from the city, instead deters inmovement to the city from its suburbs and also reduces the likelihood that migrants to the SMSA will choose the city rather than its suburbs.

14. Follain and Malpezzi (1981) infer from city-suburb differentials in hedonic values of housing that both city blight and suburban accessibility have induced suburbanization.

tion growth and encourage outmigration (Bradbury et al. 1982). Air pollution, noise, dirty and littered streets, and abandoned housing have also been related to outmovement (Speare and Long 1985). The possibility that concentrations of poor people induce further selective outmigration is important to arguments that decline will be cumulative. This does appear to be the case, but the relative roles of poverty, minority concentrations, and higher crime rates have been hard to evaluate. One study found that crime and racial disturbances were not significant in explaining outmigration differences in the 1960s, if controls for concentrations of minorities or poverty were included (Marshall 1979; Droettboom et al. 1971).

Evidence on the deterrent effects of poverty or race is particularly unclear. One study showed the location of upper-income population in 1960 more strongly deterred by high proportions of poor population within central cities than by concentrations of black population (Bradford and Kelejian 1973). But another study found race to be an influential determinant of higher rates of suburban selection among better-educated white city movers in the late 1960s. Lower-status whites were attracted to job opportunities in the suburbs but deterred by higher tax rates there, while higher-status whites were more attracted by suburban services and repelled by black concentrations. Although Frey (1980) did not explicitly control for poverty concentrations in this research, he argued in his summary that white outmigration from central cities "responds to the central city racial composition, at least outside the South; that there exists a feedback relationship between flight levels and suburb-city disparities in public expenditures . . . ; and that both of these explanations are more important in accounting for the out-movement of a city's college-educated population than for out-movement at other status levels."

Yet, in testing both relative income and racial concentrations within a simultaneous model of intrametropolitan movement for two decades, Greenwood (1981) found that race influenced white outmigration less in the late 1960s than it had in the 1950s. He therefore speculated that the repelling effect of minority concentrations had declined over time. Analyzing the changing location of population by income and race for 106 SMSAs between 1960 and 1970, Grubb (1982) also found evidence that class rather than race considerations motivated suburbanization.[15] For the

---

15. Grubb (1982, 349) concludes that "differential mobility of upper-income and white residents has been a powerful force concentrating lower-income residents and nonwhites in central cities. Since upper-income residents tend to flee cities with concentrations of poor people, the process of 'class flight' is self-reinforcing; however, the analogous process of 'white flight,' describing the tendency of whites to flee concentrations of nonwhites, is not confirmed." Yet Mills and Price, studying differences in density functions in 1970, find evidence that race was still more of a deterrent to city residence than poverty at that time (Mills and Price 1984).

early 1970s, however, Bradbury, Downs, and Small still found racial con-centrations more important than poverty as a determinant of population change. Moreover, their evidence led them to conclude that poverty in central cities did not encourage further suburbanization: "Cities with lower relative incomes were not less attractive to higher-income residents and in fact showed greater subsequent relative income growth. This . . . unexpected finding . . . suggests that the divergence between cities and suburbs may tend to disappear in the absence of other conditions leading to slower city income growth" (1982, 101).

These studies deal variously with population, migration, or income changes, using different measures of income or poverty and different models at different time periods for different metropolitan areas over a twenty-year span. Thus, one can conclude only that the relative effects of poverty and race on possible revitalization are uncertain. In some com-bination, however, they do appear to reduce the likelihood of upper-status residence in cities and thus feed into the process of cumulative self-reinforcing decline.

Proxies used to measure amenities are less often found significant than either housing or employment, although amenities do appear to attract migrants. Farley (1965) found faster growth in upper-income suburbs in the 1950s. Greenwood (1980) interpreted the positive relationship be-tween labor force suburbanization and higher suburban income growth in the 1950s and 1960s as movement toward better neighborhood amenities in the suburbs. Frey (1980) found that better-educated white movers were particularly responsive to higher levels of educational expenditures in the suburbs. In addition, the finding that having more municipalities in an SMSA encouraged central city population losses appears to support the hypothesis that movers respond positively to opportunities to choose among many jurisdictions for their desired mix of services and tax levels (Bradbury, Downs, and Small 1982; but see Schneider and Logan 1982 for evidence that upper-income movers benefit most). Evidence that city-suburban disparities in tax levels influenced migration or population de-concentration, especially for higher-status movers, is also found in several studies (Frey 1980; Grubb 1982).

Such results imply that reversing suburbanization (or promoting urban revival) through public policies would be difficult. Frey (1980) tried to compare the impact upon suburbanization of factors capable of being in-fluenced by public policy and the effect of basic structural shifts in hous-ing and employment. He estimated how much outmigration to the sub-urbs would fall if tax and service disparities between cities and their suburbs were equalized and if city crime rates and concentrations of black population were reduced. The resulting reductions in outmigration over a five-year period would be very small—generally less than 10 percent—

even in cities that had the conditions most unattractive to highly educated migrants. When Bradbury, Downs, and Small (1981) simulated whether potential public policies could reduce urban decline in Cleveland, they concluded that an all-out revitalization strategy could accomplish "substantial though not complete revival," but that such strategies would be so expensive and politically difficult that they would be unlikely to be adopted.[16]

Econometric studies thus support the perception that housing growth and economic factors have been the primary forces behind population losses and suburbanization of population from central cities. Environmental attributes which movers prefer or dislike appear to have played a secondary role, and factors that can be influenced by public policy show up as least important. The hypothesis that selectively greater outmigration by upper-income families is self-reinforcing is also supported, implying that urban decline and distress are cumulative rather than self-correcting.

Two studies of the determinants of location in cities basically concur with the results of econometric studies of suburbanization in the relative importance they find for housing, jobs, amenities, and problems; but each suggests that employment is more important in retaining or attracting upper-income residents to cities than it appears to have been in suburbanization. Studying cities in which upper-income neighborhoods had persisted over time, James (1977a) found for 1970 that concentrations of office space, expenditures on entertainment services in the city, and the relative availability of single-family homes were important in distinguishing among cities.[17] In his study of upgrading within cities, Lipton (1977) examined the characteristics of cities having increases between 1960 and 1970 in the number of central tracts with above-average education or income. He also found that office space was the single most important correlate of improvement, while concentrations of blue-collar employment in the central city appeared to deter increases. The importance for urban

16. The policies in their "all-out" revitalization strategy included job stimulus, housing rehabilitation, transit improvements, fiscal equalization, and controls on suburban growth. By comparison with their "base case," in 1990 this comprehensive package would reduce the projected 1980–90 job loss by 50%, slightly reverse changes in households from a decrease to stability, reduce city unemployment rates from 8.5% to 6.8%, increase the tax capacity of the city and its school district by 17%, and raise city per capita income by $500 (in 1977 dollars). Bradbury, Downs, and Small 1981, 156–57.

17. James (1977a) also notes that there is no evidence in the data through 1970 that city life is newly attractive to well-to-do families. Instead, the percentage of families or individuals in the SMSAs who live in cities tends to decline both with income and over time. But this pattern differs across cities. Monotonic decreases by income in the proportion of SMSA population living in the central city characterize Boston, Philadelphia, Detroit, St. Louis, and Newark. But in some cities this relationship is "U-shaped," with the city housing a higher proportion of the SMSA's upper-income residents than of the SMSA's middle-income residents. James found this alternate pattern in Washington, D.C., New Orleans, Denver, New York, and Pittsburgh.

revival of access to jobs was further supported by his evidence that improvement was more likely in cities with longer commuting distances between the central business district and the suburban fringe.

Although these studies identify factors that should be considered in evaluating chances for revival, there are still many reasons to conclude that we know relatively little about what will determine future intrametropolitan location decisions. In addition to the usual statistical limitations, the econometric studies are flawed by imperfect data and by the possibility that the models tested are time- and culture-specific. Since most of the data used are available only for several dates in the postwar period, studies can at best "explain" cross-sectional differences rather than change over time; annexation and metropolitan area growth or redefinition mean that even the available data are often not comparable over time; and crucial variables cannot be measured. Even when data are available, aggregations of all central cities in each metropolitan area or of all suburbs—defined as the non-central-city remainder of the SMSA— mask crucial detail.[18] Most basically, cross-sectional studies of differences among cities cannot evaluate the impact of national changes which affect all cities, including economic evolution, structural changes, and changes in national public policy. Nor can cross-sectional studies offer guidance about trend reversals.

In particular, despite the significance repeatedly found for variables considered proxies for economic evolution, these studies do not prove that public policies are unimportant. Both housing production and job location have been strongly influenced by federal subsidies and by local policies such as those on zoning and annexation, and public influence on these factors has burgeoned over the past several decades. Moreover, the few studies that have attempted to measure suburbanization over a longer time frame using consistent measures find evidence that suburbanization accelerated markedly in the 1950s (Mills 1972; Taeuber 1972). Although postwar prosperity undoubtedly accounts for some of this acceleration, it also is consistent with hypotheses that federal mortgage subsidies and highway construction after the war encouraged and supported suburbanization.

Suburban boundaries provide a clear example of the influence of political decisions on city distress (Norton 1979, ch. 5). Cities that are able to annex freely as fringe land is developed are likely to decentralize with

18. Research done by sociologists, social ecologists, and geographers has documented the extent of spatial variation in social class, race, and life cycle (the three dimensions usually found to be most important) among and within communities (Johnston 1971; Berry 1972; Ley 1983). Past studies have found that such differences in social status among suburbs within metropolitan areas persist over time; Logan and Schneider (1981) further show that inequality among suburbs increased between 1960 and 1970 in metropolitan areas with fragmented governmental structure.

growth and technological change (Mills 1972), and they may lose comparative advantage to other cities as they age. Status differentials among neighborhoods within such cities are also likely, but in the absence of separately incorporated suburban communities with different levels of taxes and services outside city boundaries, the dynamics underlying cumulative decline are less likely to begin.[19] Yet annexing new territory to cities or fighting annexation through suburban incorporation are political decisions. Political economists argue that state controls over city annexations at the turn of the century were imposed for political reasons. And cases such as San Antonio show that attempts to exclude poverty while seeking to control tax revenue continue.[20] Indeed, the Reagan administration is now arguing that since cities are creatures of the states, responsibility for city problems should be returned to states.

Other biased policies can also worsen urban decline. Federal subsidies for homeownership and highways are usually cited, along with tax code biases toward new construction rather than toward maintenance and rehabilitation (Vaughn 1980; HUD 1980a). Local decisions also contribute, as in growth controls or large-lot zoning in suburban areas to exclude the poor (Downs 1973, 1979). Jurisdictional fragmentation at the local level additionally reinforces tendencies to help the poor in their place of residence, thus usually continuing their relative concentration in central cities. Busing to achieve school integration has been cited as another public policy that hurts cities by inducing white flight (Coleman 1978).[21]

Alternative Interpretations

Although much evidence is inconsistent with expectations drawn from simplified models of intrametropolitan location and evolution, these mod-

19. In 1941, for example, Hoyt cautioned that the presence of "numerous independent political subdivisions . . . with differences in tax rates, zoning and municipal regulations" promotes decentralization, because of "movement of people working in the city to communities with lower taxes on metropolitan fringes" (844).

20. In a revealing variant on more typical city-suburban differences over annexation, San Antonio, Texas, was recently ordered to annex poor suburban territory along with the richer areas it was annexing. Fleischman (1977) reviews in detail the political context of decisions about annexation there since World War II.

Gordon (1977b) argues that annexation of outlying residential districts became much less common after 1910 not because of "some exogenous shift in people's preferences about suburban autonomy" but because manufacturers moving from cities wanted to avoid city taxes as well: "After industrialists joined the movement against central city extension, political fragmentation was the natural consequence" (77).

21. Coleman (1978) cites policies toward both school desegregation and crime as "egalitarian" social policies that have the unintended effect of weakening central cities. The voluminous literature and arguments on the influence of school desegregation and busing on white flight are well summarized in Clotfelter (1979).

els appear useful because they summarize the main trends of recent decades. But they are criticized for failing to describe adequately the complexity of the urban mosaic, for implying a unilateral trend of development, and for reflecting only particular cultural, economic, and institutional structures. These criticisms raise considerations that are relevant for assessing chances of revival. They direct more attention to the conditions under which revival might occur and emphasize the influence of political conflict and financial interests on the development of urban areas.

The concentric-ring theory of urban growth implies that cities evolve by growth at the fringe and deterioration in the center. But the persistence and reemergence of higher-status neighborhoods within some central cities provide striking counterexamples to these expectations.[22] Hoyt's study of the location of the rich and the poor in central cities in 1939 identified concentrations of upper-income residents in quite central locations in many cities, and other studies have documented the persistence of upper-income neighborhoods within central cities (Johnston 1971). The experience of various neighborhoods around the country, moreover, demonstrates that formerly lower-class or impoverished areas have revived. Such findings underlie alternate theories which do not consider downward filtering inevitable. Instead, areas near a strong urban core may experience stagnation and deterioration followed by upgrading and renewal: "At some point in time the land occupied by an old slum becomes too valuable to justify its use as an old slum. Its inhabitants become too weak politically to hold on to it. Property is then reacquired, leveled or rehabilitated and put to more efficient use such as high-income apartments, office buildings, or public housing" (Birch 1971). Frieden's study of old neighborhoods (1964) points up the importance of local conditions for such redevelopment. The likelihood of rebuilding old neighborhoods depends on the balance between site cost and reuse value, which varies with regional structure in terms of locational advantage, availability of alternatives, and the existing density.[23]

22. An example of the pitfalls of generalizing from cross-sectional differences can be seen in Schnore and Jones (1968). They hypothesized that an "evolutionary sequence" of urban residential patterns might exist: (1) smaller and younger central cities tend to be occupied by local elites, with suburban areas containing the lower strata. With growth and passage of time (2) the central city becomes the main residential area for both highest and lowest strata, with middle classes being overrepresented in the suburbs. (3) Finally, suburbs become the semiprivate preserve of both the upper and middle strata, while central cities are given over to the lowest stratum. (Davis [1965] had also found evidence cross-sectionally that there were fewer middle than upper class living in cities during the 1950s.) But this hypothesis was not supported by the data when Schnore and Jones looked at changes over time. It can be equally dangerous to observe revival in several cities or neighborhoods and infer that this is now the general trend.

23. Like the discussion of cost factors by Edel and Rothenberg (1972, 3) and by Bradbury, Downs, and Small, however, these theories have been more likely to consider the precondi-

The criticisms most relevant for studying revival are that conventional models with poor households in the city center are both culture specific and period specific—that they reflect only American land use patterns resulting from particular periods of development and legal constraints, and not all American cities at that. Location patterns in which richer residents live in the urban center have been shown to characterize cities in developing nations now, and American and European cities prior to the industrial revolution.[24] Schnore's work (1965, 1972) demonstrates that in the 1950s and 1960s, many urban areas in the U.S. had cities with higher-status residents than their suburbs. Downs (1972) contends that the prevalent U.S. pattern is actually atypical, and that it is mainly due to zoning that outlaws construction of new low-quality housing on the undeveloped fringes of cities. Criticisms from a Marxist perspective are most explicit in considering conventional theories applicable at best to a specific historical situation, and in arguing how and why urban form might change. Gordon (1977b, 61) argues that rather than growth being gradual and evolutionary, the basic urban form and structure in the United States have been qualitatively transformed over the past two centuries in ways that correspond to the three main stages of capital accumulation: commercial accumulation, industrial accumulation, and advanced corporate (or monopoly) accumulation.[25] Extrapolating to the future, Fainstein and Fainstein (1982) theorize that the economic system is now evolving toward international monopoly capitalism and that certain American cities may be "restructuring" toward a European model in which the rich tend to be centrally located in cities.[26]

---

tions for profitably redeveloping central land at higher densities than factors that would encourage rehabilitation of existing structures.

24. Williams (1984) reviews the "fragmentary" evidence of gentrification in Europe, noting that it is associated with clearance in Paris but with rehabilitation in London. He also observes that location patterns are "interestingly different" in Eastern Europe. There, significant levels of residential segregation in a number of cities "has produced a pattern the inverse of the classic ecological model with the wealthy at the center and the poor displaced to the periphery" (224).

25. Gordon (1977b) also discusses some of the distinguishing characteristics of urban form in each stage. The commercial cities, which also served as transport nodes, had little obvious socioeconomic residential segregation, although the poor were isolated on the outskirts. The industrial city located new segregated working-class housing districts near downtown industrial districts, while middle and upper classes tended to escape from the industrial districts. The corporate city saw the development of central business districts and political fragmentation of metropolitan areas, although cities developed in this era tend to have no centralized working-class housing districts. Watkins (1980) discusses how different cities in the United States were shaped by the stages of capitalism at their time of greatest growth and develops procedures to date the period of main growth.

26. However, Stave (1982, 185), on the basis of David Goldfield's study of the renewal of European cities, observes that "while most of the urban Europe's ancient historic centers are being preserved, the not-so-historic districts near the old centers are suffering."

The Fainsteins' discussion of the conjunction of many factors that together may restructure some cities exemplifies the dynamic perspective and attention to differences over time and among cities that Marxist explanations of urban development provide. As Richardson (1977) notes, the Marxist perspective contributes real people struggling in real time to the often sterile perspectives of conventional theory. Marxist explanations do not disagree that factors such as technology and income changes are important in influencing urban form, particularly suburbanization.[27] But Marxists argue that to understand rather than merely describe changing urban form, one must consider the uses and development of land in the context of the prevailing mode of production, both the economic system and its interaction with social and political forces. In a capitalistic society such as the United States, both the constant pressure to accumulate profits and the resulting conflicts within and between capital and labor interests form the context in which economic and political decisions about urban development are made.[28]

Thus, the needs of capital for profitability and accumulation are important in influencing the location, form, and timing of urban development. Gordon (1977, 61) argues that the process of capital accumulation has been the most important factor structuring the growth of cities, with "the transitions between stages of urban development predominantly influenced by problems of class control."[29] Harvey (1973) contends that the financial superstructure that supports and promotes large-scale suburbanization was adopted by capitalism as a way to stimulate consumption during the Depression, so that now the welfare of capitalism and suburbanization are inextricably linked.[30] Similarly, Smith (1979, 1984) hypothesizes that

27. Edel (1981) points out that some urban phenomena—e.g., fiscal weakness of local tax bases, segregation of housing markets by class—can be linked to capital accumulation through simple causation. For such phenomena, Marxist explanations are not too different from other simple economic determinisms like neoclassical economics or social ecology, although "Marxists will be more attuned to problems raised by growth and crises or to differences between the actions of different classes" than are conventional observers.

28. Analytic case studies of redevelopment in five cities (Fainstein and Fainstein, 1983) illustrate how reproduction of cities in a capitalist society depends on both private and public decisions in a complex interaction. Government plays a critical role because it helps disparate business interests to act collectively (with, however, a systematic bias toward the interests of business firms and elite institutions) and mediates conflicts among opposing social groups.

29. Edel (1981) claims, however, that although American suburbanization was instituted because of class conflicts and rising costs of social reproduction, it was not the only possible solution to urban crisis then. Instead, suburbanization was selected through class conflict, as working-class struggles eliminated other possible solutions, such as declining housing standards or the company town.

30. Sawyers (1975) discusses how suburbanization and the interests of capital accumulation interact. He argues that suburbanization became an "interactive, snowballing process"

"the need to earn profit [is] a more decisive initiative behind gentrification than consumer preference." Rather than resulting mainly from autonomous changes in consumer preferences, gentrification occurs only where rent gaps, due in large part to previous disinvestment and redlining by investors, make reinvestment of capital in inner areas profitable.

(Mis)interpretations of Marxist arguments imply that the mode of production or the needs of capital determine everything.[31] But although they argue over specifics, most Marxists agree that it is simplistic to think that urban form reflects only the needs of capital or only the influence of the class struggle.[32] Instead, the interests of capital are far from monolithic (Fainstein and Fainstein 1983), and conflicts and disagreements among differing interests within both capital and labor influence urban outcomes.[33] In addition to stressing the influence of conflicting interests on urban change, Marxists provide an important dynamic perspective as they ana-

---

in large part because of automobiles: "Once people buy cars, moving to suburbs becomes feasible. Once they move . . . they demand more roads . . . once the auto industry becomes sufficiently large, it has the political clout to force the building of more roads. Thus all of these factors feed off or and reinforce the others" (54). He argues that all these factors can be linked directly to capitalism: transportation technology is privately owned and is developed to make profits from land speculation; and preferences for land result from pressure of capitalism for consumerism and income segmentation.

31. For example, Guterbock (1980, 430), discussing theories about gentrification, says that "Marxists give primacy to economic forces, but see these as manifestations of the power of the ruling class, which builds and rebuilds the city to advance its own interests." Therefore, "the phenomena of inner-city revitalization is just one more mechanism for exploitation by the rich and middle class." City governments have a direct interest in gentrification because of their dependence on tax revenues, and city decision-making processes are dominated by industrial, commercial, realty, and construction interests.

32. Gottdiener (1983, 235) cites as "reductionist" both Gordon's explanation of suburbanization as an example of class-conflict theory, which views industrial location decisions primarily as a response to labor unrest, and Harvey's explanation that massive subsidization of homeownership was a bribe by capitalists to the working class. He argues instead: "Because specific features of development prove useful to the reproduction of capitalism, this does not demonstrate that capitalism is endowed with a teleological impulse nor that the capitalist class operates with a prescience that exceeds the bounds of credulity." Gottdiener cites approvingly Walker's consideration of both demand-side and supply-side factors in suburbanization (through the relationships between real estate investment and the cycles of capitalist accumulation), noting that the class struggle plays a role but that it is only one part of the process by which the capitalist system reproduces itself.

33. Edel (1981, 41) argues that more than one combination of institutions or policies may be compatible with accumulation, so that "working-class pressure may determine which one will emerge." Therefore, class struggle must be considered in explaining observed urban phenomena. Although specific outcomes must be consistent with accumulation to survive, the actual outcomes are not logically deducible from the existence of the capitalist mode of production or from the tendency to accumulation. Therefore, "Concrete analysis of the links involved, and the identification of opportunities for working-class intervention, become the tasks of radical urban analysis."

lyze the contradictions that arise within the urban development process.[34] Detailed studies of politics and processes underlying urban redevelopment in five American cities (Fainstein et al. 1983) provide good examples of the insights possible with this approach: these studies discuss how local circumstances, the needs of capital for access and profits, and the relative power of different classes interact to influence the outcomes of redevelopment attempts in different contexts.

These perspectives supplement conventional hypotheses about the factors influencing development over time in cities and the relative likelihood of revival or further decline. Although all would agree that the location of housing and employment opportunities are important in explaining intrametropolitan location patterns, Marxists in particular often "go beyond the explanations of autonomous preferences or tastes usually used by orthodox analysis" (Edel 1981, 38). Longer historical perspectives highlight the ways in which political structure and conflicts among different interests shape the contexts for the profit- or utility-maximizing decisions studied in conventional economic analyses. In particular, the Marxian perspectives underscore the importance of factors influencing the *supply* of new or rehabilitated housing, particularly the availability of financing and the influence of profits and speculation on decisions about real estate investments in different locations. Marxists further show how decisions of urban policymakers tend to be biased toward the interests of elites, even in cities with working-class representation (Fainstein and Fainstein 1983, ch. 7), and their contention that political decisions are embedded in the prevailing mode of production also reaffirms the potential importance of industrial transformation to future urban development.

What Have Trends in Major Factors Implied for Revival?

During the 1970s, many developments in these major determinants of intrametropolitan location suggested that distressed central cities were un-

34. As a contradiction within metropolitan development in U.S. cities, Sawyers (1975) cites the need of the ruling class of monopoly capitalism for small, geographically concentrated administrative centers, which are usually now in central business districts, "yet because of deteriorating nature of the central city . . ., [the administrative bureaucracy] must live ever-increasing distances from their jobs." He judges both urban renewal—"which expropriated the land of the poor, in town, and built luxury apartments or commercial developments" (65)—and rapid rail transit to be attempts of the ruling class to resolve this contradiction.

Similarly, Harvey (1973) argues that the direct relation between the need of capitalism to promote effective demand through suburbanization and the dynamics of urban spatial structure leads to two contradictions: "Speculative suburban development to boost profitability [is] successful only at the expense of central cities, in which financial institutions are directly involved as holders of long-term debt" (221). Also, the suburbanization associated with shaping a city as a consumption system conflicts with its efficiency as a production unit.

likely to revive. Nationally, population decentralized out from SMSAs, reversing a long pattern of net migration into metropolitan areas; regionally, selective net outmigration from the Frostbelt to the Sunbelt further weakened northern SMSAs. Intraregionally, housing and employment continued to decentralize, and distressed cities became poorer and blacker. Despite intergovernmental transfers to central cities, fiscal disparities between cities and their suburbs generally widened. Thus as decentralization continued and spread, many of the dynamics and city-suburban disparities thought to encourage cumulative decline worsened, particularly in the North.

But some national and local developments of the 1970s were more favorable to distressed cities. Although suburbanization continued, it slowed in the early 1970s from earlier rates (Bradbury et al. 1983). Higher costs of financing, building, and owning homes reduced housing construction, raising both incentives to reuse existing stock and profits from doing so. Industrial transformation from manufacturing toward advanced services proceeded, potentially strengthening central business districts and other urban employment bases. Energy prices skyrocketed, encouraging residence nearer to work or to mass transit routes. Demographic factors and complementary life-style changes increased the number of households that have traditionally chosen urban residence, while renewed interest in historic preservation focused attention and resources on older neighborhoods. Completion of long-term urban renewal projects and funding for urban parks and neighborhood rehabilitation reduced blight in many distressed cities. Such developments affected both housing and employment, the two main factors thought to influence past intrametropolitan location. They may also have increased preferences for living in cities and the profits to be made by providing housing there.[35]

Housing, Costs, and Profits

New housing was still built predominantly in suburban areas during the 1970s, but construction lagged behind household formation in the late 1970s and early 1980s. Construction levels were particularly low in the North, and excessive abandonment of central-city housing contributed to scarcity there (Berry 1982). But although growth in real income slowed, even among households with two workers, inflation plus tax incentives for homeownership made ownership particularly desirable. Higher housing costs and housing scarcity also increased condominium and cooperative

35. In addition, studies of cities with "no growth" reveal such apparently positive developments as increases in homeownership and community ties (Rust 1979). Declines in rural-to-urban migration could reduce pressures on cities to assimilate poor inmigrants (Porter 1976), although immigration from abroad increased for some cities. Newitt (1983) argues that foreign immigration can contribute to city revitalization because of the diversity and energy such immigrants contribute.

ownership; although these forms of ownership also occur in suburbs, their new popularity reduced the bias toward suburban residence previously inherent in tax subsidies for owners. Housing shortages also increased incentives to utilize, renovate, and convert existing stock: in the late 1970s, there were no net removals from the housing stock. Such pressures made older central-city housing relatively more attractive, an advantage heightened by price differentials between city and suburban housing (Malpezzi, Ozanne, and Thibodeau 1980; Lowry 1980) and sharp increases in oil prices.[36] Increasing attention to historic preservation and tax incentives for renovation of pre-1940 buildings also favored older cities.

Greater demand for city housing also increased the profitability of investing in city housing. Smith (1979) argues that gentrification reflects movement of capital, rather than people, back to cities, as policies restricting redlining together with the substantial amount of public capital invested in urban redevelopment made artificially devalued central land once again a good investment.[37]

Employment and Industrial Transformation

During the 1970s, employment in all major industries continued to decentralize from central cities and from the North to the South and West (Nelson 1984; Greenwood 1984). Industries became more "footloose" as communications technology improved and production facilities were more often sited apart from headquarters. Simultaneously, the composition of employment continued to shift toward services, particularly "high-level" services such as business, legal, and health services (Noyelle and Stanback 1983; Phillips and Vidal 1984). This transformation from "goods to information processing" has been most extensive in central cities, which attract health, education, and business support services. Noyelle and Stanback argue that such shifts in employment do not necessarily mean that goods production requires less labor, but rather that technological and organizational changes shift employment to advanced services supporting goods production. But even if the total number employed does not vary, such compositional shifts affect different cities differently. Cities

36. The sharp increases in oil prices in 1974 and 1979 caused much speculation about reviving cities, but the eventual consensus has been that adjustments would be made more in size and fuel efficiency of automobiles than in residential location (Bradbury, Downs, and Small 1981; Solomon 1980).

37. Smith (1979), like Harvey (1973, 1981), argues that financial institutions played a major role in redlining cities and directing financing to suburbs. Walker (1981) similarly argues that property capital and the land development process propelled suburbanization through land speculation, channeling capital flows and creating state support for it. Financial institutions were also important in backing suburban mortgages while redlining inner-city neighborhoods.

with branch plants may be adversely impacted as they become more dependent on decisions made elsewhere (Bluestone and Harrison 1982).
Large cities, however, may benefit. "Headquarters" functions are more
likely to locate in major cities in the urban hierarchy for access to legal,
advertising, and financial services that require contact and access and cannot be stockpiled.[38] Thus, even in many of the large distressed cities of
the Northeast, growth in health, legal, and government employment during the 1970s was sufficient to balance other employment losses (Bunce
and Neal 1983). Since the well-educated professionals who work in advanced services tend to be the "yuppies" prominent in accounts of gentrification, and since office employment in the central business district
has been related to upper-status residence, industrial transformation
should encourage residential revival as well.

Preferences for Cities

The possibility that more people are coming to prefer central-city residence has been repeatedly advanced as an explanation for gentrification.
Scholarly accounts invoke sociocultural explanations of desire for neighborhood, community, and stimulation (Laska and Spain 1980; Ley 1983;
Palen and London 1984). One version of this argument is essentially based
on compositional shifts: changes in age structure and household types
have increased the numbers and shares of groups—such as young adults
and unmarried individuals without children—with relatively high residence in cities. Other versions, even more favorable to cities, claim that
preferences for city living have increased absolutely as new value is as-
cribed to community, diversity, distinctive housing, and so on.

Over the 1970s, population and household composition definitely
changed. Later marriage, lower fertility, and higher divorce rates brought
more adult-oriented households with less concern about the child-rearing
and familial advantages offered by suburbs and more interest in the "bright
lights" of cities. The growing number of two-earner families suggests that
access to employment, shopping, services, and entertainment might be
more important in residential choices (Palen and London 1984, 259).

The "demographic factor," as Alonso terms it, is the prime mover in
this list. The maturing of the baby boom generation meant that there
were 10 million more persons aged 25–34 in 1985 than in 1975. The num-

---

38. Stephens and Holley (1980, 163) conclude: "Usually the controlling headquarters
operation is located in an economically diversified metropolitan center at or near the apex of
the urban hierarchy." Similarly, Borchert (1978, 215) argues that "large organizations shape
the evolving pattern of the nation. . . . these organizational headquarters have been major
shapers of the images of downtown districts, cities and regions. They have influenced regional differences in tax base and philanthropy."

ber of elderly persons has also increased rapidly, and cities often provide better access to services and shopping for those unable to drive.[39] Such dramatic social changes as delayed fertility, increased female labor force participation, and more adults living alone are accentuated by the sheer size of the young adult cohort. Before the post-1980 increase in interest rates, moreover, this cohort was buying homes at faster rates than earlier cohorts, despite delays in marriage and child-rearing (HUD 1982). Larry Long argues that demography may be the main cause of back-to-the-city phenomena: "A life cycle effect (persons in their 20's traditionally being attracted to cities) may be interacting with a cohort effect (more people in their 20's) to boost city populations at this age group, while other trends such as smaller households, more two-earner households and the rising prices of single family homes may keep more of this group in the cities" (1980a, 63). Similarly, Frey and Kobrin (1982) note that the decades of fastest suburbanization, the 1950s and 1960s, were characterized by familism, when fertility was high and a large proportion of households were raising children. Very different attitudes toward family and individual responsibilities now interact with the size and household composition of the baby boom to provide a possible explanation for slower suburbanization.

But compositional changes may not be the only explanation: preferences for older cities could also have increased absolutely.[40] The Bicentennial and historic preservation stimulated recognition of the amenities of older cities. Creative remodeling of distinctive houses has been both personally and financially rewarding. Attendance at cultural activities, which still tend to be located in large cities, has grown, possibly because higher educational levels have enlarged the pool of those valuing cultural attractions. And, as Hoyt noted five decades ago, development tends to move toward areas of higher status. Gentrification has spawned publicity about remodeled houses, in-town living, and exotic foods and thus conferred status on such accoutrements; and status itself tends to be self-perpetuating.

These explanations tend to be complementary rather than contradictory. For example, the sheer size of the young adult cohort increased demand for housing; explanations invoking changing values often refer to the experiences of young adults; and as high-level services expand, they are more likely to employ well-educated young professionals. Indeed,

39. Cybriwksy (1980, 32) speculates: "There are some indications that the market is broadening (beyond young well-educated professionals) to include substantial numbers of financially secure retirees who are being drawn to close-in locations by the cultural and entertainment facilities they offer."

40. For example, London and Palen (1984, 16) offer as a sociocultural explanation for gentrification: "It is entirely possible that greater proportions of our population are now developing a prourban value system. . . . If such value changes are under way, they may have a tendency to become cumulative. People often do what is vogue."

many of these factors interacting together may be necessary for revival, with none alone sufficient. Fainstein and Fainstein (1982), for example, cite demography, expansion of the service sector, the "prominence" of the city, and the opportunity for large speculative gains as all important, and they also consider the absence of the poor a prerequisite for urban revival.[41] Yet, as the next section indicates, the future course of revitalization may depend heavily on which of these explanations predominate.

Summary and Outlook

Even though older distressed cities are more likely to have lower-status populations than their suburbs and selective outmigration tends to be self-reinforcing, this review of the literature suggests that cities need not inevitably become poorer and poorer. European examples show that alternative location patterns exist in other advanced economies, and the persistence of upper-status neighborhoods within older central cities demonstrates similar possibilities in the United States. Some recent developments in housing, employment, and population favor increased demand for central-city housing, both generally and among higher-status groups. Completion of urban renewal projects that had been underway for many years and such public policies as pressures against redlining and for equal opportunity should reinforce positive developments.

But increasing population loss and distress in many cities over the 1970s implies that such developments may be inadequate to overcome factors reinforcing continued decline. Moreover, even if migration improves, the probability of further revival within cities is likely to differ, depending on which factors most influence past and future decisions of movers to and from each city. The major factors offered as explanations for past gentrification could have very different long-run implications for cities. Absolute increases in preferences for urban living, especially among higher-status groups, would be more likely to support ongoing revival over the next several decades than would preference "changes" that re-

41. Fainstein and Fainstein (1982) claim that since the mid-1970s, the downtown is again becoming a source of profit in some "prominent" cities as uses change from port, factory, and working class, to office, tourist center, and upper-class neighborhoods. Almost all cities hope to attract such activity, but only some go beyond "islands of hopeful development (most of which are publicly funded) . . . [to] a new urban core with a complete connecting fabric of structures and activities." They consider the difference to be the "context of increasing private investment" (165), with changes in demography and an expansion of the service sector as contributory causes. But to realize such development, cities have to overcome the domination of the core by impoverished racial and ethnic minorities. Moreover, the Fainsteins believe that such transformations through private investment occur only when interaction of a number of variables (e.g., suburbs' restricting growth and cities' subsidizing development) have produced opportunity for larger speculative gains through turnover of properties.

sult mainly from recent shifts in age composition. Greater preferences for stimulation, community, diversity, older housing, and historic areas might provide a basis for a lasting turnaround that spreads to many central areas.[42] But if gentrification to date stems mainly from the size of the baby-boom cohort passing through their twenties, city population and households may drop quickly as the baby "bust" ages in the 1980s and 1990s.[43]

Different reasons for choosing city housing also could have very different implications for city futures. If rehabilitation and purchase of city housing increased in the 1970s primarily in response to anticipated speculative gains, slowing inflation and slower appreciation in housing values could sharply reduce demand for inner-city development. Similarly, if city housing was increasingly chosen by households with constrained incomes because it was cheaper, such increased demand for housing might bolster cities in the short run. However, in the longer run an influx of lower-income persons could widen income and fiscal disparities between cities and their suburbs, thus worsening the pressures that induce selective outmigration and cumulative decline.

Next to major increases in preferences for cities, an ongoing transformation to an advanced service economy seems most encouraging for cities. Much of the planning associated with urban renewal and urban redevelopment is based on the hope that services will save our cities. Kasarda (1983) argues that service employment provides opportunities for revitalization now, and Sternlieb and Hughes (1983) seem to concur. However, it is unlikely that such developments would help all areas and all cities. Fainstein and Fainstein agree that worldwide transformation to an advanced economy can restructure cities, but they do not believe this will occur for all cities. Noyelle and Stanback also doubt that the economic transformation they document can help all areas. Instead, they contend that the economic transformation is causing an emerging dichotomy in U.S. urban structure, as wealth is redistributed toward cities that are "well-positioned in terms of the production and export of high level services" (1983, 226). Because of factors such as the growth of large corpora-

42. The publications (and advertisements therein) of the National Trust for Historic Preservation report on instances of rehabilitation of pre-1940 buildings all over the country.

43. Newitt (1983, 29) shows how "big cities have been benefitting from the sheer size of the baby-boom generation, and its record-breaking proportion of college graduates," but she also documents how drastically growth in the 25–34-year-old age group in the 1970s is likely to switch to decline and worse in the 1980s and 1990s for many of the older northern cities. Unless these cities do better proportionally in retaining and attracting population in the "gentrifying ages" in the 1980s than they have done in the 1970s, the numbers in these age groups "could decline by amounts ranging from 25 percent in Chicago to as much as 51 percent in Cleveland. In San Francisco, Washington, and Boston . . . there could be exceptional declines in the 24-to-34 age groups" (39).

tions, they see an evolving hierarchy of metropolitan areas, with large command and control centers particularly well positioned for continued growth but with the future less assured for SMSAs further down in the hierarchy. With the corporate complex of headquarters requiring access, specialized services, face-to-face contact, and the other advantages Hoover and Vernon first noted for downtown location, at least some cities may be aided by transformation of SMSA employment. But since the research of Noyelle and Stanback is couched in terms of metropolitan areas, it does not even follow that all *central cities* of favored SMSAs will share equally in the benefits of providing advanced services. Instead, suburbs could capture both the office industries and the upscale residences and retail opportunities that accompany them.

Distinguishing clearly among these alternative hypotheses is probably impossible. In the first place, they are often linked: the demand for home-ownership was heightened by a conjunction of the maturing baby boom, inflation, and the tax advantages of homeownership. Furthermore, as dis-cussed above, statistical techniques and data may well be unequal to the task. Nevertheless, to provide a firmer basis for speculation about future revival, I attempt, in the next two chapters, to determine not only *whether* past selective outmigration from cities has slowed or reversed, but also where and why such changes have occurred. Chapter 3 reviews national sample data on all migration to and from cities by age during the 1970s to determine the extent to which migration to cities was altered only by changes in household or age composition, particularly by the large group of young adults. Claims of newly greater preferences for cities would im-ply, alternatively, that we should observe higher rates of movement to cities (or lower rates of movement from cities) by specific age groups. In Chapter 4, I examine the characteristics of the forty large cities studied to infer which of these possible explanations appears most consistent, both logically and econometrically, with changes observed after 1970 in the proportion of movers to and within each metropolitan area who select residences in its central cities.

3. National and Regional Changes in Central-City Migration During the 1970s

Although accelerating population losses and net outmigration from individual cities imply that net outmigration from central cities had generally been under way for several decades before 1970, total migration to and from all central cities of metropolitan areas (SMSAs)[1] was not explicitly measured in the United States until estimates of net migration between 1960 and 1970 were made from 1970 census data.[2] According to these estimates, "in the 1960s central cities lost 3,400,000 persons through net outmigration, suburban rings gained in excess of 8,600,000 through net inmigration, and nonmetro areas lost 2,300,000" (Tucker 1984, 541). During the 1970s, sample data revealed some changes in migration which suggest that central cities became more attractive—or at least less unattractive—to migrants. In the second half of the decade, central cities as a group still

1. "Movement" denotes any change of residence. "Migration" is usually restricted to movement over long distances, and in the United States, it has usually meant movement across a county line. Because many suburbs are located in the same county as a central city of their Standard Metropolitan Statistical Area (SMSA), intrametropolitan movement between city and suburbs is thus, technically, often not "migration." However, "migration" is defined in this study to include intrametropolitan movement across a central-city boundary in addition to longer-distance migration to, from, or among metropolitan areas. "Movers" then include both "migrants" and those moving within a city (or among the central cities of an SMSA with several central cities) or within the suburbs of a metropolitan area. Following the standard Census Bureau terminology, suburbs are defined as the non-central-city residual of each SMSA. In most of the work reported here, each SMSA is defined as the central cities and contiguous counties included in the 1970 census definition (See U.S. Bureau of the Census 1971 or 1972 for the exact definitions of the counties and central cities of the metropolitan areas in 1970).

2. In, and prior to, the 1970 census, the customary practice in presenting data on migration was to categorize migrants moving between counties by their previous (same/different) state of residence. This procedure was followed in most 1970 census publications and in the *Current Population Reports* series. This convention does not show whether the previous residence of an inmigrant to a central city was another county of the same central city (as might occur in New York City, which has five counties), a suburb of the same SMSA, another SMSA, or a nonmetropolitan area. Since 1973, however, both the *Current Population Reports* and the Annual Housing Survey have published information on intrametropolitan flows between central cities and their suburbs.

52

lost migrants on net, but they had more inmigrants and fewer outmigrants. In spite of these favorable shifts in migration, however, deconcentration of population from cities continued.

This chapter examines national and regional migration for two periods (1970–75 and 1975–80) to ascertain why central cities attracted and retained more migrants in the second half of the decade. To infer reasons for migration changes, I consider the characteristics of the migrants of particular interest. Did central cities attract higher shares of any groups, especially higher-status migrants? Or were migration improvements due mainly to compositional effects, particularly changes in household and/or age composition (Long 1980, 66)? Changes in many of the demographic, economic, and social factors considered salient for revitalization lead us to expect that cities attracted more migrants between 1975 and 1980 than earlier in the decade.

Secondly, the selectivity of migration is studied to see if the types of people moving to and from central cities changed more than migration rates during the 1970s. Although by 1978 migration had apparently not reduced median income gaps between cities and their suburbs (Long and Dahmann 1980), trends in migration rates by education and income suggest that cities are indeed attracting and retaining more young professionals and other higher-status groups.

The review of interregional and intraregional flows in the third section of the chapter shows that cities in the Northeast and North Central regions, where distress is most common, shared in the decade's changes, but that the largest improvements occurred in the South. Finally, actual migration changes during the 1970s are compared with 1979 survey responses on residential preferences and likely migration between 1979 and 1984.

Favorable Developments in the 1970s

With the maturing of the baby boom generation and the flexing of oil-state muscles, three national developments favorable to cities in the 1970s were numerical growth in the young adult age group, spiraling energy costs and resulting inflation, and strong demand for homebuying.[3] Both the size and household formation rates of the 20–29-year-old group grew at above-average rates between 1970 and 1980; the 30–39-year-old group

3. Long (1980) discusses demographic changes over the decade; Bradbury, Downs, and Small (1982, ch. 10) summarize developments in energy scarcity and their probable effects on urban development. Although transformation to more employment in advanced services was also underway during this period, Noyelle and Stanback's detailed study (1983) only includes data on changes through 1975. Phillips and Vidal (1983) document the restructuring of metropolitan economies through 1977.

also increased in size and moved into homeownership at above-average rates. In the early years of the decade, housing supply benefitted from a boom in multifamily construction, but by the end of the decade, attempts to fight inflation through high interest rates were reducing both new construction and home sales.

As Table 3.1 shows, economic and demographic factors were more favorable for central city revitalization in 1975–80 than earlier in the decade. Growth in the 20–34-year-old group, delays in marriage, and increases in the divorce rate led to rapid household formation. The proportion of single-person households increased markedly. Fewer households had children present, in part because of decreases in children ever born. As the fertility rate dropped to a historic low in 1976, the proportion of women between 25 and 34 who were childless continued to grow. Labor force participation rose for all women, particularly among married women

Table 3.1

Selected Indicators of Changes in Population, Households, and Housing, 1970–1975 and 1975–1980

	1970–75	1975–80	
Number[a] *of*			
New households	8,100	9,500	
New housing units	10,900	9,500	
Net removals of housing units	2,800	0	
Percentage change in			
Price of existing single-family house	150	176	
Annual expenses for new single-family house	171	198	
GNP implicit price deflator	137	141	
CPI rent index	125	139	
	1970	*1975*	*1980*
Percentage of households able to afford median price new house	61.0	49.0	34.0
Percentage of primary individual households	17.0	20.0	22.0
No. of divorced per 1,000 married	47.0	69.0	100.0
Average household size	3.1	2.9	2.7
Percentage of families with child(ren) below 18	56.0	54.0	52.0
Children ever born per 1,000 women aged 18–44	1,918.0	1,645.0	1,506.0
Percentage of married couples with wife in labor force	41.0	44.0	50.0

SOURCES: HUD 1982b; U.S. Bureau of the Census 1981b.

[a] In thousands.

and those with small children, and the share of families with two workers also rose (U.S. Bureau of the Census 1976 and 1981b).

Although household formation rose in the latter half of the decade, new construction slackened. Reflecting lower supply, housing costs rose. Both the price of existing single-family homes and total expenses for buying a new house rose more quickly than inflation throughout the decade, especially in the latter half. As a result, the proportion of households able to "afford" a new single-family home dropped from 61 percent in 1970 to 34 percent in 1980 (HUD 1982b). Utilization of the stock rose accordingly: as conversions from larger residential and nonresidential units matched losses, net removals shrank from 2.8 million units in 1971–76 to zero between 1976 and 1981.

Both declines in new construction and increased utilization of existing stock made central-city housing relatively more attractive. Despite increased sales prices, tax deductions and capital gains treatment made housing a good investment, and renovating older housing offered attractive prospects of capital gains for sweat equity and little financial investment. Cities' advantages were reinforced by price differentials between city and suburban housing. Nationally, the median value of owner-occupied central-city housing was only 87 percent that of suburban housing in 1970, and during the 1970s, prices increased less in cities than in suburbs. Some of these price differentials reflect differences in quality, but hedonic indices suggest that in many central cities the price of a house was less than that of a house of comparable quality in their suburbs (Malpezzi, Ozanne, and Thibodeau 1980).

Did Migration to Cities Increase and Outmigration Decline?

According to Current Population Survey (CPS) sample data, the number of migrants into cities did increase over the decade, from 6.5 million inmigrants between 1970 and 1975 to 6.9 million in the 1975–80 period.[4] Outmigrants simultaneously dropped from 13.6 million to 13.2 million. These "improvements" for central cities in both inmigration and out-

4. The data used in this chapter are gathered in the March supplement of the Current Population Survey (CPS) and published by the U.S. Bureau of the Census as *Current Population Reports* (CPR), Series P-20. To examine comparable data for the two five-year time periods, this chapter compares unpublished Census Bureau tabulations for migration between 1970 and 1975 from the 1975 CPS with published data on 1975–80 migration (U.S. Bureau of the Census 1981c). The unpublished 1970–75 data are more comparable to the published 1975–80 data than the published 1970–75 data (U.S. Bureau of the Census 1975) because similar allocation procedures were used in each when previous place of residence was unreported. (Personal communication, Celia Boertlein, Population Division, U.S. Bureau of the Census.)

migration reduced their net outmigration from 7.1 to 6.3 million. Nevertheless, migration continued to cause central cities heavy population losses. By 1975, 11.5 percent of the surviving 1970 population had moved out of central cities on net, and by 1980 the 1975 city population had dropped an additional 10.4 percent because of migration. Immigration from abroad to cities remained essentially constant, while the extent of emigration from cities to other countries is unknown.

The decline in outmigration from cities reflected a marginal increase in retentiveness: the rate of total outmigration declined slightly (although insignificantly) from 22 to 21.7 percent.[5] The larger number of inmigrants to cities, however, appeared due only to growth in the non–central-city population "at risk of migration." The population of suburbs and nonmetropolitan areas increased almost 10 million between 1970 and 1975—in large part, of course, because of net migration from cities. But the proportion of these non-city residents moving to cities stayed essentially constant, insignificantly decreasing from 5.1 percent in 1970–75 to 5.0 percent in 1975–80. Overall, therefore, cities were apparently not attracting a higher share of residents from suburbs and nonmetropolitan areas, but only retaining a slightly higher proportion of their own residents.

Disaggregation by race, however (Table 3.2), reveals that white rates of movement to cities increased slightly, while black rates decreased. Decreased outmigration from cities was also concentrated among whites, as black outmigration increased. Together, increases in inmigration and decreases in outmigration caused white net outmigration from cities to fall more than a percentage point. In view of past racial differences in migration, the fact that the improvement for cities was concentrated among whites is doubly encouraging. It not only suggests that whites, who are more free to choose, have become more likely to choose city residences,

---

5. Using published standard errors, I find very few of the differences between the five-year periods to be significant. However, the standard error of the difference between two proportions includes a factor for the correlation between the two proportions being compared. Estimates of the magnitude of these correlations have not been made by the Census Bureau. Yet because respondents for the Current Population Survey were selected from the same sample neighborhoods for both the 1975 and the 1980 surveys, to the extent to which slowly changing neighborhood factors influence migration to and from cities the correlations are likely to be positive (personal communication, Dennis Schwantz, Statistical Methods Division, U.S. Bureau of the Census). Therefore, omitting the correlation overestimates the standard errors of the differences and thus tends to underestimate the number of significant differences. Because of this problem, the procedure adopted in reporting and discussing differences was to consider any difference that is statistically significant at the .05 level without adjustment for correlation coefficient "highly significant" (denoted by ** in the tables), and to consider differences significant at the .10 level significant (* in the tables) as well.

Table 3.2
Rates of Migration by Race for U.S. Central Cities and Remainder of United States,
1970–1975 and 1975–1980

	Central cities		Rest of U.S.	
	1970–75	1975–80	1970–75	1975–80
Total population at beginning of period (000s)	61,891.0	60,873.0	127,805.0	137,530.0
Rate of inmigration	10.5	11.3	10.7	9.6
Rate of outmigration	−22.0	−21.7	−5.1	−5.0
Net migration rate	−11.5	−10.4	5.6	4.6
White population at beginning of period (000s)	48,137.0	46,315.0	117,926.0	126,181.0
Rate of inmigration	11.7	13.0	10.4	9.3
Rate of outmigration	−25.6	−25.4	−4.7	−4.8
Net migration rate	−13.9	−12.4	5.6	4.6
Black population at beginning of period (000s)	12,507.0	13,203.0	8,605.0	9,495.0
Rate of inmigration	6.3	5.5	12.2	12.2
Rate of outmigration	−8.4	−8.8	−9.2	−7.6
Net migration rate	−2.0	−3.3	3.0	4.6

SOURCES: U.S. Bureau of the Census 1981c, and comparable unpublished tabulations from the March 1975 Current Population Survey.
NOTE: Rates are calculated as a percentage of the population of the area at the beginning of the period.

but also that suburbs became somewhat more open to blacks.[6] Only the direction of change improved, however: rates of net outmigration of whites from central cities in 1975–80 were almost four times as high as those of blacks.

Age Composition and Migration from and to Cities

Although CPS data on migration to and from cities by age are unfortunately not available by race, the age data are nevertheless useful. Because migration rates generally decline sharply with age (U.S. Bureau of the Census 1981b), the overall decrease in outmigration could result not from lower age-specific rates of outmigration, but from the aging of city population into age groups with lower migration rates. Similarly, increased inmigration could result mainly from growth in the size of the young adult base outside cities, since historically, young adults have had relatively high rates of migration into cities. If migration improvements for cities

6. Nelson (1980) further discusses the implications of past differentials and recent trends in black suburbanization.

Table 3.3
Rates of Outmigration and Net Migration by Age for Central Cities and
Remainder of United States, 1970–1975 and 1975–1980

Age at beginning of period	Central cities				Non–central cities			
	1970–75		1975–80		1970–75		1975–80	
	Out	Net	Out	Net	Out	Net	Out	Net
0–4	−28.0	−16.4	−28.3	−16.6	− 5.9	+ 7.7	− 5.2	+ 7.4
5–9	−23.5	−14.9	−21.7	−12.6	− 3.7	+ 6.5	− 3.6	+ 5.0
10–14	−16.8	− 7.6	−16.7	− 7.2	− 3.9	+ 3.2	− 3.8	+ 2.8
15–19	−26.7	− 3.0	−26.0	− 2.4	−11.8	+ 1.5	−10.6*	+ 1.1
20–24	−38.6	−18.3	−35.8**	−15.1	−12.8	+11.6	−11.7*	+ 8.5
25–29	−34.4	−22.4	−33.3	−19.6	− 6.8	+12.8	− 7.3	+10.4
30–39	−23.9	−15.0	−24.4	−14.3	− 3.9	+ 6.7	− 4.1	+ 5.7
40–49	−13.9	− 7.7	−13.2	− 6.0	− 2.8	+ 3.5	− 3.0	+ 2.5
50–59	−11.6	− 7.3	−11.4	− 6.8	− 2.0	+ 3.5	− 2.0	+ 2.9
60+	−10.0	− 6.6	− 9.6	− 5.6	− 1.8	+ 3.5	− 2.0	+ 3.4
Total	−22.0	−11.5	−21.7	−10.4	− 5.1	+ 5.6	− 5.0	+ 4.6

SOURCES: U.S. Bureau of the Census 1981c, and comparable unpublished tabulations from March 1975
Current Population Survey.
NOTE: Rates are calculated as a percentage of the original population in the area still resident in the
U.S. at the end of the period.
** Difference between the two periods significant at .05 level.   * Difference significant at .10 level.

reflect greater attractiveness of cities to particular age groups rather than
only composition effects, rates of age-specific inmigration should be higher
and those of outmigration lower.[7]

Actual changes in age-specific rates (Table 3.3) imply that the drop in
outmigration reflected a real, although marginal, increase in city "retentiveness." Over the decade, rates of age-specific outmigration from cities
decreased for all age groups except young children 0–4 and their parents,
adults 30–39. The sharpest decline (and the only significant one) occurred among young adults aged 20–24. However, these young adults
continued to leave at higher rates than any other age group, with more
than one-third moving outside of cities in each five-year period. The total
decrease in outmigration was due largely to drops in age-specific rates in
almost all age groups rather than to aging of the population. The racial
differences found for total migration imply that these improvements were
concentrated among whites.

However, the age-specific data also show that the greater number of mi-

7. For each comparison, the relevant rate is the outmigration rate of the population at
risk. Thus, the rate at which non-city dwellers are migrating to cities should be examined to
determine if cities are becoming more attractive to those living outside cities, and the rate at
which city residents are outmigrating is the appropriate rate to monitor to see if cities are
retaining higher proportions of their own residents.

grants into cities resulted in large part from changes in age composition. The numerical growth was concentrated in the young adult group, those 15–39 in 1970 and 25–49 in 1980, in which the number of inmigrants grew 12 percent. But if the rates experienced in the first half of the decade had continued, growth in the base of young adults living outside central cities should itself have increased inmigration to cities 16 percent among this group. The lower actual growth resulted from significant *drops* in migration rates into cities among the youngest adults, those aged 20–29 at the end of each period. But rates of migration from outside cities into cities did increase among the group aged 30–54. This shift is encouraging because these age groups will continue to grow in size during the 1980s.

Characteristics of Movers between Cities and Suburbs

Thus, during the late 1970s cities did attract or retain a higher proportion of many age groups than earlier in the decade. But though the changes were in the right direction, they were minimal compared to the remaining extent of outmigration. This section examines the characteristics of migrants to and from cities to see if the slight improvements in numbers were paralleled or exceeded by changes in the characteristics of movers. Unfortunately, data on socioeconomic characteristics of movers to and from cities are available only for those moving within and between metropolitan areas: the characteristics of movers between cities and nonmetropolitan areas are not distinguished.[8] Because characteristics of movers in the flows between metropolitan areas in the aggregate and nonmetropolitan areas changed very little over the decade, the discussion below assumes that city-suburban differentials in migration characteristics were little changed by the back-to-the-country movement first observed during the 1970s. However, if the highest-status groups were moving to the exurban fringes that over the decade increasingly spilled over into nonmetropolitan counties, this assumption may not hold.

Migration by Household Type

The changing mix of household types has been repeatedly cited as a reason for expecting cities to attract more people and households (Alonso 1980; Long 1980; Frey and Kobrin 1982). Single-person households have

8. Since 1973, the *Current Population Reports* have been publishing tables on migration between cities and suburbs, and on migration between metropolitan and nonmetropolitan areas. Unfortunately, however, less detail is published—or available from unpublished tabulations—on all three-way flows among cities, suburbs, and nonmetropolitan areas. Therefore, information on the socioeconomic status of movers to and from cities is available only for those moving within and among metropolitan areas.

been more prone to live in cities than other households, while husband-wife families, especially those with children, have a higher propensity to live in suburbs. Thus the declining share of husband-wife households (down in central cities from 58% of households in 1970 to 50% only five years later) and the increasing share of persons living alone might themselves lead to lower outmigration rates among city households. Furthermore, increasing female labor force participation and decreasing numbers of children born and at home are commonly expected to make cities more attractive to husband-wife households. Young, childless, two-profession families desiring access to city jobs, services, and cultural amenities have been a staple ingredient of most speculation about the revival of distressed cities (*Newsweek* 1981; Palen and London 1984).

As Table 3.4 shows, however, outmigration of households from cities to suburbs continued unchecked during the decade. Shifts in the types of households were apparently offset by changing migration rates by household type. Husband-wife families did have both higher rates of outmigration from cities and lower inmigration rates than other household types, but in spite of the relative decline in husband-wife families, the rate of household migration from cities to suburbs remained at 15.6 percent. Indeed, rates of outmigration from cities actually dropped slightly among husband-wife households, but this drop was offset by rising outmigration to suburbs among both single individuals and families with single heads.

Table 3.4
Rates of Outmigration and Net Migration between Central Cities and Suburbs, by Household Type, 1970–1975 and 1975–1980

Household type	1970–75		1975–80	
	Out	Net	Out	Net
Central cities				
All households	−16	− 9	−16	− 8
Both spouses present	−19	−13	−19	−12
Male family householder	−12	− 6	−13	− 5
Female family householder	− 9	− 4	−11	− 5
Male primary individual	−14	− 3	−15	− 3
Female primary individual	−10	− 3	−10	− 2
Suburbs				
All households	− 7	+ 9	− 7	+ 7
Both spouses present	− 5	+10	− 5	+ 8
Male family householder	− 7	+ 8	− 8	+ 5
Female family householder	− 9	+ 5	− 8	+ 7
Male primary individual	−17	+ 4	−16	+ 4
Female primary individual	−10	+ 4	−11	+ 2

SOURCE: U.S. Bureau of the Census 1981c.
NOTE: Rates represent migrants between central cities and suburbs as a percentage of the original population in cities (suburbs) that both survived 5 years and remained in an SMSA.

Nor did rates of migration from suburbs to cities shift greatly among suburban households. Migration to cities rose slightly among single women and male-headed households, but not among husband-wife families. Because of the larger suburban base, the net result of these slight changes in the two opposite flows was a slight decline in rates of net outmigration from cities for every household type other than female-headed families. As has traditionally been the case, net migration from cities remained highest for husband-wife households and higher for families than for individuals.

Outmigration among Husband-Wife Households

Both the numerical importance of husband-wife households and past speculation about their changing preferences for city residence imply that even the slight decline in their outmigration from cities deserves further attention. Was it due to the increasing incidence of couples with one or no children? Or were cities becoming more attractive to families with children? Neither appears to be the explanation. As Table 3.5 shows, outmigration rates rose slightly among childless husband-wife households, who had higher outmigration rates than any other household type by the second half of the decade. Rates of outmigration from cities also rose among husband-wife families with two children and for all non–husband-wife families with children. The only significant drop in outmigration among husband-wife families occurred for families with four or more children. Similarly, rates of migration into cities from suburbs increased only among large families.

Further disaggregation by income (Table 3.6) dispels hopes that increases resulted from preference: the decline in outmigration from cities was greatest in the lowest income group.[9] In general, having more children retards migration (Long 1972, 371), and suburban families in all income groups conformed to this pattern. The more children suburban families had, the lower their rate of moving from suburbs to cities, and this rate further decreased over the decade. But among city households, by contrast, having more children apparently increased the likelihood of outmigration from cities among husband-wife families in the highest income class. Thus the fact that the decline in outmigration from cities among husband-wife families was concentrated among those in the lowest income class with many children suggests strongly that the decline was

9. Because of inflation, the 1974 income categories by which 1970–75 migration is available are not directly comparable to the 1979 income categories used for 1975–80 migration. However, since the ratio of the 1979 to the 1974 consumer price index was almost exactly 1.5, $10,000 in 1974 dollars should be equivalent to $15,000 in 1979. Therefore, the lowest income category in Table 3.6 should be directly comparable over time. Because it is the only category for which income is comparable, significance tests were calculated only for it.

Table 3.5

Rates of Outmigration and Net Migration between Central Cities and Suburbs, by Family Type and Number of Children, for Households with Head Aged 15–54, 1970–1975 and 1975–1980

| | Central cities | | | | Suburbs | | | |
| | 1970–75 | | 1975–80 | | 1970–75 | | 1975–80 | |
	Out	Net	Out	Net	Out	Net	Out	Net
Husband-wife families								
With no own children	−23	−14	−25	−14	− 9	+12	− 8	+10
With one child	−24	−16	−24	−16	− 7	+14	− 6	+12
With two children	−24	−15	−25	−18	− 7	+10	− 4**	+11
With three children	−25	−20	−23	−16	− 4	+14	− 4	+10
With four plus children	−22	−15	−17*	− 9	− 5	+11	− 5	+ 6
Non–husband-wife households								
With no own children	−11	− 6	−11	− 4	− 8	+ 8	− 8	+ 5
With one child	−14	− 7	−15	− 8	−10	+11	−11	+11
With two children	−12	− 4	−14	− 5	−13	+ 5	−12	+ 6
With three children	−10	− 4	−14	− 8	−10	+ 6	−12	+16
With four plus children	− 7	− 2	− 8	− 2	−12	+ 6	−11	+ 5

SOURCE: U.S. Bureau of the Census 1981c.

NOTE: Rates are expressed as a percentage of those surviving to the end of the period and still residing in SMSAs who lived in central cities, or in suburbs, at the beginning of the period.

** Difference between the two periods significant at .10 level.   * Difference significant at .05 level.   ** Difference significant at .10 level.

Table 3.6

Rates of Outmigration and Net Migration between Central Cities and Suburbs for Husband-Wife Families with Head Aged 15–54, by Income and Number of Children, 1970–1975 and 1975–1980

Family income[a] and number of children	Central cities				Suburbs			
	1970–75		1975–80		1970–75		1975–80	
	Out	Net	Out	Net	Out	Net	Out	Net
<$10,000 / <$15,000								
With no children	−18	− 6	−19	− 7	−15	+ 7	−14	+ 8
With one child	−21	− 9	−19	− 9	−14	+10	−10	+ 9
With two children	−20	− 9	−20	−13	−12	+ 9	− 7*	+13
With three or more children	−23	−13	−17**	− 8	−12	+16	− 8*	+ 8
$10,000–$14,999 / $15,000–$24,999								
With no children	−19	− 9	−25	−15	−10	+ 9	− 9	+14
With one child	−26	−16	−24	−16	− 9	+15	− 7	+19
With two children	−24	−17	−26	−18	− 6	+16	− 5	+11
With three or more children	−19	−16	−17	−11	− 3	+13	− 4	+ 8
$15,000+ / $25,000+								
With no children	−26	−19	−26	−16	− 6	+15	− 6	+ 9
With one child	−24	−19	−26	−19	− 4	+14	− 4	+12
With two children	−26	−16	−27	−21	− 6	+ 9	− 4	+11
With three or more children	−28	−21	−27	−20	− 4	+12	− 3	+ 9

SOURCE: U.S. Bureau of the Census 1981c.

NOTE: Rates are expressed as a percentage of the population surviving to the end of the period and still residing in the SMSA any who lived in cities or in suburbs at the beginning of the period.

[a] Incomes are for the year previous to the survey, with the first income that of 1974 and the second that of 1979.   * Difference significant at .10 level.   ** Difference between the two periods significant at .05 level. (The significance of differences is calculated only for the lowest income category, since it is the only one directly comparable in real dollars over the 5 years.)

due, not to greater preference for cities, but to increasing difficulties in affording or finding suburban housing.

Intrametropolitan Mobility by Income for All Male Heads

These migration differences among husband-wife families in three income classes do not suggest that cities were attracting upper-income groups. But for finer income breaks available only for male-headed households, changes during the decade are somewhat more encouraging. Changes by five income categories reveal significant decreases in outmigration from cities at both ends of the income spectrum. The drop in outmigration found for married males with incomes below $6,000 (in 1979 dollars) may be forced by income and price constraints, as implied by the differentials observed among large families. But outmigration from cities also decreased among both married and unmarried males with incomes above $30,000, for whom changes may be assumed to be voluntary.[10] Furthermore, as the next sections demonstrate, evidence of increased city attractiveness among the highest income groups is consistent with differentials found by occupation and education.

Intrametropolitan Mobility by Education, Occupation, and Race

Over the past several decades, outmigration from cities has been selectively higher by education and occupational status (Pinkerton 1968). But if restructuring of cities' economic bases, white-collar employment, and reactions against excessive commuting to distant suburbs are indeed attracting higher-status groups, past socioeconomic differentials in outmigration should narrow, as apparently occurred for migration by income. Since educational and occupational data from the CPS also distinguish migration by race, they can show specifically whether status differentials changed within each racial group.

Among whites, status differentials in outmigration from cities did narrow during the 1970s in terms of both occupation and education (Table 3.7). Consistent with the gentrification hypothesis and decreased outmigration of high-income groups, the largest (and significant) drops in rates of outmigration occurred for higher-status groups—professionals and college graduates. At the other end of the socioeconomic spectrum,

---

10. Despite—or because of—the improvement in migration rates among some income groups, the total annual loss in income of city residents that can be attributed to net outmigration from cities to suburbs grew from $27 billion in 1975 to "only" $35 billion in 1980, expressed in current dollars. Thus the tax bases of central cities continue to be adversely affected by net outmigration, although the fact that the increase in losses was less than the rate of inflation during the five-year period might be considered encouraging. Sternlieb and Hughes (1981) further discuss the significance of such income and revenue losses for cities.

Table 3.7
Rates of Outmigration and Net Migration between Central Cities and Suburbs,
by Race, Occupation, and Education, 1970–1975 and 1975–1980

	Central cities				Suburbs			
	1970–75		1975–80		1970–75		1975–80	
	Out	Net	Out	Net	Out	Net	Out	Net
CIVILIAN LABOR FORCE								
Whites								
Prof. and managerial	−25	−16	−23*	−12	− 7	13	− 8	8
Sales and clerical	−19	−11	−20	−10	− 7	9	− 7	7
Crafts and operative	−19	−12	−19	−10	− 5	8	− 5	7
Laborers and service	−18	−10	−18	− 9	− 5	8	− 6	6
Unemployed	−17	− 3	−20	− 7	−10	2	−10	5
Blacks								
Prof. and managerial	−12	− 9	−12	− 8	−12	33	− 8	20
Sales and clerical	− 8	− 3	−11	− 7	−19	13	−11	19
Crafts and operative	− 7	− 3	− 6	− 1	−13	12	−13	2
Laborers and service	− 5	− 2	− 8	− 5	− 9	7	− 9	14
Unemployed	− 7	− 1	− 7	− 3	−21	2	− 6	4
YEARS OF SCHOOL COMPLETED								
Whites 25 years or older								
8 or less	− 8	− 5	−10*	− 6	− 3	5	− 4	5
High school 1–3	−14	− 8	−12**	− 7	− 4	6	− 4	5
High school 4	−19	−13	−18	−11	− 4	9	− 4	7
College 1–3	−24	−14	−24	−14	− 8	11	− 7	10
College 4 plus	−26	−18	−24*	−14	− 7	14	− 7	10
Blacks 25 years or older								
8 or less	− 4	− 1	− 3	− 2	− 8	4	− 3	9
High school 1–3	− 4	− 2	− 5	− 1	−11	10	−12	5
High school 4	− 7	− 3	− 8	− 5	−14	14	−10	14
College 1–3	− 9	− 6	− 8	− 4	−14	23	−12	12
College 4 plus	−12	− 8	−12	− 6	−13	22	−15	13

SOURCE: U.S. Bureau of the Census 1981c.
**Difference between the two periods significant at .05 level.
*Difference between the two periods significant at .10 level.

rates of outmigration rose among unemployed whites and those with less
than an elementary school education.

The evidence from declines in outmigration that cities attracted more
professional workers is reinforced by changes in suburban migration. Professionals were one of the two occupations to move from suburbs to cities
at higher rates (the other was laborers). The overall result of changes in
both intrametropolitan flows was that net outmigration from cities dropped
over the decade from 16 to 12 percent among white professionals and
from 18 to 14 percent among college graduates. Further disaggregation
by both education and age shows that the improvement among profes-

sional workers was particularly marked among young adults. Outmigration rates from cities dropped 7 percentage points among college graduates aged 25–29, and 4 percentage points among those aged 30–34 with any college experience. Net outmigration of young college graduates was halved during the decade, dropping from 20 percent to 10 percent between the two five-year periods.

Among blacks, the increase in outmigration from cities occurred mainly among middle-status workers. Outmigration rose most among high school rather than college graduates, and among sales, labor, and service workers. These slight increases are encouraging in suggesting greater access of blacks to suburban jobs, but black rates of outmigration from cities remain much lower than comparable white rates for any occupation or education level.

In sum, status differentials in net migration between cities and suburbs narrowed among both blacks and whites. Among whites, by 1975–80 the highest-status groups were only twice rather than three times as likely to leave cities as were the lowest-status groups. Differentials by status remained greater among blacks, although their rates of net outmigration were lower than whites at all status levels. But despite this welcome evidence of narrowing in the differential migration that has led to status and racial differences between cities and suburbs, at decade's end net migration was still decidedly directed out from central cities for all groups and both races.

Migration to and from Cities by Region

The national data reveal both increased migration to central cities and decreased rates of migration from them, particularly among whites. There is also some evidence that such improvements were spurred by young professionals. However, the improvements are so marginal that they are unlikely to have aided many cities appreciably. Nor can national data demonstrate that these slight upturns benefitted older, distressed central cities. Instead, the apparent improvements could be a statistical artifact of ongoing regional shifts in migration. Long-distance net migration has been directed toward the Sunbelt, particularly Texas and western states (Long 1981), and cities in these states tend to have higher proportions of both total and higher-status SMSA populations than do central cities in general. Therefore, in preparation for focusing more specifically on individual cities in Chapter 4, here we examine the available data on migration to and from cities by region. Because a higher proportion of the large cities in the Northeast and North Central regions are distressed, we are particularly interested in determining whether the national improvements in city net migration also characterized cities there.

Regional Rates of Migration by Race

CPS data unfortunately give little detail on the characteristics of migrants moving to and from cities in each region, but rates of migration to and from cities, suburbs, and nonmetropolitan areas are available by race (Table 3.8). They show that population losses from cities because of migration slowed in all regions except the West, although not necessarily in the most distressed cities in these regions. Increases in rates of white inmigration to cities over the decade occurred in every region except the West, but the decrease in outmigration from cities was apparently concentrated in the South. Expressed on the base of the original population, net outmigration rates therefore decreased in all regions but the West.

Immigration from abroad, which was highest in the West and Northeast, offset some of the city population losses caused by domestic net outmigration. Indeed, in the West the population increases resulting from immigration over the decade replaced almost half of the loss of white migrants caused by internal net outmigration. In the other three regions, however, immigration of whites from abroad to cities offset only a small fraction of the other migration losses.

Because increased black outmigration from cities was apparently concentrated in the South and West, the regional data do not point to any lessening of white-black differences in suburbanization in the more segregated northeastern and north central SMSAs. The national decrease in black inmigration to cities resulted mainly from the halving of inmigration into northeastern cities, since black inmigration into north central cities was constant and that into western cities increased. These shifts brought increased net black outmigration from northeastern and southern cities, although black rates of outmigration were still only one-half to one-fourth the rates of whites. Thus, even though blacks are now also net outmigrants from central cities, the proportion of blacks in cities is still tending to increase in all four regions as the result of faster outmigration of whites.[11]

For suburbs and nonmetropolitan areas, the remaining sections of Table 3.8 indicate that white suburbanization slowed in the South, but was still fastest there, with population gains of 14 percent between 1975 and 1980. By contrast, northeastern suburbs barely held their own: outmigration almost equaled inmigration, and immigration from abroad provided more

---

11. Long (1975) shows that white outmigration rather than black inmigration was the primary reason that proportions of black residents in central cities increased during the 1960s. The racial breakdowns shown here do not include immigrants of races other than white or black; the number of such immigrants increased markedly over the decade, especially in the West.

Table 3.8
Rates of Internal Migration and Immigration by Race and Region, 1970–1975 and 1975–1980

	Northeast		North Central		South		West	
	1970–75	1975–80	1970–75	1975–80	1970–75	1975–80	1970–75	1975–80
Cities								
Whites								
Inmigration	5.6	7.4	11.8	13.8	15.4	16.0	23.9	23.7
Outmigration	−18.3	−19.3	−28.9	−29.3	−32.0	−29.4**	−31.4	−31.7
Net migration	−12.6	−12.0	−17.1	−15.5	−16.6	−13.4	− 7.5	− 8.0
Immigration	+ 3.3	+ 2.6	+ 1.7	+ 1.3	2.5	2.2	3.2	3.6
Blacks								
Inmigration	5.3	2.7	6.8	7.0	9.5	8.9	13.4	16.6
Outmigration	− 9.4	− 8.9	− 9.7	− 8.8	− 9.5	−11.7*	−16.0	−18.4
Net migration	− 4.0	− 6.2	− 3.0	− 1.8	0	− 2.8	− 2.5	− 1.8
Immigration	+ 2.4	+ 1.9	+ 0.1	1.2	1.3	1.0	1.9	1.2
Suburbs								
Whites								
Inmigration	11.8	10.7	18.8	17.0	35.8	30.1	26.4	25.9
Outmigration	−10.8	− 9.8	−13.1	−12.9	−15.7	−16.3	−16.8	−17.5
Net migration	1.0	+ 0.9	5.7	4.1	20.1	13.8	9.6	8.4
Immigration	+ 1.2	+ 1.0	+ 1.1	0.8	2.6	2.1	2.7	2.7
Blacks								
Inmigration	18.7	14.0	25.0	22.5	26.9	35.9	26.4	36.3
Outmigration	−12.5	− 9.2	−16.5	−18.7	−15.5	−13.9	−16.8	−23.5
Net migration	6.2	4.8	8.5	3.7	11.4	22.0	9.6	12.7
Immigration	+ 2.2	+ 2.4	1.5	0.7	1.0	3.7	2.7	6.4
Nonmetropolitan areas								
Whites								
Inmigration	11.8	11.1	10.6	11.3	16.5	14.9	21.5	21.7
Outmigration	−11.1	−11.9	−10.1	−11.9	−10.5	− 9.6	−15.4	−15.8
Net migration	0.7	− 0.8	0.5	− 0.6	6.0	5.3	6.1	5.9
Immigration	+ 1.0	+ 0.8	0.9	0.6	1.2	0.9	2.6	1.9
Blacks								
Inmigration	23.7	21.1	16.1	10.6	6.0	6.1	14.8	28.2
Outmigration	−16.7	−26.7	−11.8	−16.4	− 9.4	− 7.5	−21.1	−45.3
Net migration	7.0	− 5.6	4.3	− 5.8	− 3.4	− 1.5	− 6.3	−17.1
Immigration	+ 3.8	+ 2.2	3.9	2.4	0.4	0.3	10.2	2.6

SOURCE: U.S. Bureau of the Census 1981c, and unpublished tabulations from the March 1975 Current Population Survey.
NOTE: Rates are calculated as a percentage of the original population in the area still resident in the U.S. at the end of the period.
  ** Difference between the two periods significant at .05 level.
  * Difference between the two periods significant at .10 level.

new white residents than did internal migration. Like western cities, western suburbs had high rates of population growth from white immigration, and their white population grew more than 11 percent each period from all migration. The regional data also demonstrate clearly that the much-heralded turnaround to net migration into nonmetropolitan areas is actually a phenomenon confined to the South and West.

Intraregional Exchanges

Because Sunbelt cities are generally still gaining population and are less often distressed than those in the North, it is often thought that the migration process favors them. But this advantage holds only for long-distance migration. Within regions (Table 3.9), suburbanization and decentralization from central cities were clearly underway in all regions of the country. Indeed, in terms of net migration between cities and their immediate suburbs, suburbanization was proceeding at the fastest rate in the West; it also accelerated there over the decade, because of fewer in-migrants to cities and more outmigrants. Cities in the South and in the North Central region had the next highest net rates of suburbanization, but net outmigration from these cities to their immediate suburbs dropped over the decade because of more inmigrants to cities and fewer outmigrants to the suburbs. Northeastern cities had the lowest rate of suburbanization, and net outmigration from these cities declined further during the decade as increases in inmigration exceeded those in outmigration rates.

In addition to suburbanization, in each region cities also were losing migrants to the rest of their region throughout the decade. But for each region sums of all exchanges between central cities and the rest of the same region show the position of central cities improving over the decade. In all four regions, both the number of inmigrants and the rate of inmigration to central cities from the rest of the region increased, while outmigration from cities to the rest of the region dropped. If the population of cities were altered only by interactions with their own regions, northeastern cities would have the lowest rates of net outmigration and southern cities the highest.

These results show clearly that the recent population losses of northern and north central cities, and the corresponding gains of western and southern cities, result mainly from interregional migration. At the local and regional level central cities in all four regions are experiencing decentralization of population. Thus, actions taken by local and state governments to influence the distribution of population between cities and their suburbs and exurbs cannot necessarily ensure population stability in cities.

Table 3.9

Rates of Migration for Central Cities, by Region and Distance of Migration, 1970–1975 and 1975–1980

	Northeast		North Central		South		West	
	1970–75	1975–80	1970–75	1975–80	1970–75	1975–80	1970–75	1975–80
To cities from rest of SMSA	2.0	2.6	3.7	4.4	2.5	3.2	7.3	6.8
From cities to rest of SMSA	− 5.4	− 5.6	−11.6	−10.8*	−10.8	−10.2	−13.3	−14.0
Net migration	− 3.4	− 3.0	− 7.8	− 6.4	− 8.2	− 7.0	− 6.0	− 7.2
To cities from rest of region	1.9	2.1	3.6	4.1	6.0	5.4	6.8	7.6
From cities to rest of region	− 5.9	− 5.5	− 6.3	− 6.8	−10.0	− 9.6	−10.3	− 9.6
Net migration	− 4.0	− 3.4	− 2.7	− 2.7	− 4.0	− 4.1	− 3.5	− 2.0
To cities from other regions	1.6	1.5	3.4	3.7	5.3	5.4	7.4	8.1
From cities to other regions	− 5.4	− 5.9	− 7.0	− 6.8	− 5.2	− 5.0	− 5.5	− 6.1
Net migration	− 3.8	− 4.4	− 3.6	− 3.1	+ 0.1	0.4	+ 1.9	+ 1.9
Total inmigration	5.5	6.2	10.7	12.2	13.8	14.0	21.5	22.5
Total outmigration	−16.7	−17.0	−24.9	−24.2	−26.0	−24.8	−29.1	−29.9
Total net migration	−11.2	−10.8	−14.1	−12.2	−12.1	−10.7	− 7.6	− 7.3

SOURCE: U.S. Bureau of the Census 1981c.
NOTE: Rates are calculated as a percentage of the central-city population at the beginning of the period.
* Difference between the two periods significant at .10 level.

Probable Future Migration

The marginal nature of changes in migration during the 1970s do not support claims or hopes of marked increases in absolute preferences for city living, nor do compositional changes in household types appear to have helped cities greatly. This interpretation is reinforced by responses to a 1979 question included in the national sample of the Annual Housing Survey that asked where household heads would prefer to live in five years. Reviewing the results, Long (1982, 1–2) concluded that the "responses indicate further deconcentration of population," in that "the desire to move away is inversely related to size of place" and "the bigger the place, the greater the proportion of households wanting to be someplace else." As Table 3.10 shows, in each region the proportion of household heads in the largest central cities who said that they preferred staying in the same place was lower than the regional averages. Interregional shifts from the North also seem likely to continue: indeed, if all those who reported mi-

Table 3.10

Percentage Distribution of Preferred Residence in 1984 and Likelihood of Moves, by Region, Residence in Central Cities of SMSAs over 1 Million, and Income below or above 80 Percent of SMSA Median in 1979

	Prefer same place	Want to move		Different region likely
Respondents		Move unlikely	Move likely	
Northeast				
Total region	70.4	14.0	15.6	8.5
Central cities				
<80% median income	67.9	19.7	12.4	9.0
80+% median income	64.6	18.1	17.3	11.6
North Central				
Total region	70.7	12.2	17.1	9.9
Central cities				
<80% median income	69.0	15.8	15.2	10.0
80+% median income	65.9	14.2	19.9	11.7
South				
Total region	79.5	8.2	12.3	3.8
Central cities				
<80% median income	80.9	8.7	10.4	4.4
80+% median income	69.2	10.7	20.1	7.5
West				
Total region	68.4	11.7	19.9	4.1
Central cities				
<80% median income	67.6	14.0	18.4	5.1
80+% median income	64.5	14.0	21.5	4.7

SOURCE: Special tabulations of the 1979 National Annual Housing Survey.

gration to be likely actually moved, five-year rates of outmigration from the North Central region would be markedly greater than they had been in 1975–80 (Nelson 1984).[12] Even more serious, categorizing the responses by relative income shows that both the likelihood of moving and the proportion moving to a different region were greater for upper-income city residents, especially in the Northeast and North Central regions. This finding reinforces Althaus and Schachter's warning (1983) that the New Federalism may induce migration from regions and areas with higher taxes and slower growth.

Summary

National and regional sample data on migration trends do not suggest that widespread gentrification or urban revitalization is presently likely to occur as a result of central cities' newly attracting many more migrants. Although moderate reductions in net outmigration from cities among higher-income males and higher-status whites are encouraging developments—and ones that appear to alter previous trends—they are swamped by the remaining tide of net outmigration from cities in all four regions. That outmigration, furthermore, continues to be quite selective by status and by race. The resulting population losses or slower growth of large central cities, combined with growing concentrations of poverty there,[13] demonstrate that much more drastic reversals in past migration trends would be necessary to support widespread revival; yet evidence that much of the migration "improvement" in the 1970s resulted from compositional changes in age and household types does not promise further advances at a national or regional scale. This pessimistic assessment of trends during the 1970s at the national and regional levels is underscored by responses to a 1979 survey that showed preferences for outmigration

12. Although the relationship between preferences and actual migration is often questioned, Morgan (1978) concludes his summary of research on residential preferences over the previous forty years by saying that "preferences do correlate with behavior, at least in very gross terms" (133) and that preferences for rural areas and for the West have been quite consistent between 1937 and 1973–74. Based on his 1973–74 survey, "if everyone who wanted to live elsewhere actuallly moved to the region and type of place of their choice, . . . [t]here would be growth in the Mountain, Pacific, New England, and South Atlantic states . . . [and] cities would lose 22 per cent of their populations and rural-farm areas would gain 31 per cent" (134).

13. Further detail on the increasing concentrations of poor residents in central cities, and on increasing disparities in income and poverty between cities and their suburbs, is given in Nelson (1984). As the U.S. poverty rate rose from 12.1% in 1969 to 13.0% in 1980, central-city poverty rates increased from 12.7% to 17.2% among all residents, and from 24.3% to 32.3% among black residents.

higher among higher-income city residents who considered migration likely during the 1979–84 period. The next chapter seeks to determine whether evidence of reversal in past selective outmigration is clearer for any of forty of the country's major metropolitan areas, especially their more distressed central cities.

4. City or Suburbs? Three Periods of Residential Choice in Forty Metropolitan Areas

National sample data show that central cities attracted and retained more migrants during the late 1970s than earlier in the decade. Although much of the improvement can be attributed to the large numerical increase in young adults over the decade, encouraging changes also occurred among higher-status migrants. But the national changes during the 1970s were not large enough to reverse the overall pattern of net outmigration from central cities nor to have markedly aided many individual cities. Nor can aggregate data demonstrate that distressed cities benefitted. Even though cities in the more distressed Northeast and North Central regions shared in the slight upturns, their improvements in migration could have occurred in nondistressed cities.

For forty of the largest metropolitan areas individually, therefore, this chapter utilizes migration data from three periods that span more than two decades to investigate two questions. First, when compared to changes between the late 1950s and the late 1960s in residential choice, do the slight national improvements in central-city migration during the 1970s represent a change from or a continuation of earlier trends? And, second, if improvements over earlier trends occurred, did they help any major distressed central cities? The forty large SMSAs studied are introduced by reviewing population changes in their central cities and other indicators of distress; in 1970, central cities in twenty-seven of the forty were distressed, some severely so. Yet factors such as economic base, city-suburban differences in housing prices, and attractiveness to young adults were favorable in some of these cities, so that expectations of the relative likelihood of cumulative decline versus revival differ among the twenty-seven distressed cities.

Because of the dearth of data for individual cities on complete inmigration and outmigration by socioeconomic status, most of this chapter focuses on changes in "city selection rates"—the proportion of movers to or within metropolitan areas who choose city rather than suburban residence. To determine whether cities are "attracting" more migrants, trends

are studied mainly for nonblacks, because of past constraints on movement by minorities.[1] The strengths and weaknesses of this measure are
introduced by examining average changes for the forty SMSAs. Annual
changes in city selection rates between 1974 and 1981 for the forty SMSAs
grouped by region are shown to parallel the national results for the 1970s,
since they too show improvements for cities toward the end of the decade.
Comparable data on city selection for three periods between the late
1950s and the late 1970s—1955–1960, 1965–70, and the years around
1980—demonstrates that even the slight increases of the late 1970s represented a marked improvement over earlier patterns. Average changes
over the past two decades in SMSA population distribution and city selection rates of movers for total and for upper-income nonblacks show that
migration in the 1970s became markedly more favorable for cities than
the acceleration of selective suburbanization that occurred between the
1955–60 and the 1965–70 periods covered by census data.

Changes in each SMSA's city selection rates between 1970 and 1980 are
then studied individually to assess whether migration has become more
favorable to distressed central cities, and if so, whether migration improvements were sufficient to reverse their past relative declines in per
capita income. Since selectively faster outmigration of higher-income residents has been a main cause of past declines in per capita income, purchasing power, and municipal revenue (Sternlieb and Hughes 1981),
changes in migration by income should foreshadow future changes in city
resources. Differences among the distressed cities in city selection during
the 1970s are also analyzed statistically to infer why they are occurring.

The Forty Metropolitan Areas Studied

The metropolitan areas for which equivalent data on central-city migration are available for three periods were forty of the fifty largest SMSAs in
1970.[2] In 1970, they contained 42 percent of the U.S. population and 61
percent of its metropolitan population. Since they are so large, they are
not representative of all SMSAs, but they are unrepresentative in two im-

1. Similar analysis of post-1970 changes in black migration (Nelson 1980) shows that black
rates of selecting suburban residence increased in some of these metropolitan areas, particularly among upper-income blacks. In the present study, the terms "white" and "nonblack"
are used interchangeably because almost all "nonblacks" were white in most of the SMSAs
studied.

2. The 40 SMSAs studied are all but two of those for which the Annual Housing Survey
SMSA sample results identify central cities (within 1970 boundaries) separately from the
"suburban" remainder of each SMSA (as defined in 1970). Such geographic detail is also
available for the Honolulu and Anaheim–Santa Ana–Garden Grove SMSAs, but these were
excluded as being atypical.

portant ways that make them particularly appropriate for evaluating relative tendencies toward revival or further distress. On the one hand, they tend to be old, underbounded, and distressed, with many losing population during both the 1960s and the 1970s. Most of the more distressed cities have disproportionate concentrations of poor and/or minority population, along with the sharp city-suburban disparities believed to encourage differential suburbanization and thus cumulative decline. Yet many of the factors encouraging revival (as discussed in Chapter 2) are also associated with size—cultural amenities, specialized employment and retail opportunities, historic districts and housing, educational institutions, long commuting distances, and office employment in the central business district (Lipton 1977). Size seems particularly important in establishing an area as a command and control center rather than a subordinate city in the evolving "advanced economy" (Noyelle and Stanback 1983).

Central-City Strengths and Weaknesses

As Table 4.1 shows, central cities in many of these SMSAs have been losing population for several decades. Absolute losses were most common in the 1970s, when growth slowed even in those (newer) cities with absolute growth. Although some cities have annexed suburban territory (Norton 1979), Table 4.2 shows that faster suburban growth and outmigration from central cities have reduced central-city shares of SMSA population in essentially all of these cities (the only slight exception is Sacramento between 1960 and 1970).

Table 4.2 also shows that in almost every instance white population losses have exceeded total losses, particularly during the 1970s. Furthermore, rates of white net migration during the 1960s were usually even more negative for these cities than rates of white population loss. Thus, for most cities disparities between net migration and total population losses for whites in the 1960s, combined with increasing white losses from the 1960s to the 1970s, imply that "white flight" has been accelerating rather than reversing. As Long (1975) showed, faster net outmigration by whites has been the main cause of increasing black concentrations in many cities.

Population decline is often—both popularly and in formulas—associated with distress (Burchell et al. 1981). But since 1950, selective net outmigration has increased even in cities where population growth continues. Furthermore, in almost all of the SMSAs, upper-income movers in 1970 were less likely to select city over suburban residences than the city share of SMSA population distribution would suggest: that is, there were "gaps" between city selection rates and city population shares. Thus, distress does not result from population losses or lower SMSA shares per se

Table 4.1
Rates of Population Change in Central Cities of Forty SMSAs, 1940–1980

	1970 SMSA rank	% change in total population			
		1940–50	1950–60	1960–70	1970–80
New York	1	5.9	− 1.4	1.1	−10.4
Los Angeles–LB	2	31.0	25.8	12.5	5.0
Chicago	3	6.6	− 1.9	− 5.2	−10.8
Philadelphia	4	7.3	− 3.3	− 2.7	−13.4
Detroit	5	13.9	− 9.7	− 9.5	−20.5
San Francisco–Oak	6	22.2	− 4.5	− 2.8	− 5.5
Washington	7	21.0	− 4.8	− 1.0	−15.7
Boston	8	4.0	−13.0	− 8.1	−12.2
Pittsburgh	9	0.8	−10.7	−13.9	−18.5
St. Louis	10	5.0	−12.5	−17.1	−27.2
Baltimore	11	10.5	− 1.1	− 3.6	−13.1
Cleveland	12	4.2	− 4.2	−14.3	−23.6
Houston	13	55.0	57.4	31.4	29.2
Newark	14	2.1	− 7.6	− 5.6	−13.8
Minneapolis–St. Paul	15	6.8	− 7.4	− 6.6	−13.9
Dallas	16	47.4	56.4	24.2	7.1
Seattle–Everett	17	27.0	19.1	− 2.2	− 6.2
Milwaukee	19	8.5	16.3	− 3.3	−11.3
Atlanta	20	9.6	47.1	2.0	−14.1
Cincinnati	21	10.6	− 0.3	− 9.9	−15.0
Paterson–Clif–Pass	22	4.7	6.9	1.0	− 6.2
San Diego	23	64.4	71.4	21.5	25.5
Buffalo	24	0.7	− 8.2	−13.2	−18.5
Miami	25	44.8	177.0	14.8	3.6
Kansas City	26	14.4	4.1	6.7	−11.7
Denver	27	29.0	18.8	4.2	− 4.5
San Bernardino–R–O	28	44.5	68.0	38.4	21.4
Indianapolis	29	10.4	11.5	13.6	− 4.9
New Orleans	31	15.3	10.0	− 5.4	− 6.1
Portland	33	22.3	− 0.3	2.7	− 3.6
Phoenix	34	63.3	311.1	32.4	30.9
Columbus, Ohio	35	22.8	25.4	14.5	4.6
Providence–Paw–War	36	− 1.9	− 4.3	− 4.8	− 7.3
Rochester	37	2.3	− 4.2	− 7.0	−18.1
Louisville	40	15.7	5.8	− 7.5	−17.5
Sacramento	41	29.8	39.3	32.7	7.2
Fort Worth	43	56.9	27.8	10.4	− 2.1
Birmingham	44	21.8	4.6	−11.7	− 5.5
Albany–Schen–Troy	45	3.7	− 6.8	− 8.4	−16.8
Oklahoma City	50	19.1	33.2	13.0	9.5

SOURCES: Bogue 1953; U.S. Bureau of the Census 1963, 1971, and 1981b.

but rather from a growing imbalance between needs and resources. As we saw in Chapter 2, when cities differentially lose upper-income population, employment opportunities, and financial base, concentrations of poor and minority population grow (Kain 1979), and cities cannot assimilate inmovers (Bradbury, Downs, and Small 1982) because there are fewer jobs available and fewer resources to deal with their needs.

Much research suggests that such "functional decline" often accompanies population loss (Bradbury, Downs, and Small 1982). Between 1960 and 1970, relative income slipped in relation to the United States as a whole in all but two of these cities, and concentrations of poor and minorities generally increased. Table 4.3 presents some of the indicators that have been related to distress (Bunce and Goldberg 1979; Burchell et al. 1981; Fossett and Nathan 1981). For different purposes, distress has been measured by such indicators as population loss, unemployment, poverty, crime, employment loss, fiscal problems, and old housing in different combinations; but different measures are highly consistent in ranking the same cities as badly distressed (Burchell et al. 1981). The table shows the quintile ranking of these cities in terms of distress in 1970 (I is most distressed, V least), based on a comparison of sixty-six large cities with a factor index developed at the Department of Housing and Urban Development (HUD) to evaluate targeting formulas for the Community Development Block Grant program (Bunce and Goldberg 1979).[3] Altogether, twenty-one of the forty SMSAs have central cities in the two most distressed

3. The distress index is based on city rankings on three factors derived from a factor analysis of 13 indicators of socioeconomic problems in 1970. The factors and the variables that load heavily on them are

   1. Poverty: low income, poor persons, overcrowded housing, and housing lacking plumbing.
   2. Age and decline: pre-1940 housing stock, population loss, slow growth in retail sales, persons over age 65, female-headed households, and low education.
   3. Density: population density, crime, nonwhite population, renter households, and female-headed households.

Because the relative ranking assigned a city depends not only on the indicators used but also on the number and characteristics of the cities compared, the rankings reported here were based on comparing 66 large cities. They were chosen to include all of the 52 central cities in the 40 SMSAs studied here and all others with 1970 population above 150,000 whose distress has been ranked by either Fossett and Nathan (1981) or in the different distress rankings reviewed and summarized by Burchell et al. (1981). For the SMSAs with multiple central cities, a distress score was calculated separately from data for each city, and a composite score for the multiple cities calculated by weighting the separate scores by the 1970 population of each city. Some of the multiple central cities differed quite markedly in distress. For example, Warwick is much less distressed than either Providence or Pawtucket, and Clifton much less distressed than Paterson or Passaic.

Table 4.2
Changes in SMSA Share and White Population, 1960–1980, and Net Migration by Race,
1960–1970, for Central Cities of Forty SMSAs

	City SMSA share		% change white pop.		Est. net migration	
	1960	1970	1960–70	1970–80	White	Black
New York	73	68	− 9	−29	−14	38
Los Angeles–LB	47	45	−17	5	− 3	30
Chicago	57	48	−19	−32	−24	14
Philadelphia	46	40	−13	−23	−17	7
Detroit	44	36	−29	−51	−33	20
San Francisco–O	42	35	−17	−28	−18	29
Washington	37	26	−39	−18	−40	9
Boston	22	19	−17	−25	−18	39
Pittsburgh	25	22	−18	−23	−20	− 6
St. Louis	36	26	−32	−34	−34	− 0
Baltimore	52	44	−21	−28	−24	10
Cleveland	46	36	−26	−33	−33	− 1
Houston	66	62	26	8	9	26
Newark	24	21	−37	−40	−40	23
Minneapolis–SP	54	41	− 9	−19	−17	46
Dallas	61	54	14	−11	6	36
Seattle–Everett	54	41	− 7	−14	−11	21
Milwaukee	58	51	−10	−23	−19	35
Atlanta	48	36	−20	−43	−27	18
Cincinnati	40	33	−17	−23	−27	− 2
Paterson–C–P	24	21	− 9	−24	−13	46
San Diego	56	51	17	8	5	39
Buffalo	41	34	−21	−31	−24	12
Miami	31	26	14	−10	14	− 9
Kansas City	44	40	0	−20	− 7	16
Denver	53	42	− 0	−20	− 9	34
S. Bernardino–R–O	28	27	34	4	22	NA
Indianapolis	71	67	7	−11	−11	15
New Orleans	69	57	−18	−27	−23	− 4
Portland	46	38	0	−10	− 2	22
Phoenix	66	60	31	18	17	22
Columbus, Ohio	62	59	11	− 2	− 3	12
Providence–P–W	29	23	−18	−12	−12	21
Rochester	44	34	−17	−31	−23	68
Louisville	54	44	−14	−23	−24	10
Sacramento	31	32	24	−10	15	65
Fort Worth	62	52	4	−15	− 2	20
Birmingham	47	41	−15	−28	−25	−17
Albany–S–T	42	36	−11	−15	−15	6
Oklahoma City	63	57	9	5	− 4	12

SOURCES: U.S. Bureau of the Census 1971 and 1981b.

Table 4.3

Indicators of Distress in Central Cities of Forty SMSAs Ranked by Size of SMSA in 1970

	(1) City / U.S. PCI ratio		(2) City age	(3) 1970 % old housing	(4) 1970 % poor	(5) 1970 % black	(6) 1970 distress rank	(7) City / suburb PCI ratio 1973	(8) City / suburb Disparity index 1970
	1959	1969							
New York	124	118	1830	62.1	14.6	21.2	II	88	−1
Los Angeles–LB	141	126	1960	32.1	12.8	16.5	III	104	−1
Chicago	124	109	1900	66.6	14.3	32.7	II	85	−4
Philadelphia	101	96	1800	69.5	15.1	33.6	II	82	−4
Detroit	108	102	1930	61.8	14.6	43.7	I	94	−5
San Francisco–O	146	129	1950	62.5	14.4	20.5	II	102	−4
Washington	129	123	1940	47.0	16.2	71.1	I	96	−5
Boston	103	99	1800	77.2	15.4	16.3	I	78	−5
Pittsburgh	105	98	1880	74.4	15.0	20.2	II	102	−5
St. Louis	97	87	1870	73.8	19.7	40.9	I	81	−4
Baltimore	100	92	1840	59.9	18.1	46.4	I	73	−5
Cleveland	100	90	1920	73.4	17.1	38.3	I	70	−5
Houston	111	108	1970	16.8	14.5	25.7	IV	115	1
Newark	96	79	1910	68.4	22.2	54.2	I	71	−5
Minneapolis–SP	120	110	1900	65.9	10.6	4.0	III	102	−4
Dallas	119	118	1970	18.1	13.4	24.9	IV	115	1
Seattle–Everett	134	127	1950	47.3	10.1	6.5	V	105	−1
Milwaukee	113	102	1900	55.0	11.2	14.7	III	85	−3
Atlanta	104	101	1960	30.3	19.9	51.3	II	97	−5
Cincinnati	110	100	1850	59.2	17.0	27.6	II	103	−4
Paterson–C–P	110	104	1880	63.9	12.5	17.4	II	79	−5
San Diego	124	112	1970	21.7	11.0	7.6	V	107	2

(continued on next page)

80

Table 4.3 (continued)

	(1) City/U.S. PCI ratio		(2) City age	(3) 1970 % old housing	(4) 1970 % poor	(5) 1970 % black	(6) 1970 distress rank	(7) City/suburb PCI ratio 1973	(8) City/suburb Disparity index 1970
	1959	1969							
Buffalo	103	92	1900	85.7	14.8	20.4	II	122	−5
Miami	99	90	1950	29.9	20.4	22.7	I	81	−5
Kansas City	117	106	1920	51.5	12.6	22.1	III	85	−4
Denver	122	113	1950	41.0	13.5	9.1	IV	110	−3
S. Bernardino–R–O	113	100	1960	20.1	12.5	7.4	V	113	−2/+3
Indianapolis	109	110	1970	40.0	9.4	18.0	V	110	2
New Orleans	94	86	1840	49.4	26.3	45.0	I	98	−2
Portland	123	113	1950	57.2	12.6	5.6	IV	108	−3
Phoenix	108	104	1970	11.1	11.6	4.8	V	109	3
Columbus, Ohio	101	96	1950	39.0	13.2	18.5	IV	96	−1
Providence–P–W	99	100	1880	68.1	13.4	4.9	III	102	−3
Rochester	111	103	1920	79.5	12.0	16.8	II	91	−4
Louisville	95	83	1930	53.3	17.0	23.8	II	91	−3
Sacramento	133	108	1970	27.6	14.1	10.7	IV	115	−1
Fort Worth	105	103	1950	26.7	13.4	19.9	IV	103	0
Birmingham	84	82	1950	42.0	23.9	42.0	I	95	−3
Albany–S–T	107	104	1910	78.2	12.4	7.9	III	105	0
Oklahoma City	107	103	1960	29.1	14.0	13.7	V	106	1

DATA DEFINITIONS AND SOURCES: (1) Ratio of city to U.S. per capita income—ACIR 1965, 1977; (2) City age, defined as the most recent decade in which city rates of population growth exceeded the national average growth rate—Watkins 1980; (3) 1970 percentage of city housing built before 1940–1970 population census data used by Bunce and Goldberg 1979; (4) 1970 percentage of city population with income below U.S. poverty line—ibid.; (5) 1970 percentage of population that was black—U.S. Bureau of the Census 1971; (6) 1970 distress rank (in quintiles)—Bunce and Goldberg 1979 (see also n. 3 to ch. 4); (7) 1973 ratio of city to suburb per capita income—ACIR 1977; (8) 1970 city-to-suburb disparity index—Bradbury, Downs, and Small 1982 (see also n. 5 to ch. 4).

81

Table 4.4
Favorable Characteristics for Central Cities of Forty SMSAs

Cities by 1970 distress rank	(1) 1970 SMSA size rank	(2) SMSA net migration	(3) City / suburb ratio		(4) Median commuting time (min.)	(5) SMSA economic type[a]	(6) 1975 bank rank	(7) Cultural rank
			Hedonic rent	Value				
QUINTILE I								
Newark	14	−12	86	70	21	Fcnl SSC	32	34
St. Louis	10	−1	85	93	20	Regl DSC	10	22
Washington	7	9	110	99	25	Natl SSC	16	2
Baltimore	11	0	94	75	24	Regl DSC	18	14
New Orleans	31	7	106	100	21	Regl DSC	23	26
Miami	25	15	100	100	22	Regl DSC	30	27
Cleveland	12	−8	82	79	22	Regl DSC	24	8
Detroit	5	NA	88	77	21	Fcnl SSC	12	15
Boston	8	0	96	79	20	Regl DSC	6	5
Birmingham	44	2	108	100	21	Subr DSC	54	63
QUINTILE II								
Atlanta	20	15	105	98	23	Regl DSC	9	30
Chicago	3	−1	98	87	23	Natl DSC	2	4
Buffalo	24	−13	100	74	18	Mfg	28	13
Philadelphia	4	−1	96	91	22	Regl DSC	7	7
Pittsburgh	9	−12	115	100	19	Fcnl SSC	14	16
New York	1	0	89	99	29	Natl DSC	1	1
Cincinnati	21	0	101	100	21	Regl DSC	19	19
Louisville	40	−7	100	90	20	Fcnl SSC	35	44
Paterson–C–P	22	−4	83	92	20	Fcnl SSC	54	167
San Francisco–O	6	8	113	107	21	Natl DSC	3	6
Rochester	37	−3	105	83	18	Fcnl SSC	54	25
QUINTILE III								
Albany–S–T	45	−12	110	100	18	Gv–Ed SSC	39	46
Providence–P–W	36	−7	93	100	17	Mfg	43	28
Kansas City	26	6	102	93	20	Regl DSC	8	23
Milwaukee	19	2	98	83	19	Fcnl SSC	26	12
Los Angeles–LB	2	10	103	109	20	Natl DSC	4	3
Minneapolis–SP	15	5	93	91	19	Regl DSC	17	10

Table 4.4 *(continued)*

Cities by 1970 distress rank	(1) 1970 SMSA size rank	(2) SMSA net migration	(3) City / suburb ratio		(4) Median commuting time (min.)	(5) SMSA economic type[a]	(6) 1975 bank rank	(7) Cultural rank
			Hedonic rent	Value				
QUINTILE IV								
Denver	27	18	98	96	19	Regl DSC	13	9
Columbus, Ohio	35	1	94	90	20	Regl DSC	39	61
Fort Worth	43	18	107	100	19	Regl DSC	20	11
Houston	13	27	107	107	22	Regl DSC	11	20
Dallas	16	18	106	100	21	Regl DSC	5	11
Sacramento	41	16	100	92	18	Gv–Ed SSC	54	51
Portland	33	22	104	90	19	Regl DSC	22	42
QUINTILE V								
S. Bernardino–R–O	28	20	100	100	16	R&Rec	54	72
Oklahoma City	50	18	100	100	18	Subr DSC	32	48
Indianapolis	29	3	100	92	21	Regl DSC	35	31
San Diego	23	12	108	100	20	Ind–Mil	43	18
Phoenix	34	23	104	100	19	Regl DSC	27	50
Seattle–Everett	17	20	107	100	21	Regl DSC	15	17

DATA DEFINITIONS AND SOURCES: (1) Rank of SMSA by size in 1970—U.S. Bureau of the Census 1971; (2) Net migration for SMSA, 1975–80, of independent adults younger than 30—Greenwood 1984; (3) City-to-suburb ratios of hedonic rents and values, mid-1970s—Malpezzi, Ozanne, and Thibodeau 1980; (4) Median commuting time in minutes from home to work in SMSA, mid-1970s—Annual Housing Surveys for 1974, 1975, or 1976; (5) SMSA economic type—Noyelle and Stanback 1983; (6) 1975 bank rank, based on number of correspondent relationships with banks in the other 66 cities identified in the SMSA Annual Housing Surveys—Bartelt 1985; (7) Cultural rank in terms of cultural facilities—Boyer and Savageau 1981.

[a] Abbreviations are as follows: Fcnl SSC —Functional Specialized Service Center
Regl DSC —Regional Diversified Service Center
Natl SSC —National (Scale) Specialized Service Center
Subr DSC —Subregional Diversified Service Center
Mfg —Manufacturing Production Center
Gv–Ed SSC—Government–Education Specialized Service Center
R&Rec. —Resort–Retirement Consumer–Oriented Center
Ind–Mil —Industrial–Military Production Center

quintiles, and most of those in the third quintile have also been categorized as distressed in other rankings.[4] Except for Houston and Dallas,
all the central cities in the twenty largest SMSAs are in the three most
distressed quintiles. (I refer to cities in the first quintile as "most distressed," and to those in the first and second quintiles together as "more
distressed." "Distressed" refers to all twenty-seven cities in the most distressed three quintiles.) Differences in distress among these cities conform to common generalizations: larger cities in the Northeast and North
Central regions have a high incidence of distress, and distress is correlated
with population loss, a low share of SMSA population, city-suburban income disparities, and city age. As discussed below, distress is also correlated with greater "gaps" between city selection rates and city population
shares.

Selective outmigration of upper-income residents and employment opportunities is induced by many of the conditions characterizing distress,
such as older infrastructure and housing and population loss. But it is particularly likely when there are marked city-suburban disparities in income, taxes, services, available housing, and poverty (Frey 1980). Such
intrametropolitan disparities are measured in Table 4.3 by the 1973 ratio
of city-to-suburban per capita income, and by an index, varying from −5
to +5, that summarizes differences in crime, poverty, old housing, income, and employment.[5] Only in three of the distressed southern cities—
New Orleans, Louisville, and Birmingham—are city-suburban disparities
not −4 or −5.

Yet, as Table 4.4 shows, many of these distressed cities also have characteristics prominently mentioned as contributing to revitalization. (Cities
are ranked by distress in the table to facilitate discussion of differences in

4. For example, Fossett and Nathan's Urban Condition Index ranked Minneapolis in the
most distressed quintile among 55 large cities in 1960, Kansas City in the second, and Milwaukee in the third. Bradbury, Downs, and Small (1982) compared 153 cities on five indicators of decline: Los Angeles and Providence each scored −2 on their −5 to +5 scale.

5. The "city-suburb disparity" index shown was derived by Bradbury, Downs, and Small
(1982, 48–67). Differences between 153 large cities and their 121 SMSAs were calculated for
five elements:

　　1. City minus SMSA unemployment rate, 1975;
　　2. City minus SMSA violent crime rate, 1975;
　　3. City/SMSA ratio of per capita income, 1974;
　　4. City/SMSA ratio of percentage of population poor, 1970; and
　　5. City minus SMSA percentage of old housing, 1970.

All cities were then ranked on the basis of each component, and then each distribution was
divided into thirds, with scores of −1, 0, and +1, respectively, going to cities in the most
disadvantaged, middle and least disadvantaged thirds of the distribution for each component. A score of −5 thus indicates that a city's relation to its SMSA was in the "bottom" third
of the distribution relative to other cities and their SMSAs on each of the five components.

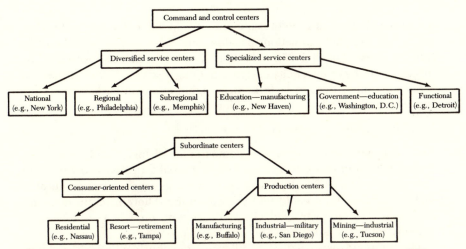

Figure 4.1. Classification Scheme for the 140 Largest SMSAs. SOURCE: Hanson 1982, adapted from Noyelle and Stanback 1983.

terms of distress.) Although more than half of the distressed cities were in SMSAs with no net inmigration of young adults between 1975 and 1980, many had above-average commuting times and central-city housing which in the mid-1970s was, in Lowry's words, "relatively a bargain." As shown in the final column of the table, many in addition were major centers of cultural activities. Perhaps most striking is the information about economic base. Many of the large old distressed cities are national or regional diversified service centers (DSCs), thought to have better prospects for future growth than more specialized service centers (SSCs) such as functional nodes dependent on particular industries or cities dependent on manufacturing or military contracts.[6] If position with respect to the production and export of advanced services—including education, government, and corporate support activities—will indeed increasingly determine future economic development (Noyelle and Stanback 1983), the extent to which an area is a "command and control center" should also influence its likelihood of gentrification and future revitalization, in large part because of the well-educated workers required by such an economic base (Kasarda 1982). Figure 4.1 summarizes this urban hierarchy and ex-

6. Hanson (1983, 38–39) summarizes the continuously evolving new hierarchy of metropolitan areas as follows: "The new urban system is characterized by the growing dominance in corporate and producer services of a relatively small number of national and regional 'command and control' centers. In these centers, strategic economic and political decisions are made that affect both these cities and the rest of the urban system. The centers contain high concentrations of corporate and government headquarters, producer services, and higher education and cultural resources. The remaining urban areas are more specialized in their economic functions, which tend to be subordinate to the decisions made in the com-

plains the characterization of economic base in Table 4.4; the table's data on rank in banking transactions provides one concrete measure of rank in the hierarchy (Bartelt 1985). Whether advantages such as position in the urban hierarchy or lower city costs are helping distressed cities attract and retain migrants, despite factors encouraging cumulative decline, is the important empirical question considered in this chapter.

Possible Futures for Distressed Cities

Even if economic restructuring, demographic changes, and cost incentives might help distressed cities revive, probabilities of recovery differ among these cities. Disadvantages and advantages such as those indicated in Tables 4.3 and 4.4 could interact with quite different implications for the twenty-seven distressed cities, depending on which factors most strongly influence migration and city selection.

The ten most distressed cities differ in city-suburban disparities, housing price differentials, commuting time, and economic base. In terms of net migration, differences among SMSAs are mainly regional. Due to net outmigration of young adults, the baby boom is less likely to have helped northern SMSAs, but net migration was positive for the southern SMSAs, particularly Washington. Newark and Cleveland had the greatest intra-metropolitan disparities, with extremely distressed cities but affluent suburbs, and Baltimore's disparities were almost as great. The distressed Southern cities, New Orleans and Birmingham, differed least from their suburbs, since poverty rates were relatively high in both. Selective migration within SMSAs mirrored these differences: for most of these distressed cities upper-income movers were only two-thirds as likely to select cities as the city population share might predict. Intrametropolitan differences in housing prices seem greatest for cities with other intra-metropolitan disparities: Newark, Baltimore, Detroit, Cleveland, and Boston offered the greatest bargains for owned housing. Despite large city-suburban disparities, Washington's housing was not competitively priced. Washington, Boston, and Cleveland stand out for their cultural opportunities, and commuting times were longest in Washington and Baltimore.

In terms of economic base, six of these ten SMSAs are regional diversified service centers (DSCs), serving as regional nodes in the command and control hierarchy. Washington is the nation's only national government-education "control" center, but because it is very distressed, with

---

mand and control centers, and they can be grouped by their primary orientation as consumer service centers or productions centers."

Following Noyelle and Stanback (1983), who developed this classification, I use the term "node" to mean "service center."

high intrametropolitan disparities and no apparent housing cost advantage, its experience during the 1970s is of particular interest. Newark and Detroit are functional centers whose welfare is tightly linked to particular industries, and Birmingham is a subregional node.

Weighing such factors, Newark and Detroit might be predicted to be the least likely of the most distressed quintile to revive: they are very distressed, with extreme city-suburban disparities and relatively specialized economic bases. Only if housing bargains are important incentives to movers might they attract more residents. The regional DSCs, by contrast, might attract more investment and migrants because of their specialized service activities. If so, New Orleans should retain more movers in the center city than other nodes because of lower disparities in conditions between city and suburbs. Washington's housing costs and sharp city-suburban disparities should deter central-city residence, although cultural opportunities and commuting burdens might encourage it.

The eleven cities in the second quintile of distress are in SMSAs that are equally diverse in economic base, with three of the four national DSCs (New York, Chicago, and San Francisco), three regional DSCs, four functional nodes, and a manufacturing center. All these cities lost population during the 1970s, and only Atlanta and San Francisco were in SMSAs with net inmigration of young adults between 1975 and 1980. All eleven cities were more distressed than their suburbs, with the disparities greatest for Paterson and Atlanta. New York and Louisville (although very different otherwise) were the only two for which the disparity index was not −4 or −5. City selection rates reflected these disparities, with gaps varyings from 70 to 90 percent of city population shares. Only in Buffalo, Rochester, and Chicago were owned home values less than 90 percent of equivalent suburban homes; rental units in most cities were as expensive as equivalent suburban units. New York stands out as the preeminent cultural and banking center, and also for its excessive commuting time. Chicago and San Francisco add cultural advantages to their position in the national hierarchy, but in San Francisco central-city housing is correspondingly more expensive.

If previous distress, population losses, and city-suburb disparities are important predictors of cumulative decline, continued suburbanization would appear likely in all, especially Pittsburgh, Buffalo, and Atlanta. Housing-cost differentials appear insufficient to overcome city problems in most of the cities, although in New York commuting time should provide strong incentives to live closer to work. If position in the command and control hierarchy aids city revitalization, the national and regional nodes would be more likely to recover than functional nodes or manufacturing centers.

The six cities in the third quintile are less distressed than the others. However, all but Albany-Schenectady-Troy have city-suburb disparities, and all but Los Angeles have had both population losses and selective out-migration. Several have been judged severely distressed in other rankings (Burchell et al. 1981; Fossett and Nathan 1981), and all are relatively distressed compared to smaller cities (Bunce and Neal 1984).

Based on the factors considered, Kansas City and Minneapolis-St. Paul appear weakest in this quintile because of their relatively great city-suburban disparities, but their economic role as DSCs and their housing cost advantages provide offsetting strengths. Net inmigration, marked housing bargains, and cultural facilities are all positive for Milwaukee, and inmigration and cultural and service facilities could outweigh high housing costs for Los Angeles. The combination of net outmigration, city-suburban disparities, a manufacturing base, and no cost advantages in owned housing make Providence-Pawtucket-Warwick appear to have less chance for revival than other cities in this quintile. However, these cities were almost alone in having relative gains in per capita income between 1960 and 1970.

City Selection Rates and City Shares of SMSA Population

Because gathering and processing data is always more difficult for out-migrants than for inmigrants, statistics on complete outmigration from cities are rare; obtaining such measures over time for comparable geographic units by income or education is even more difficult. Even the decennial population censuses have not provided complete data in the past on gross outmigration from cities by migrant characteristics other than race.[7] The 1960 and 1970 census data used here are the best available for the purpose of comparing trends over time. For both censuses, the *Mobility for Metropolitan Areas* volumes tabulated mobility over the previous five years within, to, and from individual large metropolitan areas by characteristics such as age, race, education, and income. City and suburban residence were further distinguished for movers within and to each SMSA, but not for migrants from each SMSA. All migrants into each central city were thus identified, but measuring complete outmigration from either central cities or suburbs is impossible because only outmovement from each city to its suburbs (or from the suburbs to the central city) is explic-

---

7. Estimates of 1960–70 net migration by race were prepared after the 1970 census for all major SMSAs and their central cities by the residual method. However, "as a residual value, the net migration component reflects the net effect of any errors in the data used, such as differential undercounting in the 1960 and 1970 censuses, boundary changes, improper allocation of births and deaths by place of residence and many others. . . . Many cities have annexed territory during the past decade, and the shifts resulting from annexation are thrown into the migration component" (U.S. Bureau of the Census 1971, 117). No estimates or measures of net migration by income are available.

itly shown. Changes in SMSA or city boundaries between 1960 and 1970 provide a further disadvantage: they mean that data are only directly comparable over the decade for some of these cities and metropolitan areas.[8]

Because of this study's concern with reviving distressed cities, changes in migration are studied by income rather than by education, the other indicator of status available. For four years around 1980 (1978, 1979, 1980, and 1981), data were drawn from Annual Housing Survey (AHS) SMSA samples to define the same groups of migrants as 1970 census data.[9] The AHS covers cities and SMSAs as defined in 1970, so geographical comparability is not a problem in studying changes during the 1970s. The income categories are also directly comparable: the AHS family income cutoffs were chosen to equal $10,000 in 1969 dollars.[10]

Since complete information on outmigration is unavailable from these data, trends in movement to and from cities are measured by the propor-

8. The census data for individual SMSAs were taken from table 4 of the *Mobility for Metropolitan Areas* (U.S. Bureau of Census 1963) and table 15 of U.S. Bureau of Census (1972). It should be noted that the racial information is not strictly comparable over time. In the 1960 census volumes, information by income was not available by race, but total mobility was disaggregated into white and nonwhite. In 1970, data on the migration of the Negro and non-Negro population aged 16+ by income were available. The Annual Housing Survey data show intrametropolitan movement for people in households with black or nonblack heads. An additional problem with the 1960–70 comparisons is that in 26 of the 40 SMSAs the boundaries of particular SMSAs and cities changed between 1960 and 1970 as additional counties were added to SMSAs and cities annexed new territory. Both the Annual Housing Survey data and the 1970 census data, however, refer to the 1970 boundaries of SMSAs and central cities.

9. The Annual Housing Survey was taken nationally annually between 1973 and 1981 by the Bureau of the Census for the Department of Housing and Urban Development. Beginning in 1974, 60 of the largest SMSAs were also surveyed on a rotating basis—first 20 each year, and then, after 1977, 15 each year. The "1980" SMSA data studied here come from surveys taken in 1978, 1979, 1980, and 1981. Published reports on the housing and personal characteristics of "recent movers" (i.e., those moving in the past year) are found in Series H-170, "Housing Characteristics for Selected Metropolitan Areas," of the *Current Housing Reports,* published by the Bureau of the Census (1978, 1979, 1980, and 1981a). The published data on the central city/non–central city origins and destinations of movers cover only households that had the same head before and after the move, a group which constitutes about 70% of total households. To include all households and thus measure all population to be comparable with published 1970 census data, the tabulations reported here were drawn from the AHS microdata computer tapes.

10. To compare trends in constant incomes, the cutoffs between higher and lower family income brackets were defined to equal $10,000 in 1969 dollars, which was the cutoff in the 1970 published reports that was the closest to the actual 1969 median family income. The published 1960 cutoff of $7,000 in 1959 dollars roughly equals $10,000 in 1969. The AHS cutoffs could be chosen more precisely; with change in the CPI used as the deflator, they were as follows: $17,800 in 1978, $19,800 in 1979, $22,500 in 1980, and $24,800 in 1981. The AHS data were also tabulated to show migration by number of persons by family income to be comparable to the published 1970 data.

tion of movers to and within the SMSA who choose city over suburban residence. These "city selection rates"[11] are defined as

$$\frac{\text{Movers to and within the SMSA choosing the central city}}{\text{All movers to and within the SMSA}} \times 100.$$

Since these rates vary with the relative location of housing opportunities within each metropolitan area, they necessarily differ among SMSAs, and they tend to decline over time as new housing is built in suburban areas. Therefore, we are concerned not with absolute differences among SMSAs but with different trends in city selection rates in comparison with each city's share of SMSA population, ideally within SMSAs that had constant city and SMSA boundaries. If no suburbanization were occurring, city selection rates of movers might be "expected" to equal the city share of total SMSA population. Whether trends and levels in city selection rates differ by income is also important. Cities that retain and attract upper-income movers at the same rate as their share of total SMSA population are less likely to develop poverty concentrations. But when upper-income movers select cities at lower rates than lower-income movers and than the city share of SMSA population (which I term a "gap" between selection and city share), suburbanization accelerates and income disparities between cities and suburbs widen.

Figure 4.2 introduces this measure by showing annual changes between 1974 and 1981 in city selection rates of all movers, and of movers with family income above $10,000 (in 1969 dollars), for the forty SMSAs studied here, grouped by region. The proportions of total and upper-income SMSA population residing in these central cities each year are also graphed.

Annual Changes by Region, 1974–1981

Like the five-year migration trends studied in Chapter 3, these annual rates show city selection increasing in the late 1970s. Paralleling the marginal nature of the national improvements, however, the annual data suggest some recovery after 1977 or 1978 to earlier levels rather than major gains over the entire period. In all four regions, the share of SMSA population living in central cities declined over the 1970s, with the rate of decline showing toward the end of the decade. City selection rates dropped more sharply (and erratically, because of sampling error) than population shares until 1977 or 1978, but then increased in all regions outside the West. Some increase also occurred among higher-income movers, most markedly in the South.

The figure clearly illustrates that higher-income groups have been less

11. See Frey (1978 and 1979b) for detailed discussion of this measure and its usefulness in studying intrametropolitan migration.

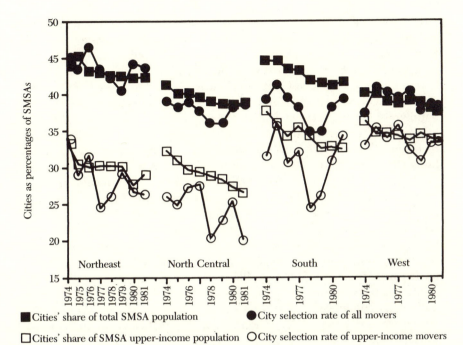

■ Cities' share of total SMSA population   **●** City selection rate of all movers

□ Cities' share of SMSA upper-income population   **○** City selection rate of upper-income movers

Figure 4.2. Central City Percentage Shares of Metropolitan Population and Movers by Income, 1974–1981, for Forty SMSAs Grouped by Region.

likely than the total population to live in or move to central cities in all four regions. The percentage-point difference in shares and selection rates between total and upper-income population is greatest in the northeastern and north central regions and least in the West. Regions have quite different "gaps" between the proportion of movers selecting cities over suburbs and the percentage of SMSA residents in cities. In no region do city selection rates of upper-income movers equal the "expected" level of the city share of SMSA population, although the gap is smallest in the West. Acknowledging differences by income, we might at least expect city selection rates of upper-income movers to approximate city shares of *upper-income* SMSA population (or even exceed them, since movers tend to be younger than the total population and younger adults tend to prefer cities). In the Northeast and West, city selection rates of both upper-income and total population did at least approximate their relative intrametropolitan population shares over the period. But in the north central and southern regions even this more conservative expectation was not met. Instead, city selection rates were lower than city population shares, implying that suburbanization was rapid.

The regional differences also illustrate the relation between distress and city selection rates of upper-income movers that are markedly lower than corresponding city shares of metropolitan population. The regions with high gaps between the two—the Northeast and North Central—have a higher incidence of distressed cities, while the West has the lowest. As might be expected in view of the role of greater upper-income outmigration in cumulative decline, on the city level as well, the gaps between actual upper-income city selection rates and the rates that would be expected if selection corresponded to city-suburban population distribution are correlated with distress. As the regional averages show for the 1970s, in both 1960 and 1970 city selection rates of upper-income movers were lower than those of lower-income movers in all SMSAs studied except San Diego, San Bernardino, and Phoenix. In 1960, the ratio between selection rates of upper-income movers and each city's share of SMSA population varied from 57 percent in Miami, 63 percent in Newark, 65 percent in Washington, and 66 percent in Detroit to 100 percent (that is, no disparity) in Dallas, Houston, Phoenix, and San Bernardino. Rankings of cities in terms of this gap between observed and "expected" city selection rates of upper-income movers were significantly correlated with the 1970 distress scores on which the rank for these cities given in Table 4.4 were based.[12]

Average Changes over Two Decades, 1960–1970 and 1970–"1980"

Both the national data of Chapter 3 and the annual trends in city selection rates of Figure 4.2 imply that suburbanization slowed only slightly in the 1970s. With data for city selection rates from the 1960 and 1970 censuses, however, we can explicitly compare the slight changes during the 1970s against experience over the previous decade. This comparison reveals that even stability during the 1970s represents a remarkable improvement over earlier trends toward suburbanization, and that increases in city selection signify a marked reversal of previous tendencies. Between 1955–60 and 1965–70, the proportion of movers selecting city residence had almost universally declined in the large SMSAs studied, regardless of levels of distress in their central cities.[13] During the 1970s, however, de-

12. The Spearman rank correlation between distress in 1970 and this "gap" between expected and observed city selection during 1955–60 would be .79 if the three furthest outliers were excluded. Indeed, Indianapolis, the furthest outlier, should be excluded, because by 1970 the city had greatly changed its boundaries by annexing almost all of Marion County. The other two outliers were New Orleans and Birmingham, which, like many southern SMSAs, have relatively low city-suburban disparities because of high levels of poverty throughout the SMSA.

13. For 20 of these cities (5 per region), I earlier documented in detail the changes in city selection rates between 1960, 1970, and the mid-1970s, of white movers by age, education,

spite continued net suburbanization of population, the proportion of movers selecting city homes increased in more than half of the SMSAs studied, with some of the greatest proportional increases in city selection occurring in distressed cities.

Table 4.5 summarizes averages of the changes for the forty SMSAs on which these conclusions are based. Between 1960 and 1970 there had been marked declines both in the proportion of SMSA population living in central cities and in the proportion of movers selecting city residence during the previous five-year period. Averages for the forty studied SMSAs, as well as national or regional totals showing this effect, reflect in part the offsetting effects of SMSA expansion and of annexation of new territory by central cities, and thus are not directly comparable over time. But as the bottom two sections of Table 4.5 indicate, such declines also characterized the two subsets of the studied SMSAs that had few or no boundary changes between 1960 and 1970. In both groups, on average, central cities' shares of upper-income and total SMSA population dropped more quickly than did their shares of lower-income population, thus reducing per capita income, revenue, and purchasing power. City selection rates of upper-income movers were lower than their share of SMSA population at the beginning of the period, while poorer movers were selecting city residence at "expected" rates—in proportion to their residential distribution within SMSAs. In the fourteen SMSAs with constant boundaries, declines in city population during the 1960s thus resulted almost completely from greater selection of suburbs by upper-income movers. When the eleven SMSAs with minor boundary changes are added, averages for these twenty-five SMSAs (bottom section of the table) show that SMSA expansion also contributed to decreasing city population shares for both income groups. For both income groups, however, disparities between city selection rates and city shares narrowed over the decade.

By contrast, between 1970 and "1980" (i.e., 1978–81; see note to Table 4.5), the average drop in city shares of SMSA population was much less than it had been over the 1960s. This can be seen most directly by comparing changes between decades in suburbanization rates for the fourteen SMSAs with constant boundaries. Moreover, average city selection rates of movers no longer declined in the 1970s. Instead, they were stable for the complete group of SMSAs and increased slightly for SMSAs with constant boundaries. This stability in city selection rates meant that by "1980" white movers were more likely to choose central-city residence than their

---

and income (Nelson 1981). The origin of movers to and within the SMSAs is also distinguished as city, suburb, or outside the SMSA. Like the Current Population Survey data presented in Chapter 2, my analysis for those cities indicates that upturns in city selection rates after 1970 were most likely among movers who had been city residents (i.e., there was less outmigration and more retention than previously) and least likely among suburban residents.

Table 4.5
Average City Shares of SMSA Population and City Selection Rates of Movers
for Total and Nonblack Population, by Family Income in 1969 Dollars
(Percentages)

	Total population		Nonblack population	
	1960	1970	1970	"1980"[a]
40 STUDIED SMSAS				
Total population				
City share of SMSA	48	39	34	29
City selection rate	46	38	32	32
Family income of <$10,000				
City share of SMSA	52	47	39	36
City selection rate	52	47	38	39
Family income of $10,000+				
City share of SMSA	43	34	31	23
City selection rate	39	31	28	22
14 SMSAS WITH NO 1960–70 BOUNDARY CHANGES				
Total population				
City share of SMSA	40	33	27	24
City selection rate	38	33	26	27
Family income of <$10,000				
City share of SMSA	45	43	35	32
City selection rate	45	44	34	34
Family income of $10,000+				
City share of SMSA	34	27	24	18
City selection rate	30	25	22	17
25 SMSAS WITH FEW OR NO 1960–70 BOUNDARY CHANGES				
Total population				
City share of SMSA	46	36	30	26
City selection rate	44	35	28	29
Family income of <$10,000				
City share of SMSA	51	46	36	33
City selection rate	50	46	36	36
Family income of $10,000+				
City share of SMSA	40	30	27	20
City selection rate	36	28	24	19

[a]"1980" refers to 1978, 1979, 1980, or 1981, depending on the year in which each SMSA was surveyed by the Annual Housing Survey.

(end-of-period) population distribution would have predicted. Although equivalent data do not exist prior to 1960, in view of past suburbanization it is highly likely that this is the first time in many decades that such has been the case.

The averages for the three groupings of SMSAs also imply, however, that improvements in total city selection rates were mainly due to lower-income movers, rather than to a new attractiveness of cities to upper-income groups. Both city selection rates and city shares continued to decline among upper-income whites in the 1970s. Yet the gaps between rates and shares did narrow for upper-income movers, raising the possibility of future stability even among these movers. The regional data of Figure 4.2, moreover, imply that by 1981 upper-income city selection rates approximated city upper-income population shares in all regions except the North Central states. To determine whether distressed cities benefitted from these post-1970 improvements, we next focus on the changes between the 1965–70 and "1980" periods that can be compared within the constant 1970 boundaries of individual SMSAs and cities.

How Post-1970 Changes in City Selection Rates Differ for Forty SMSAs

Changes after 1970 in city selection rates for the forty SMSAs (Table 4.6) parallel the averages in showing greater upturns in city selection among all nonblack movers than among upper-income movers. As the first column of the table shows in ratio form, within 1970 boundaries, city shares of SMSA white population declined in almost all of these areas.[14] Nevertheless, city selection rates for all white movers rose between 1970 and 1980 for twenty-three of the forty SMSAs (col. 2). Distressed cities shared in such increases: upturns were most common for cities in the third and second distress quintiles and least likely for the fourth quintile. Selection also increased after 1970 for five of the ten cities in the most distressed quintile, including the three most distressed cities. Yet city selection rates plummeted more than 20 percent over the decade in four cities, and three of them—New Orleans, Detroit, and Atlanta—were distressed.

14. The only cities with increases over the decade in share of SMSA white population within the 1970 city (and SMSA) boundaries were Los Angeles and Washington. The table shows the relative (ratio) changes in share, since a given percentage point decrease will be more serious the lower the 1970 base. For example, Detroit's loss of 10 percentage points implied that its 1980 share of the SMSA's nonblack population was only 56% that of the 1970 share, while for Dallas an "equivalent" decline of 10 percentage points still meant that its 1980 share was 80% of its earlier share. Considering the relative changes more meaningful than percentage point differences, I have presented the information about changes in city selection rates in the table in ratio form.

Table 4.6

Changes after 1970 in City Selection Rates of Whites for Forty SMSAs, and 1980 "Gap" of Observed / Expected Upper-Income Selection Rates

Cities by 1970 distress rank	"1980"/1970 ratio of city shares of SMSA population	"1980"/1970 ratio of city selection rates			Gap	
		All whites	Upper-income	Lower-income	1980 level	1980–70 difference
QUINTILE I						
Newark	95	147	56	119	34	−25
St. Louis	76	112	73	96	64	− 3
Washington	121	173	161	170	91	22
Baltimore	76	86	66	87	56	− 8
New Orleans	73	76	57	89	68	−18
Miami	101	90	59	91	43	−31
Cleveland	86	102	68	92	54	−14
Detroit	56	64	45	55	56	−14
Boston	98	139	91	120	74	− 6
Birmingham	64	90	76	89	102	17
QUINTILE II						
Atlanta	58	61	44	64	55	−18
Chicago	84	91	65	88	59	−18
Buffalo	82	101	79	93	74	− 6
Philadelphia	89	98	73	100	58	−12
Pittsburgh	85	119	37	134	36	−46
New York	97	112	110	98	98	11
Cincinnati	85	114	96	114	102	12
Louisville	80	107	70	103	68	−10
Paterson−C−P	101	128	60	146	42	−28
San Francisco−O	101	124	84	126	59	−12
Rochester	83	113	82	100	72	− 1
QUINTILE III						
Albany−S−T	84	120	83	107	74	− 2
Providence−P−W	90	123	130	111	120	37
Kansas City	93	105	81	120	74	−12
Milwaukee	84	98	80	99	83	− 4
Los Angeles−LB	107	112	108	111	98	2
Minneapolis−SP	85	110	77	95	65	− 7
QUINTILE IV						
Denver	76	84	70	84	71	− 6
Columbus, Ohio	97	109	88	114	83	− 8
Fort Worth	77	71	58	76	66	−22
Houston	72	81	62	99	80	−14
Dallas	80	98	72	116	87	− 8
Sacramento	85	103	73	106	67	−11
Portland	79	88	58	98	56	−21
QUINTILE V						
S. Bernardino−R−O	89	98	82	110	88	− 8
Oklahoma City	101	110	114	107	107	12
Indianapolis	89	107	87	117	98	− 2
San Diego	96	96	86	103	89	−10
Phoenix	79	84	70	90	84	−11
Seattle−Everett	86	102	77	107	66	− 8

SOURCE: Ratios derived from a comparison of data from U.S. Census 1972b and Annual Housing Survey tabulations.

But changes in the selection rates of upper-income movers (col. 3) were much less encouraging. In most cases—for both distressed and less distressed cities—improvements in total city selection rates were due either to upturns among lower-income rather than upper-income movers, or to changes in city population composition. In only three central cities did upper-income city selection rates both rise and increase more than lower-income rates: New York, Providence-Pawtucket-Warwick, and Oklahoma City. Washington and Los Angeles were the only other cities in which upper-income rates rose, with Washington recording a spectacular percentage increase from a low base. For cities in the third quintile of distress, upper-income rates either rose or were nearly stable (i.e., declined less than 20% over the decade as the city share of SMSA population also dropped). But only five of the remaining twenty-one more distressed cities—Cincinnati, Boston, San Francisco, Rochester, and Buffalo—achieved such "stability." Moreover, in Boston and Rochester, as in Washington slightly and many others markedly, the decade's change in total city selection rates was higher than that for either lower- or upper-income movers. This fact implies that the increase in total rates resulted in part from compositional changes—growing proportions of lower-income nonblacks in these cities—a development in itself likely to hinder "revival."

In contrast to these few instances of improvement or stability, the situation of the remaining distressed cities definitely worsened. In the other fourteen of the twenty-one more distressed cities, upper-income city selection rates dropped more than 20 percent over the decade. Seven cities had decreases of more than 40 percent: Pittsburgh, Atlanta, Detroit, Newark, New Orleans, Miami, and Paterson-Clifton-Passaic. Even worse for these seven and several others is evidence that decline is accelerating. The final two columns of Table 4.6 show the extent of the gaps in "1980" between upper-income city selection rates and city shares of total SMSA white population, and the decade's percentage point changes in these gaps. Pittsburgh, Miami, Newark, and Paterson-Clifton-Passaic were clearly worst off in terms of both levels and changes in gaps. In 1980, their upper-income movers were only 30 to 40 percent as likely to select city residence as the population distribution would imply, and this ratio had dropped sharply over the decade. At the encouraging end of this spectrum, the decade's changes in gap were positive for Providence, Washington, Birmingham, Cincinnati, and New York. Providence's gap in 1980 was particularly heartening: upper-income movers were 20 percent *more* likely to choose the central cities of Providence, Pawtucket, and Warwick than the cities' share of metropolitan population would suggest.

Finally, if we compare all cities, these measures imply that disparities between distressed and nondistressed cities are widening. In contrast to the sharp declines in upper-income selection found for many of the more distressed cities, of cities in the two least distressed quintiles only Portland and Fort Worth had drops as large as 40 percent.[15]

Determinants of Changing City Selection Rates

This closer look at recent changes in city selection in twenty-seven distressed cities demonstrates that most failed to attract more upper-income movers either absolutely or proportionally during the relatively favorable conditions of the 1970s. Although city selection rates of upper-income nonblack movers dropped less rapidly than did city shares in almost half of the distressed cities, thus narrowing the gap between present share and movers' choices, actual upturns in city selection rates were quite rare. The most favorable interpretation that can be drawn from these trends is that five of the twenty-seven cities attracted higher proportions of upper-income movers, while eight maintained the status quo rather than continuing to decline at earlier rates. But in the other fourteen cities conditions deteriorated further.

With regard to differences among cities in favorable and unfavorable factors, the pattern of changes (weakly) supports claims that economic restructuring can help slow or reverse differential upper-income outmigration; at least this hypothesis appears to explain the actual changes better than either demographic or cost alternatives. Since three of the five national nodes (New York, Los Angeles, and Washington) had upturns, while San Francisco was "stable," it appears that restructuring economic bases is aiding distressed cities at the hierarchy's apex to overcome cumulative outmigration (see Table 4.7). But through 1981, regional nodes other than Boston and Cincinnati were apparently not helped, and functional nodes did not benefit.[16] The sharp declines in city selection experienced by Atlanta and Miami despite young adult inmigration seem to rule out the possibility that the baby boom alone can revitalize otherwise deteriorating cities, while continued declines for Newark, Detroit, and Buffalo—in contrast to improvements for New York and San Francisco—suggest that intrametropolitan differences in relative housing costs are not sufficient incentives for revival either.

To evaluate formally the relative roles of factors hypothesized to influence "back-to-the-city" movement in the actual 1970–80 changes in city selection rates for distressed cities, the income-specific ratios reported in Table 4.6 were regressed against a variety of independent variables. As I

15. Such sharp decreases in city selection suggest that distress may be worsening in these two cities.

16. Obviously, however, several of these functional nodes, especially Detroit and Pittsburgh, are dependent on industries that were seriously affected by economic conditions in the late 1970s and early 1980s.

Table 4.7
Patterns of Change in City Selection Rates of Upper-Income Movers, 1970–1980,
for Distressed Cities by Economic Type

Downturn	Stability	Upturn
	National Diversified Service Centers	
Chicago	San Francisco	New York
		Los Angeles
		Washington
	Regional Diversified Service Centers	
Atlanta	Boston	Cincinnati
Baltimore	Kansas City	
Cleveland	Minneapolis–	
Miami	St. Paul	
New Orleans		
Philadelphia		
St. Louis		
	Subregional Diversified Service Center	
Birmingham		
	Functional Specialized Service Centers	
Detroit	Rochester	
Louisville	Milwaukee	
Newark		
Paterson		
Pittsburgh		
	Government-Education Specialized Service Center	
	Albany	
	Manufacturing Centers	
	Buffalo	Providence

noted in Chapter 2, four major types of hypotheses have been advanced to explain why central cities might newly attract more movers: "advanced service" economies, cost and transportation constraints, demographic factors, and increased preferences for city living. To weigh the relative importance in the actual outcomes of these four possible explanations for upturn versus factors implying continued decline in the more distressed cities, I tried to select independent variables to measure each factor. Table 4.8 lists the variables used and their hypothesized positive or negative influence on upturns in city selection by higher-income movers. Cumulative decline, for example, is expected to be more likely in the most distressed cities, especially in cities most different from their suburbs. Scores on the need index used to rank cities by distress were used to measure the first possibility, and the Bradbury index, the second. Another measure

Table 4.8

Independent Variables and the Hypothesized Direction of Their Relation to the Ratio of "1980" to 1970 City Selection Rates of Upper-Income Nonblack Movers

Measures of city distress and city/suburban disparities

NEED70A (−): Factor score measuring relative need of each city on dimensions related to poverty, age of housing, and crime, developed by Bunce and Goldberg (1979).

CSDSPI (−): Summary index prepared by Bradbury, Downs, and Small (1982) of city-suburban disparities in income, poverty, crime, old housing, and unemployment.

CSINCR (+): Ratio of city-to-suburban per capita income in 1973 (ACIR 1977).

GAP72 (?): Ratio of actual city selection rate of upper-income movers in 1965–70 to the "expected" rate based on the 1970 proportion of SMSA nonblack population living in the central city. If disparities between observed and expected rates tend to be self-equilibrating, one would expect upturns to be more likely the lower this ratio and thus a negative relationship. But if differentially greater upper-income outmigration is self-reinforcing, the relationship will be positive.

Measures of advanced service economies

PPROF (+): Proportion of employed SMSA residents in 1970 in professional or managerial occupations (U.S. Bureau of the Census 1972a).

PGOVEMP (+): Proportion of employed SMSA residents in 1970 in government (ibid.).

PSER (?): Proportion of employed SMSA residents in 1970 in service industries (ibid.).

PWR (+): Proportion of employed SMSA residents in 1970 in wholesale and retail trade (ibid.).

PPASPG (+): The sum of PPROF and PGOVEMP.

BANKI2 (+): Index of rank of city in terms of number of correspondent banking relationships received from banks in each of 66 cities. The index is constructed so that the expected relationship is positive by assigning each city the negative value corresponding to its rank: e.g., New York, −1; Albany, −39, etc. (Bartelt 1985).

Measures of cost constraints favoring city housing

HVALCS (−): City-suburban ratio of value for a standard single-family house in the mid-1970s, derived from hedonic indices of housing value and rent developed by Malpezzi, Ozanne, and Thibodeau (1980).

HRNTCS (−): City-suburban ratio of rent for a standard rental unit in the mid-1970s, derived as above.

JTWTIME (+): Median minutes for commuting for the SMSA, as reported by the Annual Housing Survey in the mid-1970s (U.S. Bureau of the Census 1978, 1979, 1980, 1981a).

Measure of demographic factors

MIG829 (+): SMSA net migration rate, 1975–80, of independent adults aged 29 or less in 1980 (Greenwood 1984).

Measures of city attractiveness

ARTIND (+): Rank of each SMSA in terms of cultural facilities as determined by the *Places Rated Almanac*. Index varies from −1 for New York to −167 for Paterson–Clifton–Passaic, but Paterson's value was reassigned to be −50. Boyer and Savageau 1981.

AGEDUM1 (+): Age of city dummy for cities whose last decade of above-average population growth occurred before 1880 (Watkins 1980).

AGEDUM2 (−): Age of city dummy for "industrial-era" cities whose last decade of above-average growth occurred between 1890 and 1940.

highly correlated with distress was the city-suburban disparity in 1973 per capita income (a more precise measure of one of the five factors summarized by the Bradbury index). Since the 1970 "gap" between observed and expected selection rates (the ratio of city selection rates of upper-income movers during 1965–70 to the city share in 1970 of total white SMSA population) is also correlated with distress, I included it in the regression to determine explicitly whether differentially greater outmigration by upper-income groups tends to be self-perpetuating. If outmigration is self-equilibrating, upturns should be *most* likely in cities with the greatest past gaps between population distribution and mover selection.

Since Noyelle and Stanback's ranking of SMSAs with regard to position in a national hierarchy of an evolving advanced services economy is based on a variety of measures that are hard to summarize, several possible measures were tested. The 1970 proportions of SMSA residents employed in services, in professional occupations, in wholesale or retail trade, or in government were used in various combinations. The proportion of workers who were professionals seems more suitable than the proportion in services because of the emphasis Noyelle and Stanback place on advanced services' supporting corporate headquarters.[17] Such advanced services include personnel located within central offices of major firms (even though by industry these people might be categorized in "manufacturing" or some other nonservice industry) and exclude most employment in personal services. Although government employment may be a less secure employment base, it is one that grew markedly during most of the 1970s, and it has been strongly tied to central-city employment (Harrison 1974). To attempt to quantify Noyelle and Stanback's important notion of hierarchy, which is also relevant to explanations that stress the role of capital investment in gentrification (Smith 1979), cities were ranked by the number of correspondent relationships maintained by banks located within them.[18]

Whether city housing was cheaper than equivalent suburban housing was measured by hedonic indices developed for rent and value in the mid-1970s in all of the studied SMSAs (Malpezzi, Ozanne, and Thibodeau 1980). Although I first assumed that the relative values of owned housing

17. In a conversation discussing these and other alternatives, Thierry Noyelle agreed that this measure was probably the most appropriate one for which consistent data were available for all of the SMSAs studied.

18. As part of research on the influence of the urban hierarchy on changes in housing and neighborhood conditions, Bartelt (1985) derived indices of city rank in terms of the number of correspondent banking relationships received from banks in each of the 59 SMSAs included in the Annual Housing Survey SMSA samples. The ranks used here were based on correspondent links in 1975; Bartelt calculated a similar ranking for 1929 and found a high level of stability in ranks between the two years.

would be more pertinent to upper-income movers while relative rents were more likely to influence the selection decisions of lower-income movers, the results suggest that differences in rent were more salient for both groups. As in Table 4.6, excessive commuting was measured by mean time to work in each SMSA during the mid-1970s.[19]

The net rates of migration in 1975–80 of adults who were below thirty in 1980 were used to measure the role of the young adult cohort, which is both the most important demographic factor usually cited and the one that varies greatly among SMSAs. Finally, since quantifying whether changing preferences for city living contributed to migration reversal was difficult, two approaches were tried. Under the assumption that most cultural activities are located in central cities rather than in their suburbs and that relative status in cultural activities is correlated with many of the other amenities—specialized shops and restaurants, night life, and so on—that might attract migrants and higher-status residents (James 1977), each city was assigned the rank its SMSA received with respect to cultural facilities in the *Places Rated Almanac* (Boyer and Savageau 1981). Secondly, information on the most recent decade during which city rates of population growth exceeded the average national growth rate (Watkins 1980) was used to prepare two age-of-city dummies. Because of increasing interest in historic preservation, cities last growing quickly before 1880 were hypothesized to attract upturns, while those with most recent growth between 1890 and 1940–roughly the period of industrialization—would not. Newer cities were the control.

To focus on the determinants of selection increases or further deterioration in distressed cities, only the twenty-seven SMSAs with the most distressed cities were included in these regressions. Stepwise procedures were used to identify those variables contributing significantly to explained variance. Because of the ratio form and the resulting somewhat skewed distributions of the dependent variables, both linear and log-linear equations were estimated. Since both formulations identified the same variables as most important, only the linear results are reported in Table 4.9.[20]

Although the variables available to measure several factors were less

19. Another variable considered was city employment–population ratios, to serve as an indicator of the drawing power of central-city employment. According to Richard Forstall of the Census Bureau, city employment–population ratios have been increasing over time, as population decentralizes more rapidly than employment. However, the 1980 journey-to-work data needed for this measure were not available for this research, and the published 1970 data are inaccurate because of errors in allocation.

20. Results of similar regressions on all 40 SMSAs identify the same variables as important but explain less of the total variance.

Table 4.9
"Best" Explanations of Determinants of 1970–1980 Changes in City Selection Rates
of Nonblack Movers in Twenty-seven SMSAs with Distressed Cities:
Significant Coefficients from Stepwise Regression

	Ratio of 1980 to 1970 City Selection Rates[a]	
Independent variable	Upper-income whites	Lower-income whites
PPASPG (% of employed SMSA residents in 1970 in professional occupations or working for government)	0.0247** (0.8600)	0.0141** (0.5560)
HRNTCS (city-surburban ratio of hedonic rent for a standard rental unit in the mid-1970s)	−1.4070** (−0.4850)	
GAP72 (ratio of actual city selection rate of upper-income nonblack movers to "expected" rate: the 1970 % of SMSA population in the city)	1.0050** (0.3370)	
MIG829 (rate of SMSA net migration, 1975–80, for adults with age <30)		−
ARTIND (SMSA rank in cultural facilities)	+	−0.0029* (−0.0690)
Intercept	0.4970	0.4570
R^2	0.5630	0.3280
$\bar{R}^2$	0.5050	0.2720

NOTE: Plus (+) or minus (−) indicates the next (insignificant) variable to enter the stepwise regression and its sign.

[a] Numbers in parentheses are standardized regression coefficients, comparing the relative effect on the dependent variable of each independent variable.

* Significantly different from 0 at .05 level.

** Significantly different from 0 at .01 level.

than ideal, the results imply that advanced service economies were the most important determinant of upturns among upper-income movers, with relative housing bargains in cities next most important. The standardized regression coefficients show clearly that the proportion of residents employed in professional or managerial occupations or in government, a proxy measuring advanced services, is most (positively) related to changes in city selection rates for both income groups. Relative bargains in rent for city housing were next most important in attracting or retaining more upper-income migrants: relatively lower costs for central-city housing induced selection upturns. Yet the results also imply that the process of cumulative decline is hard to reverse and that selection upturns will be most difficult for distressed cities with past differential white flight. Although other measures of city distress and city-suburban disparities had high negative partial correlations with upturns once advanced service employment and housing costs were controlled, the 1970 gap between expected and observed selection best explained the remaining variance. After controlling for the effects of these three most important variables, cultural facilities and net inmigration of young adults had modest positive relations to upper-income upturns.

The results for lower-income movers were less conclusive, partly because there was less variation among cities, but several interesting patterns emerge. A high share of advanced service employment in 1970 was also most important in increasing central-city selection rates by lower-income whites, but the roles of cultural attractiveness and young adults were reversed from those observed for higher-income movers. Although the relationship is weaker, lower-income upturns tended to occur in cities with fewer cultural facilities and relative outmigration. Relative city-suburban costs did not play a significant role, so my hypothesis that lower-income upturns were mainly due to cost constraints is not supported. The difference between upper-income and lower-income equations in the signs of migration and cultural facilities suggests, however, that lower-income upturns were more likely to occur in cities that were less attractive to upper-income movers. Such increasing differentiation by income among cities is consistent with Noyelle and Stanback's hypothesis of "an emerging dichotomy" in U.S. urban structure.

Evaluating the Current Effects of Migration

Because of constraints upon free residential choice by blacks, whether central cities have become more attractive to migrants over time has been examined only for nonblacks. But although studying trends is appropriate to determine whether basic migration processes are becoming more or less favorable to cities, trends cannot show whether current migration levels and differentials support revival. Did the large percentage increase in upper-income white selection in Washington, for instance, increase per capita or total income resources in the District of Columbia? Or does the fact that whites are only a small fraction of the District's population mean that city income losses are nevertheless continuing? Similarly, what are the impacts on Portland and Fort Worth of large decreases in city selection rates among upper-income movers? Are they likely to join the ranks of distressed cities?

To judge whether the migration improvements that occurred in distressed cities were sufficient to support positive changes in population and/or per capita income in these cities, this section examines complete information from the 1980 census of population on the net effects of *all* migration between 1975 and 1980—both out and in—by all households, with blacks now included as well.[21] Special tabulations from 1980 census microdata files show net migration "rates" for each city that express net outmigration or inmigration as a percentage of the 1980 population by income.[22] From these measures we can infer not only which cities lost or gained population because of net out- or inmigration, but also the impact of migration upon city per capita incomes that resulted from the balance within each city among upper- and lower-income movers of all races.[23] The situation most conducive to citywide revival would be net inmigration among all income groups, with higher rates of inmigration among upper-income migrants, since this pattern would increase both population and per capita income. At the other extreme, the worst case would be net outmigration among both income groups, with higher outmigration rates among upper-income movers, since this would cause further population and income losses in the city and probably also increase city-suburban fiscal disparities.

Figure 4.3 displays the relative performance of the twenty-seven distressed cities with respect to such net migration "rates" for both total and upper-income population (on the bottom axis) against the 1970–80 changes in upper-income city selection rates (on the left axis). Since each of these distressed cities had net outmigration for both groups, the net-migration axis is mainly negative, extending from −100 percent to +10 percent.

According to these measures of net migration for all movers, Los An-

21. These complete measures of all migration to and from these cities explicitly measure for the first time flows from each city to areas beyond its SMSA by income. They show that higher-income residents of cities in the Northeast and North Central regions had somewhat higher outmigration to destinations beyond the SMSA than did either lower-income residents of cities in these regions or residents of cities in the South and West.

22. Tabulations for 64 cities and SMSAs of complete inmigration and outmigration between 1975 and 1980 were prepared by Greenwood (1984) for three income categories from Sample B of the 1980 Public Use Sample. Since these tabulations come from 1980 census data, the cities and metropolitan areas are defined in terms of their 1980 boundaries. Therefore, the 1980 data for Houston cover a larger territory than either the 1970 census or the AHS data, and in 1980 Dallas and Fort Worth become two central cities in one metropolitan area. The "rates" are based on the known end-of-the-period population, so net outmigration rates can (and do) drop below −100%. Losing more than 100% of population through migration seems impossible, but such a rate means that the excess of outmigrants over inmigrants between 1975 and 1980 was greater than the remaining 1980 population in that category. The three 1979 income categories (<$12,720, $12,720–$31,799, and $31,800+) were chosen to be comparable in current dollars to the 1969 cutoffs of $6,000 and $15,000 used in the published 1970 volume (U.S. Bureau of the Census, 1972b). Since migration rates tend to fall with income and origins were coded for only 8% of the migrants, in some cases the sample base is uncomfortably small for the highest income group.

23. Changes in the income of continuing city residents obviously also affect the income distribution and city per capita income, and differences among cities in birth and death rates influence total rates of population change. However, only the effects of migration are considered here.

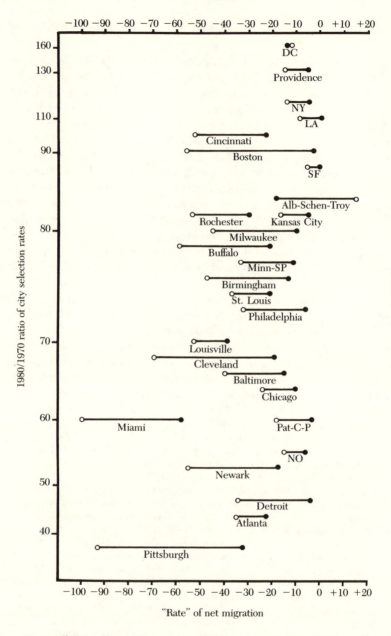

Figure 4.3.   Net Migration, 1975–1980, as a Percentage of 1980 Population for Upper-Income (○), and Total Movers (●), in Twenty-Seven Distressed Cities, versus 1980/1970 Ratio of City Selection Rates of Upper-Income White Movers. SOURCE: 1975–1980 net migration data from the 1980 Census (Greenwood, 1984).

geles was the only city in which total inmigration to the city essentially balanced total outmigration between 1975 and 1980: its net migration rate was −0.5 percent. All of the other distressed cities clearly lost population from net outmigration. Expressed as percentages of 1980 population, net outmigration rates were less than 10 percent for nine of the twenty-seven, but considerably greater for the others. Miami had the worst net out-migration, losing, on net, migrants equalling 55 percent of her 1980 population; for Louisville and Pittsburgh, migration exchanges caused losses exceeding one-third of 1980 population.

The net impacts of migration on income are reflected in this figure by the direction and extent of disparities between total and upper-income migration rates. Migration possibly increased per capita income in Al-bany-Schenectady-Troy, which had net inmigration among the highest-income group despite the cities' overall net outmigration. Among the cities with outmigration for both total and upper-income groups, lower outmigration by upper-income than by total migrants would tend to raise per capita income, whereas faster outmigration by upper-income migrants would induce losses in both income and population. Thus, Washington was the only other distressed city in which net migration patterns (slightly) supported increases in income. Over the 1975–80 period, the District ex-perienced net outmigration among both total and upper-income migrants, and thus lost population. However, since net outmigration rates were marginally less among upper-income movers (−11%) than among the population as a whole (−12%), the migration process tended to slightly increase per capita income in the city. Moreover, in a pattern that sup-ports the significance of Washington's large increase between 1970 and 1980 in city selection rates of upper-income whites, this income balance was attributable to white migration. Net outmigration rates were lower among middle- and upper-income whites (−4% and −8%, respectively) than among either lower-income whites (−12%) or blacks. For blacks, in-come differentials were more typical: middle- and upper-income blacks, with outmigration rates of 19 percent, were more likely to leave the city than lower-income blacks.

Albany-Schenectady-Troy and Washington, however, were the only dis-tressed cities for which migration had positive or neutral effects on in-come. In all of the other cities net outmigration rates of upper-income groups exceeded those of the total population, so that migration flows on net caused losses in both population and income. The situation was com-paratively better in those cities with low rates of net outmigration and small differences in outmigration rates by income—particularly San Fran-cisco and Los Angeles. New York, Providence, New Orleans, Kansas City, and Patterson-Clifton-Passaic also had relatively small disparities by in-come together with relatively low levels of net outmigration. Although they had greater outmigration, differences by income were also moderate in Chicago, St. Louis, Minneapolis-St. Paul, and Atlanta.

In the remaining cities, wide disparities between total and upper-income outmigration rates imply that migration seriously reduced city income resources during the late 1970s. Miami was also worst off in this regard, especially since the −101 percent outmigration rate graphed is for middle-income movers (the net outmigration rate for upper-income movers was an astounding 142% of the upper-income 1980 population).[24] Outmigration among Rochester's upper-income group was also very high (−117%). In Pittsburgh and Cleveland, outmigration rates of upper-income migrants were three times those of the total population. Boston's wide disparity reflects the difference between a net outmigration of 58 percent among upper-income population versus net inmigration of 1 percent for the lowest-income group (and inmigration of 12% for the youngest age group, those less than 30 in 1980).

This comparison of the effects of migration in the late 1970s against the direction of change during the 1970s suggests that the seven cities in the upper right corner (Washington through Kansas City) were best off in the late 1970s. Their relatively low rates of net outmigration were balanced by income group so that income losses were not excessive, and their 1970–80 selection rate changes imply that migration among upper-income movers was improving or stable. As the case of Washington demonstrates, however, even having the sharpest improvements between 1970 and 1980 were insufficient to reverse net outmigration.

In spite of their relative stability in city selection rates, the group of cities in the center of the figure—Cincinnati, Boston, Rochester, Milwaukee, Buffalo, Minneapolis-St. Paul, and Birmingham—are apparently losing upper-income groups and thus income resources decidedly faster than population.

The prospects for revival seem particularly bleak for the distressed cities with sharp drops in city selection rates. As Figure 4.3 shows, over half also had much higher net outmigration for the highest-income group, and the trend data imply that such relative upper-income losses were worsening. Miami and Pittsburgh were apparently worst off, with net outmigration rates above 90 percent among upper-income movers. Combinations of differential net outmigration and sharp declines in upper-income selection also are not auspicious for Cleveland, Newark, and Detroit. For Philadelphia, Baltimore, New Orleans, and Atlanta—cities which have received much publicity about gentrification[25]—the pattern is also nega-

24. The 142% rate was not graphed because it seemed extreme and the sample size of movers was low. However, it may be "accurate" because it is consistent with Miami's levels and pattern of higher outmigration by education.

25. Articles in Laska and Spain (1980) and Stegman (1979) review the evidence of gentrification in these cities.

tive. Although these cities had smaller income disparities among migrants during the 1975–80 period than some of the other cities, the drops in city selections rates imply that the differentials may increase. Substantively, then, these net migration results reinforce the impression fostered by general drops in selection rates all too clearly. Rather than attracting more upper-income movers over the decade, most distressed cities experienced continued or accelerated flight among upper-income groups. Such developments presage further declines in city resources and widening of city-suburban disparities, not revival.

The Outlook for Less Distressed Cities

Although my emphasis has been on evaluating the possibility of revival for distressed cities, information such as that presented in Figure 4.3 also provides an opportunity to probe the implications of changes in city selection rates for less distressed cities. As noted above, sharp decreases in city selection rates were less common for them: only Portland and Fort Worth had drops greater than 40 percent among upper-income movers. (Houston's drop of 38% appears almost as serious, but, as discussed below, it is not.) But only Oklahoma City had an increase in upper-income city selection, and by 1980 five of the thirteen cities had "gaps" such that upper-income city selection rates were less than 80 percent of that expected from city shares of SMSA population.

As Figure 4.4 shows by superimposing results for the less distressed cities on the previous figure, net migration rates were consistent with distress rankings in showing more favorable migration patterns for these thirteen less distressed cities.[26] With the glaring exception of Columbus, which experienced net outmigration of 68 percent among the highest-income group, these cities tend to lie to the right of the figure. Three of the thirteen—San Diego, San Bernardino-Riverside-Ontario, and Phoenix—were in the highly advantageous situation of having net inmigration for both total and upper-income groups, with higher inmigration among the upper-income population. Oklahoma City and Houston also had net inmigration among the total population, along with low rates of outmigration among upper-income movers.

Net outmigration rates and income disparities were pronounced only for four of the less distressed cities in addition to Columbus: Indianapolis, Seattle, Sacramento, and Portland. All five had markedly greater outmigration among upper-income movers, so they are clearly losing both population and per capita income. These cities seem in the most danger of

26. Since the less distressed cities tended to have more positive rates of net migration, the figure is shifted 10 percentage points to the left. Only 12 sets of migration rates are shown for the 13 cities, since Dallas and Fort Worth were combined into the same SMSA by 1980.

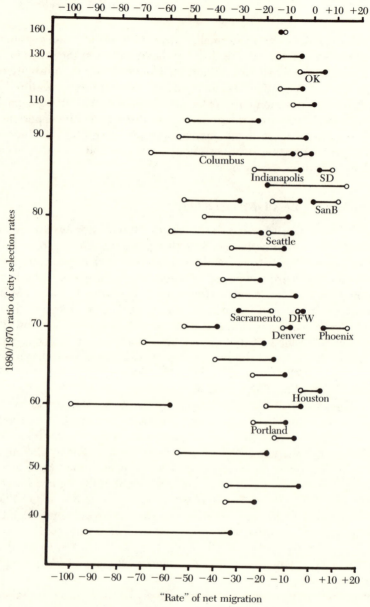

Figure 4.4. Net Migration, 1975–1980, as a Percentage of 1980 Population for Upper-Income (○), and Total Movers (●), in Forty Cities, with Nondistressed Cities (Identified) Compared to Distressed Cities versus 1980/1970 Ratio of City Selection Rates of Upper-Income White Movers. SOURCE: 1975–1980 net migration data from the 1980 Census (Greenwood, 1984).

succumbing to the process of self-reinforcing selective outmigration and increasing city distress.

Houston requires separate discussion. Its relatively favorable net migration rates for the 1975–80 period seem inconsistent with its sharp drop in upper-income city selection rates over the decade. However, in Houston's case (alone) this inconsistency is probably due to differences in boundaries resulting from annexation between 1970 and 1980. The city selection rates derived from Annual Housing Survey data suggest that upper-income selection was decreasing sharply within *1970* city boundaries. But since Houston annexed territory extensively, it is likely that many of the upper-income residents that moved beyond its 1970 limits still lived within the 1980 central-city boundaries. In fact, the extent of Houston's drop in upper-income city selection rates within 1970 boundaries, especially in contrast to its stability within those boundaries in city selection rates among lower-income movers and its favorable net migration experienced within 1980 boundaries, is quite instructive. It graphically illustrates how outward growth alone could siphon off higher-status movers from a central city, even a nondistressed central city, if that city could not annex the developing territory.

Summary

This chapter has asked whether any distressed cities were aided by the slight improvements in migration during the 1970s revealed in national data. Examining only city selection rates, which are unable to assess the extent or effects of outmigration from each city to destinations beyond its SMSA, we have looked at trends between the late 1950s and the years around 1980 for forty of the largest SMSAs. Annual data between 1974 and 1981 for these SMSAs grouped by region parallel the regional CPS data discussed in Chapter 3 in showing improvements in the late 1970s following earlier decline, with the greatest improvement occurring in the South. Changes over *two* decades, moreover, demonstrate clearly that even the slight improvements found in the 1970s represent a definite break from earlier trends. Between 1955–60 and 1965–70 city selection rates had dropped in every one of the SMSAs studied (except Los Angeles, which changed boundaries), with these drops almost always sharper among upper-income movers. But direct comparison for those SMSAs with the same boundaries in three different time periods demonstrates that changes in city selection rates improved from an average five-percentage point *loss* during the 1960s to a one-percentage point *gain* in the 1970s.

Yet in most cases such improvements in city selection rates were concentrated among lower-income movers. Increases among upper-income

movers either did not occur in the most distressed cities or were insufficient to revive them. Only five of the twenty-seven large distressed central
cities studied had increases in city selection rates among upper-income
white movers, and only in Washington and Albany-Schenectady-Troy
were improvements in migration possibly sufficient to slow past relative
declines in median per capita income. Even in Washington, furthermore,
the marginal nature of the income reversal over a decade in which many
conditions were considered favorable for central cities reinforces rather
than satisfies concerns about the fragility of possibilities for reviving distressed cities.

5. Gentrification within Distressed Cities

In contrast to nearly universal declines in city selection rates between 1955–60 and 1965–70, between the late 1960s and 1980 city selection rates of white movers to and within metropolitan areas rose or remained nearly stable in over half of forty large SMSAs. National evidence of some improvement in migration for central cities during the 1970s is thus reinforced within a longer time frame: indeed, stability and turnarounds after 1970 seem particularly striking when contrasted to the general earlier declines. Distressed cities shared more than proportionally in the improvements in total city selection of nonblacks during the 1970s. However, in almost all cities, the post-1970 upturns were due more to lower-income than to upper-income white movers. Indeed, in many areas outmovement of upper-income movers accelerated after 1970.

Documenting improvements in migration for distressed central cities demonstrates that selective outmigration can slow and that cumulative decline need not proceed inevitably. But while showing that cities vary in degree of recovery from previous selective outmigration provides a basis for evaluating which cities have recently become more attractive to movers, evidence that past outmigration trends have decelerated or reversed does not prove that migration improvements actually support gentrification or revival in distressed cities. Yet this hypothesized relationship is the basis of my claims that comprehensive analysis of trends in migration provides an appropriate means of assessing the probable extent and location of gentrification to date and that tracking changes in city selection rates in the future can monitor progress toward revival. Accordingly, to measure local upgrading and gentrification explicitly, in this chapter I examine changes at the census-tract level between 1970 and 1980 in ten of the distressed cities. I wish not only to test the hypothesized relation between selection upturns and gentrification but also to explore some persistent questions about the consequences of gentrification.

Focusing on cities in which selection trends and net migration patterns suggest that gentrification and revival might have been more extensive over the decade, I first ask whether upturns or relative stability in city selection rates among movers was indeed related to income growth at the neighborhood level within cities. Do differences among cities in the number and proportion of neighborhoods with above-average income growth conform to expectations based on differences among these cities in the decade's changes in city selection rates and their relative gaps between city selection and population shares?

After identifying neighborhoods with above-average income growth within these cities, the chapter explores some important issues about the impacts of gentrification on cities and their residents, especially the possibility that poorer residents may be hurt more than helped thereby. The extent and effects of displacement resulting from neighborhood upgrading understandably cause most controversy. Unresolved questions here include the extent to which lower-income residents have been forced from neighborhoods experiencing gentrification, whether displacement from such reinvestment is more extensive than that resulting from abandonment of housing in declining housing markets, and whether displaced households find better or worse housing and neighborhoods.[1]

Many other issues need further study. For example, the number of neighborhoods affected by upgrading is still in question. Most studies have focused only on particular neighborhoods within cities or on neighborhoods near city centers, and the only studies which have examined entire cities have found few neighborhoods with the kinds of changes in income and population composition that gentrification has been presumed to engender (Chall 1983–84; Baldassare 1984). It is also not clear that upgrading has necessarily been most likely in lower-income neighborhoods. Long and Dahmann (1980, 5), for example, speculate that rather than reflecting gentrifying lower-income neighborhoods, publicized instances of neighborhood upgrading may reflect "isolated improvements in 'pockets of plenty,' accompanied by continued declines elsewhere." The location of upgraded neighborhoods within cities is also in question. The general expectation (Lipton 1977; Smith 1979) has been that gentrification is most likely near the center of the city. Palen and London (1984), for example, claim that gentrification has occurred mainly in areas with distinctive housing and access to central business districts (CBDs); they question whether upgrading can or will extend to the many "gray areas" with working-class housing. But since most research has focused on areas near CBDs, there have been few comprehensive investigations of the location of gentrifying areas throughout cities.

---

1. As defined by Grier and Grier (1978), displacement occurs if "the move [is] necessitated by housing or neighborhood-related factors beyond the household's control, and . . . these factors make continued occupancy infeasible." Thus, moves caused by increased housing costs should be considered displacement, but eviction for cause should not.

These issues cannot be completely resolved here. But after income change in census tracts between 1970 and 1980 has been measured to estimate where upgrading and gentrification occurred, data on changes in income, population, and poverty by census tract are studied to investigate the following questions about the intracity effects of migration improvements:

1. Were improvements in total or upper-income selection rates at the city level over the past decade related to gentrification, that is, to above-average income growth in poorer tracts? Or did income growth occur mainly in upper-income tracts while the rest of the city became poorer, so that within cities development was uneven?

2. What were the impacts of gentrification on population distribution, population loss, and the poor population? Were poor people "displaced" from gentrifying tracts to new concentrations of poverty? Did gentrification, as commonly thought, lead to disproportionate population losses? Can anything be said about the extent of relative displacement and population loss resulting from thinning out or housing abandonment in relation to that attributable to reinvestment?

3. Where in each city did different types of changes occur? Were neighborhood upgrading and gentrification concentrated near central business districts? Were they located near past large-scale urban renewal projects and other areas with public investment? If some tracts are becoming poorer, are they spatially concentrated or dispersed? Are they more distant from the city center?

The Ten Cities Studied

Because of the difficulties of matching census tracts over a decade and assembling data for a large number of tracts, I did not study all forty cities at the census-tract level of geographic detail for this chapter. Instead, ten distressed cities (indicated in boldface in Table 5.1) with some evidence of improvement or stability in migration during the 1970s were chosen to represent a range of levels of distress in 1970 and some variety in the degree of post-1970 upturns among upper- and lower-income movers. Of necessity, those chosen had few changes in tract definition over the decade.[2]

2. The cities chosen do include ones in which there were "splits" in census tracts over the decade, but not ones in which tract boundaries had changed. The procedure followed for split tracts was to combine the 1980 information for the two (or three) new tracts that were equivalent to the 1970 census tract. For counts of population and poverty, this procedure is straightforward; to calculate median incomes, the median family income shown for each 1980 tract was weighted by the tract's number of families to calculate a weighted 1980 median family income for the area of the 1970 tract.

Table 5.1

Changes in City Selection Rates and Expectations about Relative Income Growth in Census Tracts within Ten Distressed Cities

Distressed cities ranked by distress quintile, 1970	1970–80 change in city selection rates among movers			"1980" gap: obs./exp. CSRs	1970–80 change in gap	1975–80 SMSA net migration	Rank in above-av. income growth	
	All white movers	Upper-income	Lower-income				Expected	Actual
Newark	**147**	**56**	**119**	**34**	**−25**	**−6**	**10**	**10**
St. Louis	112	73	96	64	−3			
Washington	**173**	**161**	**170**	**91**	**22**	**0**	**1**	**1**
Baltimore	86	66	87	56	−8			
New Orleans	76	57	89	68	−18			
Miami	90	59	91	43	−31			
Cleveland	**102**	**68**	**92**	**54**	**−14**	**−7**	**9**	**9**
Detroit	64	45	55	56	−14			
Boston	**139**	**91**	**120**	**74**	**−6**	**−4**	**3**	**4**
Birmingham	90	76	89	102	17			
Atlanta	61	44	64	55	−18			
Chicago	91	65	88	59	−18			
Buffalo	**101**	**79**	**93**	**74**	**−6**	**−6**	**7**	**8**
Philadelphia	**98**	**73**	**100**	**58**	**−12**	**−2**	**8**	**6**
Pittsburgh	119	37	134	36	−46			
New York	112	110	98	98	11			
Cincinnati	**114**	**96**	**114**	**102**	**12**	**−1**	**5**	**5**
Louisville	107	70	103	68	−10			
Paterson–C–P	128	60	146	42	−28			
San Francisco–O	**124**	**84**	**126**	**59**	**−12**	**0**	**4**	**2**
Rochester	113	82	100	72	−1			
Albany–S–T	120	83	107	74	−2			
Providence–P–W	**123**	**130**	**111**	**120**	**37**	**−2**	**2**	**7**
Kansas City	105	81	120	74	−12			
Milwaukee	98	80	99	83	−4			
Los Angeles–LB	112	108	111	98	2			
Minneapolis–SP	**110**	**77**	**95**	**65**	**−7**	**0**	**6**	**3**

New York and Los Angeles were excluded because hand-coding data for their many tracts exceeded the resources available for this research.

Of the fifteen most distressed cities, all with upturns in total city selection rates are studied here except St. Louis and Pittsburgh, which had tract boundary changes. Philadelphia was included because of its near stability in total rates, and Providence because of its strong upturn among upper-income movers. Cincinnati, San Francisco, and Minneapolis–St. Paul were added to extend the range of distress of the cities studied, and because their upturns in selection are consistent with other reports of gentrification (Gale 1984; Lipton 1977).

Although these cities are all distressed, they nevertheless differ greatly in degree of distress, population change, housing costs, and economic base. Furthermore, Lipton's study (1977) of changes in central tracts between 1960 and 1970 revealed marked differences then among six of these cities. Washington and Boston were characterized as having strong cores in 1960 and improvements over the following decade. Minneapolis and San Francisco showed overall decline between 1960 and 1970 within a two-mile radius of the CBD in the number of tracts with high median family income or educational attainment, but improvement within or directly adjacent to the CBD. Cleveland and Newark had "deteriorating or stagnant cores during the sixties" (Lipton 1977, 139).

Measuring Above-Average Income Growth and Gentrification

In this chapter both neighborhood upgrading in general and gentrification in lower-income tracts are defined for each tract in terms of above-average growth between 1970 and 1980 in median incomes, since, as Baldassare concludes, "rising income seems to be the most dependable indicator of revitalization" (1984, 92). The measures of tract income available for this research from 1970 and 1980 decennial census data were the median income of families and unrelated individuals in 1969 and family median income in 1979. Since for all SMSAs nationally these median incomes changed 251 percent in current dollars, for the tracts studied here increases above 270 percent are defined as "above-average." Such high rates of income growth are assumed to reflect some mixture of upgrading resulting from relative inmovement by higher-income persons or from the above-average income growth among continuing residents that Clay (1979) has termed incumbent upgrading.[3]

3. Declines in both household size and the proportion of households that are families, together with the presumed importance of singles in gentrifying neighborhoods, mean that changes in median family income are a less appropriate measure of improved neighborhood status and resources than changes in household or per capita income would be. However, the median income of families and unrelated individuals in 1969 was the only summary measure of income available on the 1970 tract-level data base from which this research was

Because "gentrification" commonly connotes upgrading in previously poor and deteriorating areas, the operational measure of gentrification is further restricted to tracts that were lower-income in 1970. Thus, gentrification is measured as having occurred for tracts which had both 1969 median incomes below the national metropolitan average of $8,431 ("lower-income tracts") *and* 1970–80 changes in median income above 270 percent. For several reasons, this approach may misstate the number of tracts and persons affected by gentrification. First, it is often observed that gentrification is spatially restricted, occurring on a block-by-block basis rather than neighborhood-wide (Spain 1982). Second, this definition basically identifies above-average percentage growth in tracts with below-average income. In some tracts with extremely low income bases, "above-average" increases could result from atypical occurrences and/or increases in income that are small in absolute terms.[4] Finally, as discussed below, changes in household composition over the decade complicate any single comparison of medians. To provide one measure of the sensitivity of the cutoff chosen, growth rates above 290 percent are distinguished from those above 270 percent.

Expectations about Income Growth in These Cities

Reversals or deceleration since 1970 in trends in city selection rates among higher-income movers imply a slowing in the selective outmigration that has contributed to financial, employment, and fiscal distress of cities. Therefore, I expect increases or stability in these selection rates to be associated with improvements in income within neighborhoods of the affected cities, either through gentrification of poorer neighborhoods or

---

drawn, while for 1980 median family income was the most comparable measure available when this research began.

A further question concerns my comparison of income growth rates in tracts against *national* averages. Most other studies (Lipton 1977 and 1984; Chall 1984; Gale 1984) that have examined income growth have used SMSA-specific measures of income growth or level as the standard of comparison. Lipton (1984, 12), for example, compared 1969 and 1979 median family incomes for tracts within 20 cities with their SMSA medians and found that "only Newark has a greater percentage of tracts with incomes above the SMSA average in 1979 than in 1969" (its increase was from zero to one percent!). I decided to use a national comparison for two reasons. One was to make my results more comparable across the 10 cities studied. Second, SMSA-specific comparisons may underestimate the extent of improvement in cities, especially in SMSAs in which the suburbs are so prosperous that SMSA median incomes are well above the national average.

4. In Minneapolis, for example, a local planner noted that several of the poorest tracts that had above-average income growth were located in a neighborhood with a public housing project that had been losing population and households. He speculated that the income "growth" occurred because larger households had more difficulty finding alternative housing and therefore were more likely to be still living in the project in 1980, while smaller households with lower total income had been more likely to move out.

through further upgrading of areas with above-average incomes. It is less obvious that post-1970 upturns in city selection rates that occurred only along lower-income movers might be related to upgrading. Nevertheless, evidence that city housing is attracting a higher proportion of movers than formerly should reflect a tighter SMSA housing market, and thus more neighborhood upgrading than in cities in which all city selection rates continue to drop. Thus, other factors being equal, upgrading in different neighborhoods in distressed cities should be directly related to the extent of improvement in city selection rates.

Other factors definitely influence both supply and demand for city housing, however, and these factors differ across the ten cities. Therefore, the number of neighborhoods with above-average income growth cannot be expected to vary only with the extent of reversal. At the very least the "gap" in 1970 between the actual distribution of population between cities and their suburbs and the proportion of all movers or upper-income movers choosing the city (the gap shown in Chapter 4 to deter upturns) should be relevant in evaluating the impact of trend reversals. The greater the previous gap, the greater the upturn needed to slow or reverse past selective outmigration. Demand for housing by blacks and rates of gross and net migration to each SMSA also importantly influence aggregate housing demand. In an SMSA with high levels of outmigration and low inmigration, "increases" in city selection could have little effect if there were few inmigrants. Housing-supply factors would also be relevant. The construction of new middle- or upper-income housing in cities during the decade would contribute to income growth in particular tracts,[5] but such income growth would not reflect gentrification in its common connotation of private upgrading of existing housing.

Despite the obvious importance of such factors, the small number of cities studied here precludes even crude statistical controls for *ceteris paribus* conditions. Therefore, before examining the data I have first ranked the ten cities in terms of the degree of above-average income growth that I would expect if increases in city selection among all movers and upper-income movers are indeed important. The expected rankings, in the seventh column of Table 5.1, are based on the degree of upturn in total selection as long as selection rates by upper-income movers have also increased or been stable. When two cities seem similar in upturns, I expect more upgrading in the one with a lesser gap in 1970.

If turnarounds in selection rates are indeed related to neighborhood upgrading since 1970, Washington, D.C., should show the most improve-

---

5. White's research (1980), for example, concludes that by 1970 urban renewal had significantly increased the proportion of tract residents with higher status and incomes near city cores in Chicago, St. Louis, and Cleveland.

ment across city tracts of the ten cities examined here. Although between 1965 and 1970 higher-income nonblack movers had been only two-thirds as likely to choose central-city homes in the District as the distribution of white residents then would have implied, by 1981 strong improvement in both upper-income and total selection rates had almost closed the earlier gap. Furthermore, the city's net migration balance from 1975 to 1980 implied that per capita income was stable or increasing, and there was (slight) net migration into the SMSA, especially among young adults. (However, as Chapter 4 showed, Washington's high proportion of black population apparently attenuated the effect on citywide changes of the large selection upturn among nonblacks).

Similarly, the marked turnaround in both upper-income and total city selection rates in Providence-Pawtucket-Warwick implies that neighborhoods in the central cities of that SMSA should rank high in above-average income growth, although if neighborhood upgrading occurred, it could have been located in Warwick rather than in the more distressed cities of Providence or Pawtucket. Table 5.1 therefore ranks the Providence area second, even though relatively low levels of gross migration to and from the SMSA suggest a rather sluggish housing market.

My hypothesis that upturns in both total and upper-income city selection rates are important predictors of gentrification implies that upgrading should be next most likely in Boston, San Francisco, and Cincinnati. All three had upturns in total selection rates and near stability among upper-income movers. Table 5.1 ranks them third, fourth, and fifth in the order of their upturns in total selection rates. Although Cincinnati's lesser gap and less distressed status in 1970 might imply that it should rank above Boston, San Francisco should have been aided by its more favorable net migration balance.

Actual versus expected upgrading in Minneapolis–St. Paul will further test the relative importance of selection improvements versus SMSA-wide net migration. Both its greater selection gap in 1970 and its lesser turnaround suggest less neighborhood upgrading than in either Cincinnati or Boston. Therefore, Table 5.1 ranks Minneapolis–St. Paul sixth, although its much less distressed status and net inmigration of young adults to the SMSA should be positive factors.

Buffalo, Philadelphia, and Cleveland are similar in being quite distressed, in having large selection gaps in 1970, and in maintaining levels of city selection during the 1970s only among lower-income movers as rates dropped further for higher-income movers. If stability in total but not higher-income selection rates is associated with income improvement in central city tracts, the ranking of 1970–80 changes in city selection rates implies an ordering of Buffalo, Philadelphia, and Cleveland; and this ranking also matches the differences among the cities in 1970 gap. Yet Philadelphia's ranking might be higher because the Philadelphia SMSA's net migration balance was less unfavorable.

Finally, despite its large percentage improvement in total selection rates (from a small base), Newark seems worst off. Its drastic drop in higher-income rates, in addition to a large 1970 selection gap and net SMSA outmigration, imply that neighborhood upgrading should be least likely there.[6]

How Widespread Was Above-Average Income Growth?

As Table 5.2 shows, the ten cities varied widely in the proportion of 1970 population in tracts with subsequent above-average income growth over the decade. With tracts weighted by the 1970 population, above-average income growth was most widespread in Washington, where income grew at rates above 270 percent in tracts with more than half of the 1970 population. Upgrading was also quite prevalent in San Francisco and Minneapolis–St. Paul, occurring in tracts housing 44 and 30 percent, respectively. Boston and Cincinnati came next: roughly one-fifth of their 1970 population lived in tracts that experienced above-average income growth in the 1970s. But above-average growth was decidedly less common in the remaining five cities. In Philadelphia and Providence, only tracts housing about one-tenth of the 1970 population qualified. And in Buffalo, Cleveland, and Newark, above-average income growth was quite uncommon, occurring only in tracts housing less than 8 percent of the 1970 population.

If the more stringent (but also arbitrary) cutoff of income growth above 290 percent were used to define neighborhood upgrading, the proportion of the population affected would shrink accordingly, although the ordering of the cities is similar. Only 2 or 4 percent of the 1970 populations of Newark and Cleveland lived in tracts with such rapid income growth, and this proportion was also below 10 percent in Philadelphia, Providence, and Buffalo. Yet Washington and San Francisco still qualify as having experienced substantial upgrading. Washington remains in first place with 42 percent, and San Francisco had one-third of its 1970 population in tracts with such high income growth. Even with the stricter criterion, Washington, San Francisco, Minneapolis–St. Paul, and Boston had substantial proportions of population living in tracts experiencing upgrading.

6. In September 1984, however, the *New York Times* reported that young artists, priced out of lower Manhattan, were beginning to move to Newark.

Table 5.2

1970 Distribution of Population among Tracts with Below- and Above-Median Incomes by Rate of 1970–1980 Percentage Change in Tract Median Incomes for Ten Distressed Cities, Ranked by Percentage of 1970 Population Living in Tracts with Above-Average Income Growth

	Rate of 1970–80 change in tract median incomes					1970 population in tracts with above-average income growth	
	<190%	190–229%	230–269%	270–289%	290%+	270%+	290%+
Washington							
Lower-income tracts	14	21	17	11	49		
1970 population	90,100	127,100	75,900	60,200	218,400	278,600	218,400
% share of city pop.	12.1	17.1	10.2	8.1	29.4	37.5	29.4
Upper-income tracts	0	3	8	2	19		
1970 population		23,100	48,300	6,300	94,900	101,200	94,900
% share of city pop.	0.0	3	6.5	0.9	12.8	13.6	12.8
Total % of city pop.						51.1	42.1
San Francisco							
Lower-income tracts	9	10	21	12	44		
1970 population	33,000	35,300	127,200	63,300	199,600	262,900	199,600
% share of city pop.	4.6	5	17.9	8.9	28.1	36.9	28.1
Upper-income tracts	1	9	28	4	7		
1970 population	800	51,900	148,400	25,300	26,800	52,200	26,800
% share of city pop.	0.1	7	20.9	3.6	3.8	7.3	3.8
Total % of city pop.						44.3	31.8
Minneapolis–St. Paul							
Lower-income tracts	6	28	42	9	51		
1970 population	13,500	90,100	139,100	35,900	150,000	185,900	150,000
% share of city pop.	1.8	12	18.9	4.9	20.4	25.3	20.4
Upper-income tracts	0	27	27	5	5		
1970 population		144,400	124,100	21,000	17,200	38,200	17,200
% share of city pop.		20	16.9	2.9	2.3	5.2	2.3
Total % of city pop.						30.5	22.7

(continued on next page)

Table 5.2 *(continued)*

	Rate of 1970–80 change in tract median incomes					1970 population in tracts with above-average income growth	
	<190%	190–229%	230–269%	270–289%	290%+	270%+	290%+
Boston							
Lower-income tracts	27	31	22	8	30		
1970 population	109,500	118,300	84,400	22,400	109,100	131,500	109,100
% share of city pop.	17.6	19	13.5	3.6	17.5	21.1	17.5
Upper-income tracts	5	16	4	1	1		
1970 population	20,300	129,100	21,300	7,600	1,900	9,500	1,900
% share of city pop.	3.3	21	3.4	1.2	0.3	1.5	0.3
Total % of city pop.						22.6	17.8
Cincinnati							
Lower-income tracts	15	29	21	6	16		
1970 population	37,000	111,700	88,700	21,600	49,700	71,300	49,700
% share of city pop.	8.1	24	19.3	4.7	10.8	15.5	10.8
Upper-income tracts	3	18	8	2	1		
1970 population	19,900	81,300	35,800	6,000	7,300	13,300	7,300
% share of city pop.	4.3	18	7.8	1.3	1.6	2.9	1.6
Total % of city pop.						18.4	12.4
Philadelphia							
Lower-income tracts	70	75	22	8	44		
1970 population	441,300	481,500	101,000	51,800	147,000	198,900	147,000
% share of city pop.	22.8	25	5.2	2.7	7.6	10.3	7.6
Upper-income tracts	26	78	17	1	6		
1970 population	154,800	487,500	53,200	2,300	15,500	17,800	15,500
% share of city pop.	8.0	25	2.8	0.1	0.8	0.9	0.8
Total % of city pop.						11.2	8.4
Providence–Pawtucket–Warwick							
Lower-income tracts	7	15	16	3	7		
1970 population	38,600	61,700	69,100	12,700	22,800	35,500	22,800
% share of city pop.	11.7	19	20.8	3.8	6.9	10.7	6.9

(continued on next page)

Table 5.2 *(continued)*

	Rate of 1970–80 change in tract median incomes					1970 population in tracts with above-average income growth	
	<190%	190–229%	230–269%	270–289%	290%+	270%+	290%+
Upper-income tracts	3	22	4	0	0	0	0
1970 population	8,600	104,800	13,400	0	0	0	0
% share of city pop.	2.6	32	4.1	0.0	0.0	0.0	0.0
Total % of city pop.						10.7	6.9
Buffalo							
Lower-income tracts	16	33	11	3	8		
1970 population	83,100	214,000	56,500	9,000	23,700	32,700	23,700
% share of city pop.	18.2	47	12.4	2.0	5.2	7.2	5.2
Upper-income tracts	0	8	4	0	1		
1970 population		45,100	20,800	0	3,600	3,600	3,600
% share of city pop.		10	4.6	0.0	0.8	0.8	0.8
Total % of city pop.						8.0	6.0
Cleveland							
Lower-income tracts	51	52	22	3	13		
1970 population	191,500	211,900	65,400	9,800	29,900	39,700	29,900
% share of city pop.	25.7	28	8.8	1.3	4.0	5.3	4.0
Upper-income tracts	13	36	3	1	0		
1970 population	40,000	178,500	13,500	5,100	0	5,100	0
% share of city pop.	5.4	24	1.8	0.7	0.0	0.7	0.0
Total % of city pop.						6.0	4.0
Newark							
Lower-income tracts	45	27	10	1	4		
1970 population	197,300	68,800	35,900	1,900	6,200	8,100	6,200
% share of city pop.	51.6	18	9.4	0.5	1.6	2.1	1.6
Upper-income tracts	6	9	2	0	0		
1970 population	31,800	34,600	5,700	0	0	0	0
% share of city pop.	8.3	9.1	1.5	0.0	0.0	0.0	0.0
Total % of city pop.						2.1	1.6

NOTE: "Upper" and "lower" income tracts are defined here as those whose 1970 median income was above or below the national metropolitan average of $8,431.

Actual Versus Expected Rankings

Comparing the actual with predicted rankings (see Table 5.1) shows that differences among these ten distressed cities in the proportion of 1970 population in tracts with above-average income growth were closely related to variations in the extent of reversal or slowing in past selection trends, although the unexpectedly poor showing of Providence-Pawtucket-Warwick suggests strongly that upturns by upper-income movers are not by themselves as critical as I had hypothesized. Four of the five cities with upturns or stability in upper-income selection were among the top five in local income growth, while at the other end, three of the four cities expected to have least improvement were least improved. The relationship was not perfect. Income growth at the neighborhood level was markedly less in Providence and greater in Minneapolis–St. Paul than I had predicted from the selection changes; San Francisco and Philadelphia also ranked above my expectations.[7] These disparities between actual and expected rankings confirm the need to consider other factors, particularly rates of gross migration and net migration to or from each metropolitan area. The direction of the disparities—with the three cities with balanced net migration ranking first through third and Philadelphia moving above Buffalo—suggests that net migration definitely influences the extent to which changes in city selection rates translate into improvements at the tract level. On the whole, nevertheless, changes in city selection rates do correspond to differences among these cities in the proportion of city population living in tracts with above-average income growth.

Gentrification of Lower-Income Tracts?

To determine whether income growth reflects gentrification or only "isolated improvements in pockets of plenty" (Long and Dahmann 1980), Table 5.2 also distinguishes tracts by whether their 1970 median income was above or below the national metropolitan average of $8,431 ("upper" or "lower" income tracts.) Measures of income growth by initial income level show whether income growth occurred mainly in higher-status areas, which was the tendency observed by Hoyt (1966) between the 1930s and the 1960s, or if "turnaround," or gentrification, took place in poorer neighborhoods. The results show clearly that when above-average income growth occurred during the 1970s, it more often took place in lower-

---

7. Part of the explanation for San Francisco's higher ranking in this chapter is probably because Oakland is omitted from the examination of census-tract-level changes. The census and AHS migration data both referred to San Francisco and Oakland combined. If Oakland, which is poorer and more distressed than San Francisco, also had less favorable migration changes, the total measured would be below those occurring for the city of San Francisco alone.

income than in upper-income tracts in all cities. When neighborhood income rose at above-average rates, gentrification of poorer tracts was more common than further income gains in "pockets of plenty." Furthermore, the ranking of these cities in terms of the percentage of population living in gentrifying tracts is essentially the same as that resulting from comparing the proportions of city population living in all tracts with above-average income growth. The only difference is that under 270 percent cutoff, Providence has a slightly higher proportion of population in "gentrifying" tracts than does Philadelphia.

Although the ranking of these cities by percentage of population in gentrifying tracts closely approximates that expected from migration changes, it is nevertheless somewhat surprising in comparison with publicity about gentrification. Philadelphia's low ranking, in particular, differs from popular perceptions (Smith 1979; Laska and Spain 1980). The ranking in Table 5.2 is based on the proportion of population living in tracts with above-average income growth, because this measure is most relevant to ascertaining the extent to which neighborhood improvements are contributing to citywide revival. But the amount of attention given gentrification probably is related more to the absolute numbers of residents affected. In terms of absolute numbers, Philadelphia's larger size made it third among these cities in number of persons living in lower-income tracts with subsequent gentrification; both Boston and smaller Cincinnati had fewer people in affected tracts. This ranking corresponds more closely to publicity and common perceptions about cities and gentrification, but the disparity raises questions about the validity of past generalizations that gentification is more common in larger cities.

Even or Uneven Development?

A recurring debate about gentrification has centered on its impact on residents and neighborhoods within cities. Will gentrification "yield healthy, diverse communities with a mix of age, race, and income or merely dislocate elderly, poor, and black residents" elsewhere, within or beyond the city (Solomon 1980b, 22; Sumka 1980; Fainstein and Fainstein 1983)? Some light on this question comes from examining income changes in each city outside of gentrifying tracts. If most nongentrifying tracts had income growth rates that were close to national averages, this would suggest that gentrification was aiding cities without accelerating decline (or disproportionately shifting poor residents) elsewhere within the city. But if income growth was sharply below average in many nongentrifying tracts, improvements in gentrifying areas could be occurring at the cost of less investment and interest in other neighborhoods and/or displacement of poorer residents. Determining whether rates of income change were similar or uneven is also relevant for the cities with little gentrification, and as Table 5.2 shows, Buffalo, Cleveland, and Newark themselves differ substantially in the proportion of tracts with severely lagging income growth. Nevertheless, my discussion of this issue focuses on the seven cities with gentrification in tracts with at least 10 percent of city population.

To distinguish changes in income that were below-average, Table 5.2 identifies tracts with income changes that were less than 190 percent, 190–229 percent, and 230–269 percent over the decade. Growth less than 190 percent is clearly below average, but the 190–229 percent category is presented separately because income changes in this range may in some instances represent average growth. Because median *family* incomes changed only 207 percent in current dollars over the decade, changes between 190 and 230 percent could reflect average growth in income in those tracts in which most households were families at both periods. Therefore I define only growth rates less than 190 percent to be sharply below average.

With this approach, the seven cities experiencing gentrification fall into three categories. In San Francisco and Minneapolis–St. Paul, substantial gentrification occurred without below-average income growth being common in other tracts. In both cities, less than 5 percent of the 1970 population lived in lower-income tracts that clearly became poorer, and growth rates of 230–269 percent were more common than slower growth.[8] Cincinnati and Providence had less gentrification overall, but they also had relatively few tracts with below-average income growth.

In Philadelphia, Washington, and Boston, however, much higher proportions of the nongentrifying poor tracts became relatively poorer over the decade. The disparity between gentrification and below-average growth was greatest in Philadelphia, where 43 percent of the 1970 population in nongentrifying lower-income tracts lived in tracts with income growth below 190 percent and only 10 percent lived in tracts that experienced growth as "high" as 230–269 percent. Even more disappointingly, Washington reveals strong evidence of decidedly uneven development within the city. Its top performance in gentrification and its above-average growth in per capita income would ideally imply that poverty decreased, city revenues increased, and life improved throughout the city. Instead,

---

8. In the San Francisco and Minneapolis–St. Paul SMSAs, however, as well as in Washington, D.C., equivalent analysis of relative shifts among central cities and counties in each SMSA shows some evidence that poor population shifted from the city to the suburbs at above-average rates. In Washington, that shift in poor population led to above-average reconcentration in Prince Georges County. In the San Francisco and Minneapolis–St. Paul SMSAs, county-level data do not show reconcentration of poor people to be occurring within any particular county.

31 percent of the population of nongentrifying tracts lived in tracts with income growth that was sharply below-average, and a growth of 190–230 percent was more common than one of 230–270 percent. Although above-average income growth was common, even in lower-income tracts, these favorable developments did not spread evenly. Almost all of the tracts that were upper-income in 1970 had at least average growth in income. But of the poorer nongentrifying tracts, lower-income tracts that became relatively poorer housed more people than did lower-income tracts with average income growth. Boston had less gentrification than Washington overall, but exhibited similar disparities among lower-income nongentrifying tracts.

The Impacts of Gentrification

In the light of such phenomena as conversions of boarding houses to single-family homes and upgrading of single-room occupancy hotels, in addition to secular declines in household size, population loss is expected to accompany gentrification (Spain 1982). Those concerned about displacement from homes and neighborhoods further claim that gentrification displaces poor residents to other, less attractive or accessible areas (Hart1979b, Fainstein et al. 1983). Others, however, argue that more poor people are displaced by abandonment of buildings than by gentrification (HUD 1981) and that gentrification may actually improve lower-income housing opportunities if increased demand for inner-city housing deters abandonment and supports maintenance of the housing stock. Yet analyzing which effect predominates is complicated by simultaneous declines in household size, population decentralization, and changes in the incidence of poverty over the decade.

Like most large cities, all of these cities lost population between 1970 and 1980 (cf. Table 4.1). Loss rates varied from 6 percent in San Francisco and 7 percent in Providence to 24 percent in Cleveland, and they ranged between 12 and 18 percent in the other seven cities. Changes in the extent and incidence of poverty were more diverse. In San Francisco, the number of poor people fell more rapidly than did the total population, so that the city's poverty rate dropped. Washington, Minneapolis–St. Paul, Providence, Cincinnati, and Cleveland also had decreases in poor population, but poverty rates rose because the total population had still greater losses. In Boston, Philadelphia, Buffalo, and Newark, the number of poor grew despite decreases in total population. The poverty rate rose most sharply in Newark, from 23 percent to 32 percent; and it increased five percentage points in Buffalo, Cleveland, and Philadelphia.

To identify relative shifts in both total and poor population in gentrifying tracts apart from citywide changes in population and poverty, I examined the 1970 distributions of the total and poor populations among different types of tracts and relative shifts over the decade in these distributions. As detailed below, this approach suggests that contrary to common expectations, in most of these cities gentrifying tracts did *not* have higher rates of population loss than did their cities generally. Furthermore, when relative population losses from gentrifying tracts did occur, they were decidedly smaller than those resulting from "thinning out." However, above-average net relocation of the poor does appear to have occurred in the seven cities with the most gentrification. Each gentrifying city except San Francisco had higher than average losses of poor population from gentrifying tracts and corresponding above-average relative increases of poor population in other nongentrifying lower-income tracts; San Francisco had above-average losses of poor population from its upper-income tracts with high income growth. Again, however, such differential shifts were smaller than the average population losses that occurred.

Table 5.3 details the percentage distributions of total and poor population in 1970 and their subsequent redistribution on which these conclusions are based. The seven cities with at least 10 percent of their population in gentrifying tracts are ranked in terms of relative neighborhood upgrading. As in Table 5.2, "gentrifying" tracts are defined as lower-income tracts with income growth above 270 percent. Lower-income tracts, however, are further divided into those with 1970 poverty rates above and below 25 percent ("poor" and "lower income" tracts, respectively) to track the (relative) relocation of poor residents from tracts with and without poverty concentrations in 1970 and thus determine if new poverty concentrations are forming. To treat these distinctions briefly, the following discussion refers to "poor, lower-income, or upper-income" tracts, (based on 1970 poverty and income status) that are "lagging, average, or gaining" in income status (based on growth rates in current dollar median incomes) over the decade. Because of their low levels of gentrification, Buffalo, Cleveland, and Newark are not included in the table, but population changes in their poor tracts provide a standard of comparison about the results of "thinning out." Since these three cities had overall rates of population loss between 18 and 24 percent over the decade and shares of city population in their poor tracts dropped an additional 5–8 percent, it appears that population losses as high as 25–30 percent over a decade did result from "thinning out" as population shifted out of poor, declining tracts.[9]

9. Smith (1984) cautions strongly that losses due to abandonment should not be in any way be considered "normal."

Table 5.3

The Relative 1970 Distribution of Total and Poor Population in Seven Cities among Tracts Classified by 1970 Poverty Rates and Median Income and by 1970–1980 Change in Median Incomes, and the 1970–1980 Percentage Point Changes in These Distributions

	Distribution of total population among tracts with income change of				Distribution of poor population among tracts with income change of[d]			
	<190%	190–269%	270%+	All tracts	<190%	190–269%	270%+	All tracts
Washington, D.C.								
Poor tracts[a]								
1970 % share	3.5	7.4	9.8	20.7	7.0	14.1	19.0	40.1
1970–80 change	0.3	-0.3	-1.1	-1.1	**2.1**	-0.4	-7.8	-6.1
Lower-income tracts[b]								
1970% share	8.6	19.9	27.7	56.2	8.3	18.0	24.8	51.1
1970–80 change	-0.2	-0.5	0.1	-0.6	**4.3**	**3.5**	-3.5	4.3
Upper-income tracts[c]								
1970 % share	0.0	9.6	13.6	23.2	0.0	4.0	4.9	8.8
1970–80 change	0.0	0.1	1.5	1.6	0.0	**0.6**	**1.2**	1.8
San Francisco								
Poor tracts								
1970 % share	2.8	3.5	5.2	11.5	7.3	7.5	10.9	25.7
1970–80 change	-0.8	0.1	0.1	-0.6	-1.6	-0.2	0.1	-1.7
Lower-income tracts								
1970 % share	1.8	19.4	31.7	52.9	2.3	21.7	31.7	55.7
1970–80 change	0.1	-0.1	-1.2	-1.2	**1.2**	**2.1**	-3.8	-0.5
Upper-income tracts								
1970 % share	0.1	28.2	7.3	35.6	0.1	14.4	4.1	18.6
1970–80 change	0.0	1.6	0.2	1.8	0.0	**2.6**	-0.4	2.2
Minneapolis–St. Paul								
Poor tracts								
1970 % share	0.5	3.1	4.7	8.3	1.6	8.8	15.3	25.7
1970–80 change	-0.1	-0.4	0.1	-0.3	**0.1**	-1.5	-2.5	-4.0
Lower-income tracts								
1970 % share	1.4	28.1	20.6	50.0	1.9	32.0	22.5	56.3
1970–80 change	0.5	-0.9	0.0	-0.5	**1.8**	**4.6**	-3.2	3.3

(continued on next page)

Table 5.3 (continued)

	Distribution of total population among tracts with income change of				Distribution of poor population among tracts with income change of[d]			
	<190%	190–269%	270%+	All tracts	<190%	190–269%	270%+	All tracts
Upper-income tracts								
1970 % share	0.0	36.5	5.2	41.7	0.0	15.7	2.3	18.0
1970–80 change	0.0	0.8	0.0	0.8	0.0	1.3	-0.6	0.7
Boston								
Poor tracts								
1970 % share	2.7	8.1	7.4	18.3	5.4	17.8	15.0	38.1
1970–80 change	-0.4	-1.6	1.5	-0.5	-0.6	-5.6	-5.1	-11.4
Lower-income tracts								
1970 % share	14.9	24.6	13.4	52.9	15.0	21.0	14.4	50.4
1970–80 change	-1.3	-0.7	2.4	0.5	3.9	3.1	0.7	7.7
Upper-income tracts								
1970 % share	3.3	24.1	1.5	28.9	1.6	9.2	0.7	11.5
1970–80 change	0.1	-0.1	0.1	0.1	1.3	2.1	0.2	3.6
Cincinnati								
Poor tracts								
1970 % share	5.6	13.8	4.2	23.6	13.7	33.7	7.9	55.2
1970–80 change	-1.1	0.8	-0.4	-0.7	-1.2	0.3	-2.4	-3.4
Lower-income tracts								
1970 % share	2.4	29.9	11.3	43.7	2.2	23.8	7.9	33.9
1970–80 change	-1.3	0.5	0.9	0.1	-0.6	4.1	-1.1	2.5
Upper-income tracts								
1970 % share	4.3	25.5	2.9	32.7	1.4	8.6	1.0	10.0
1970–80 change	-3.3	3.5	0.3	0.6	-0.9	2.0	-0.2	0.9
Philadelphia								
Poor tracts								
1970 % share	10.2	5.8	5.5	21.5	23.4	13.5	11.3	48.2
1970–80 change	-1.5	-0.8	-0.7	-3.0	-2.1	-3.7	-3.9	-9.7
Lower-income tracts								
1970 % share	12.6	24.9	4.0	41.5	12.5	22.2	3.8	38.5
1970–80 change	-0.1	-0.1	0.3	0.1	6.0	1.7	-1.1	6.7

(continued on next page)

Table 5.3 (*continued*)

	Distribution of total population among tracts with income change of				Distribution of poor population among tracts with income change of[d]			
	<190%	190–269%	270%+	All tracts	<190%	190–269%	270%+	All tracts
Upper-income tracts								
1970 % share	8.0	28.0	0.9	36.9	2.7	10.2	0.4	13.3
1970–80 change	1.0	2.0	0.0	3.0	**1.7**	1.3	-0.1	3.0
Providence–Pawtucket–Warwick								
Poor tracts								
1970 % share	1.4	8.3	3.2	12.9	3.3	19.3	7.1	29.7
1970–80 change	-0.3	-1.3	0.2	-1.4	**-0.1**	-3.5	-0.4	-4.0
Lower-income tracts								
1970 % share	10.2	31.0	7.6	48.8	10.4	35.8	7.7	53.8
1970–80 change	-2.6	0.0	0.3	-2.3	**2.0**	0.0	-0.3	1.7
Upper-income tracts								
1970 % share	2.6	35.7	0.0	38.3	1.1	15.4	0.0	16.5
1970–80 change	0.3	3.4	0.0	3.7	**0.8**	1.5	0.0	2.3

[a]"Poor" tracts are those with 1970 poverty rates above 25%.

[b]"Lower-income" tracts are those with 1970 poverty rates below 25% and 1970 median incomes below the national metropolitan average of $8,431.

[c]"Upper-income" tracts are those with 1970 median incomes above the national metropolitan average of $8,431.

[d]Percentage-point changes in italics are those for which the rate of relative loss of poor population (see n. 10 to this chapter) was at least 10 percentage points more negative than the rate of relative change of total population in that category of tracts.

Percentage point changes in boldface are those for which the rate of relative gain of poor population was at least 10 percentage points more positive than the rate of relative change of total population there.

Population Redistribution within Each City

When tracts are considered only in terms of their 1970 income and poverty status, over the decade the percentage point shifts (in col. 4 of Table 5.3) show that total population in each city shifted slightly out from tracts with high 1970 poverty rates ("poor" tracts) into tracts with higher income. When tracts are further identified by the different rates of income growth occurring during the decade (cols. 1–3), in cities other than Washington and San Francisco the population shifts from poor tracts are shown to be associated less with gentrification than with thinning out, possibly from housing abandonment, in "lagging" tracts with below-average income growth. Higher population losses were common in those poor tracts with lagging or average income change, while gentrifying poor tracts had lower relative population loss or relative gains. Boston and Providence display this pattern most vividly, with population relatively shifting out from both poor and lower-income lagging tracts and into both poor and lower-income gentrifying tracts. San Francisco and Minneapolis–St. Paul also had shifts from lagging poor into gentrifying poor tracts, while Cincinnati and Philadelphia had relatively greater population shifts from poor, lagging tracts than from gentrifying tracts. Washington was the only city with both large population shifts out from gentrifying poor tracts *and* relative increases in population in poor, lagging tracts.

Looking at tracts at the upper end of the income spectrum, in each city other than Boston (which saw remarkably little shifting among tracts in the three 1970 income categories), upper-income tracts gained relative shares of city population most rapidly. In most cities with relatively high neighborhood upgrading, both categories of lower-income tracts lost population while upper-income tracts gained. Such shifts were most marked in Philadelphia, where the poorest tracts' share of city population dropped from 22 percent to 19 percent and the upper-income tracts gained three percentage points.

Relocation or Displacement of the Poor?

As the right side of Table 5.3 indicates, in most of these cities the location of poor population shifted more drastically than that of total population. Although losses from nongentrifying poor tracts among both poor and total population show that thinning out was occurring, both the origins and the destinations of the above-average net shifts of poor population are consistent with claims that poor residents were being disproportionately displaced from gentrifying tracts. In each city other than San Francisco, poor residents shifted from gentrifying tracts at higher rates than did total population.[10] Disparities between total and poor shifts were the most marked in Boston, in which the share of the city's poor population living in the poor and lower-income gentrifying tracts *fell* by one-sixth even though the relative share of total city population in these tracts was *growing* by one-fourth. Washington and Philadelphia had marked losses of poor population from gentrifying tracts while total population shares remained stable. Measuring the net shifts as a fraction of the gentrifying tracts' original share of poor population, the incidence of such relocation was greatest in Philadelphia and Washington, and outmovement of poor from gentrifying tracts that had had poverty concentrations in 1970 was also high in Boston and Cincinnati. Such net relocation of the poor population cannot be directly equated with displacement defined as forced moves (Grier and Grier 1980). But it does confirm that the poor were being differentially displaced from gentrifying tracts in some cities. It also provides a basis for estimating the net impact of displacement on relocation of the poor population within these cities over the decade and identifying the types of tracts that the poor were leaving and entering.

Tracts with disproportionately high losses of poor population (i.e., with shifts at least 10 percentage points more negative than shifts of total population for that category) have those shifts highlighted in italics on the right side of Table 5.3; for tracts with disproportionate gains of poor population, shifts are shown in boldface. These disproportionate losses and gains show that within each city other than San Francisco poor persons disproportionately shifted from gentrifying tracts to tracts with slower income growth. In Minneapolis–St. Paul, Cincinnati, and Philadelphia, as well as San Francisco, there were also disproportionate shifts of poor population out from those upper-income tracts with income gains. The destination tracts were usually not those with poverty concentrations in 1970 (except in Washington, Minneapolis–St. Paul, and Providence). Yet the fact that many of the lower-income tracts that gained poor persons were in the category with sharply below-average income growth suggests that new concentration of poverty are forming, especially in Washington, Boston, Philadelphia, and Providence. Such patterns are consistent with the claim that "lower class areas of converting old cities may experience further 'decline' and devalorization as they absorb this (displaced) population" (Fainstein and Fainstein 1982, 186).

Relative shifts of poor population into tracts that had had above-average income in 1970 also occurred in most cities, implying that some downward

10. Comparisons such as these are based on "rates" of relative loss or gain, calculated as the percentage-point shift from or to the category divided by the 1970 percentage share of population in the category.

filtering of housing was taking place, and thus presumably that some lower-income households were gaining better housing. In each city, the relative growth of poor population in upper-income tracts was greater than that of total population. Only in Providence, however, was the proportion of the poor population shifting into tracts that had been upper-income in 1970 slightly higher than that shifting into other lower-income tracts.

The Location of Change within Cities

Where within these cities did such changes occur? Research and speculation on gentrification typically regard it as being most likely in older, historic neighborhoods with good access to downtown (Lipton 1977; Palen and London 1984). Palen and London, indeed, claim that the ultimate effects of urban revitalization on the economic health of cities depend on whether upgrading can spread to "grey" working-class areas. Smith's thesis (1979) that a rent gap is a prerequisite for capital reinvestment also predicts that gentrification will begin near the central business district (CBD). Displacement, conversely, is expected to force the poor farther from desirable and accessible downtown land (Fainstein and Fainstein 1982). As Harrison (1974) pointed out, because of the radial nature of much public transportation, living farther from the center of the city can reduce access not only to services and employment within the city, but also to (the increasing) employment opportunities in the suburbs.

Aside from Lipton's studies of tracts within two miles of CBDs, however, few studies have examined the location of changes throughout cities.[11] To examine such questions, I mapped the location of tracts with extreme changes in income and poverty for all tracts in each of the ten cities. The results confirm that gentrification to date has been spatially concentrated, typically occurring near each city's downtown core. Gentrifying tracts and upper-income tracts with above-average income growth are also often found near past concentrations of wealth, underscoring the importance of "location, location, location" and of status considerations.

Furthermore, for each city other than San Francisco, these maps reveal evidence of displacement and reconcentration of poverty that confirm the implications of the greater intracity shifts by poor population shown by Table 5.3. Although poverty rates often dropped markedly within or near gentrifying tracts, they nevertheless rose sharply elsewhere. The neigh-

---

11. Chall (1983–84) uses 1970–80 changes in income to examine all tracts in New York City. With his measures, he finds gentrification to be generally confined to areas south of Fourteenth Street in Manhattan and to a few neighborhoods in Brooklyn.

borhoods with increases in poverty rates were often adjacent to gentrifying tracts, but located farther from the urban core, on less "prime" real estate.

For the five cities with more than 100,000 population in gentrifying tracts, the maps of census tracts in Figures 5.1–5.5 show the relative location of tracts with different levels and changes in median income and in poverty rates. They show where gentrification occurred with respect to the CBD and the relative location of income growth versus new concentrations of poverty.

Two maps are included for each city. The first indicates which lower-income tracts had above-average income growth—that is, gentrification—and which had sharply below-average growth. The second focuses on changes in poverty rates, highlighting all areas in which poverty rates either fell or rose by more than 10 percentage points. For reference, each of the maps uses cross-hatching to show the location of CBD, and identifies by diagonal lines the "poor" tracts that had poverty rates above 25 percent in 1970 and the "upper-income" tracts with above-average median incomes in 1970. In almost all these cities in the locations of poor, lower-income, and upper-income tracts in 1970 resemble the traditional simple models of urban structure in which the poorest tracts lie near the city center while income increases with distance. But the locations of upper-income, lower-income, and poor tracts also reflect sectoral development and many special circumstances, including the persistence (or more recent development) of some central upper-income tracts.[12]

To explain the maps, I shall first describe in some detail the patterns and changes they show for San Francisco, which had much gentrification but the least apparent displacement (Fig. 5.1). In both the income and poverty maps for all cities, diagonal lines sloping up to the right show for reference the location of the poor tracts, while diagonal lines sloping up to the left show the location of upper-income tracts; the remaining "lower-income" tracts with poverty rates below 25 percent lack diagonal lines. In San Francisco, these references lines show that almost all of the northeast sector of San Francisco, except for a few tracts along the waterfront to the north, had below-average median incomes in 1969, while higher incomes were concentrated to the west and south. The poorest tracts were clustered near the cross-hatched CBD and in the southeast corner of the city. In the first map (Fig. 5.1a), areas with solid shading are those with high or low rates of change in median income between 1970 and 1980. Gentrifying lower-income tracts, those with rates of 1970–80 income change above 270 percent, are represented by dark shading, and "lagging" lower-income

---

12. White's (1980) maps of changing locations by status within Chicago, Cleveland, Detroit, and St. Louis reflect such special circumstances, particularly urban renewal efforts.

tracts with income growth below 190 percent have lighter shading. As Fig. 5.1a shows, almost all of the lower-income tracts had growth above 270 percent; indeed, most of the tracts located around and to the west of the CBD had income growth about 290 percent. Very few city tracts had below-average growth: the only relative concentrations of "lagging" tracts were on the western edge of the CBD and in the southeast corner of the city. The map details income-growth rates only for lower-income tracts, but almost all of the upper-income tracts had average or above-average rates of income growth as well.

The second map for each city shows how changes in income affected changes in poverty rates. In the poverty maps, the darker shading again denotes relative improvement, since it represents tracts with decreases in poverty rates, while the lighter shading shows tracts in which poverty rates increased by 10 percentage points or more. In San Francisco (Fig. 5.1b), income changes were associated with drops in poverty of 10 percentage points or more in five of the "poor" tracts, three to the southeast and two near the CBD. Although not many tracts had sharp increases in poverty, poverty rates did increase more than 10 percentage points in four central tracts adjacent to earlier poverty concentrations, including several with average income growth. Beyond the center, poverty rates did not change greatly over the decade.

With this introduction, I shall cover the remaining cities more quickly. Fulfilling its reputation as the vanguard of gentrification, Washington (Fig. 5.2) had both extensive gentrification and other above-average income growth in much of the city, together with clear evidence that the poor relocated from gentrifying areas into new and more distant concentrations of poverty. The reference diagonals show that in 1970 upper-income areas were generally located on the fringes of the city, except for the southwest urban renewal area south of the mall and the CBD. Poor tracts were predominantly located near the core, stretching north from the CBD and to the east around Capitol Hill. Between 1970 and 1980, income growth was above average, and often above 290 percent, in almost all tracts north of the Anacostia River, including many of the poor tracts that had had poverty rates above 25 percent in 1970. Almost all of the upper-income tracts in the prosperous sector west of Rock Creek Park also had growth rates above 290 percent. The income map (Fig. 5.2a) clearly shows the prevalent gentrification of Dupont Circle, at the northwest corner of the CBD, and of the tracts surrounding Capitol Hill, to the east of CBD. The poverty map (Fig. 5.2b) documents the corresponding sharp decreases in poverty that occurred to the east and north of Capitol Hill and northeast of the CBD. Gentrification clearly has spread from its early outpost on Capitol Hill (Gale 1976, 1984), while wealthy areas in Georgetown and other tracts west of Rock Creek Park have anchored continued

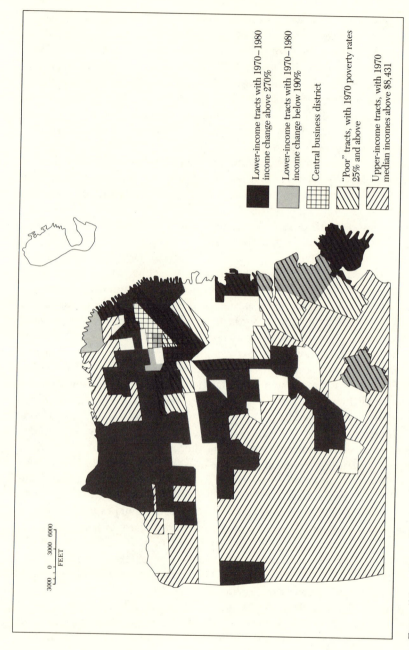

Legend:

Lower-income tracts with 1970–1980 income change above 270%

Lower-income tracts with 1970–1980 income change below 190%

Central business district

"Poor" tracts, with 1970 poverty rates 25% and above

Upper-income tracts, with 1970 median incomes above $8,431

3000 0 3000 6000
FEET

Figure 5.1a. Census Tracts in San Francisco Classified by Median Income and Poverty Rates in 1970 and by 1970–1980 Change in Median Income.

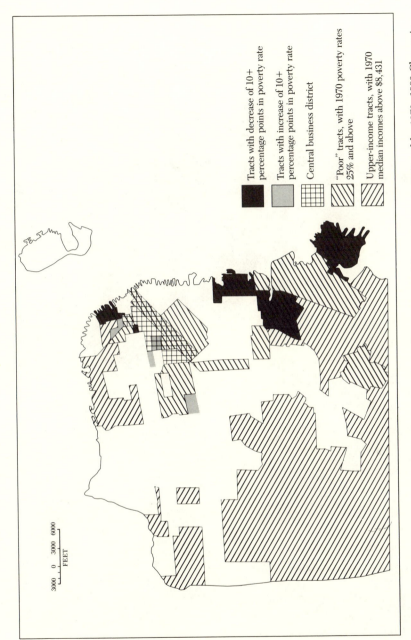

Legend:

- Tracts with decrease of 10+ percentage points in poverty rate
- Tracts with increase of 10+ percentage points in poverty rate
- Central business district
- "Poor" tracts, with 1970 poverty rates 25% and above
- Upper-income tracts, with 1970 median incomes above $8,431

FEET
3000 0 3000 6000

Figure 5.1b. Census Tracts in San Francisco Classified by Median Income and Poverty Rates in 1970 and by 1970–1980 Change in Poverty Rates.

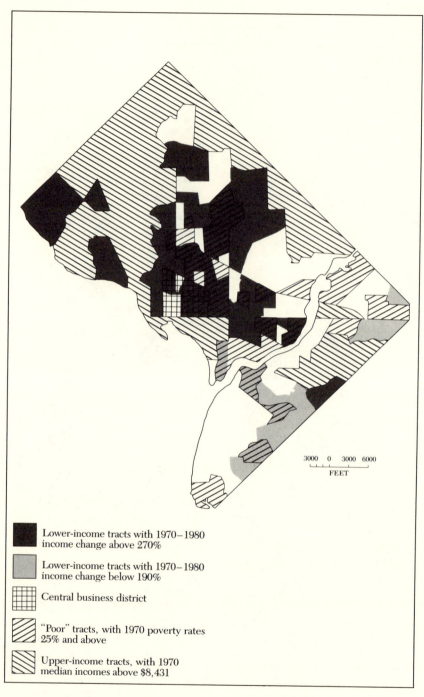

Figure 5.2a.   Census Tracts in Washington, D.C. Classified by Median Income and Poverty Rates in 1970 and by 1970–1980 Change in Median Income.

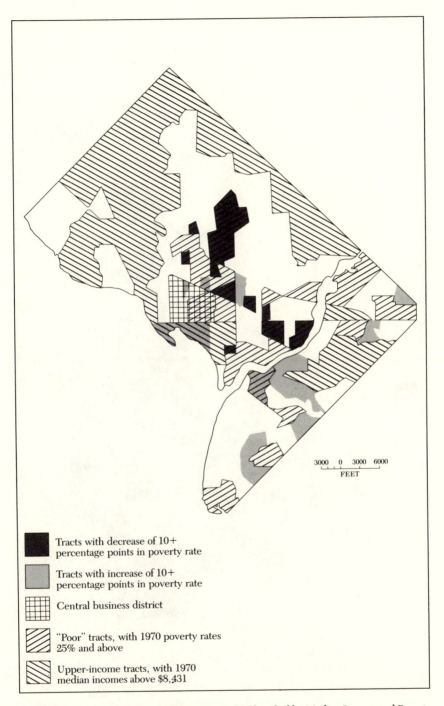

Tracts with decrease of 10+
percentage points in poverty rate

Tracts with increase of 10+
percentage points in poverty rate

Central business district

"Poor" tracts, with 1970 poverty rates
25% and above

Upper-income tracts, with 1970
median incomes above $8,431

3000   0   3000   6000
FEET

Figure 5.2b.   Census Tracts in Washington, D.C. Classified by Median Income and Poverty
Rates in 1970 and by 1970–1980 Change in Poverty Rates.

141

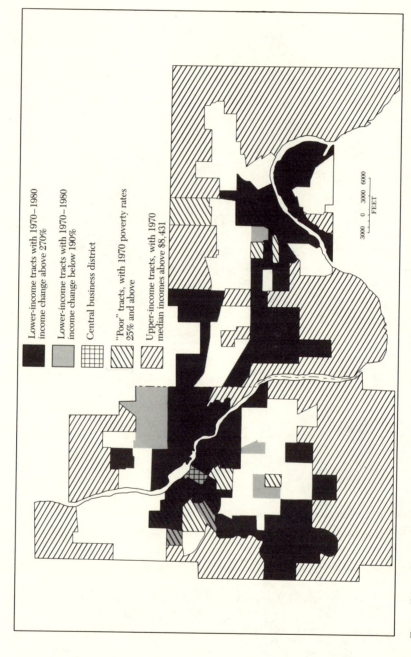

Legend (on map):
- Lower-income tracts with 1970–1980 income change above 270%
- Lower-income tracts with 1970–1980 income change below 190%
- Central business district
- "Poor" tracts, with 1970 poverty rates 25% and above
- Upper-income tracts, with 1970 median incomes above $8,431

3000 0 3000 6000
FEET

Figure 5.3a.   Census Tracts in Minneapolis-St. Paul Classified by Median Income and Poverty Rates in 1970 and by 1970–1980 Change in Median Income.

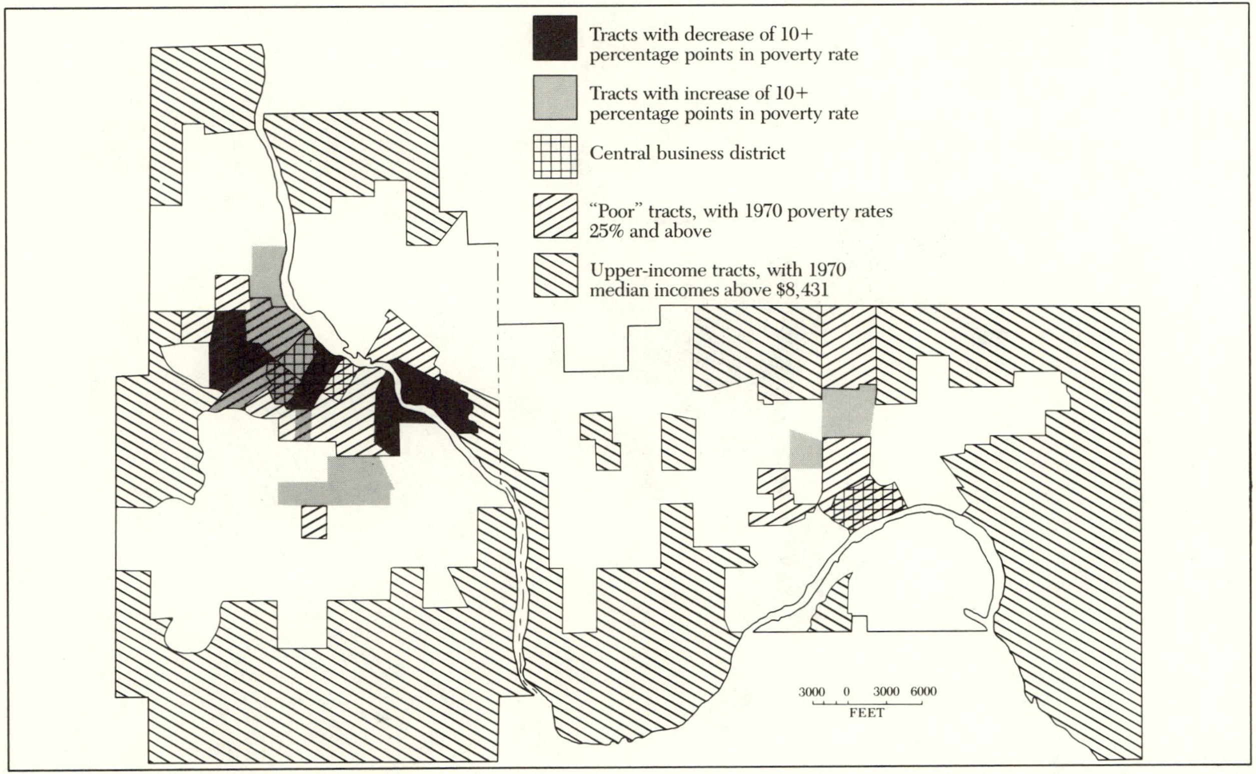

Tracts with decrease of 10+ percentage points in poverty rate
Tracts with increase of 10+ percentage points in poverty rate
Central business district
"Poor" tracts, with 1970 poverty rates 25% and above
Upper-income tracts, with 1970 median incomes above $8,431
3000 0 3000 6000
FEET

Figure 5.3b. Census Tracts in Minneapolis-St. Paul Classified by Median Income and Poverty Rates in 1970 and by 1970–1980 Change in Median Income.

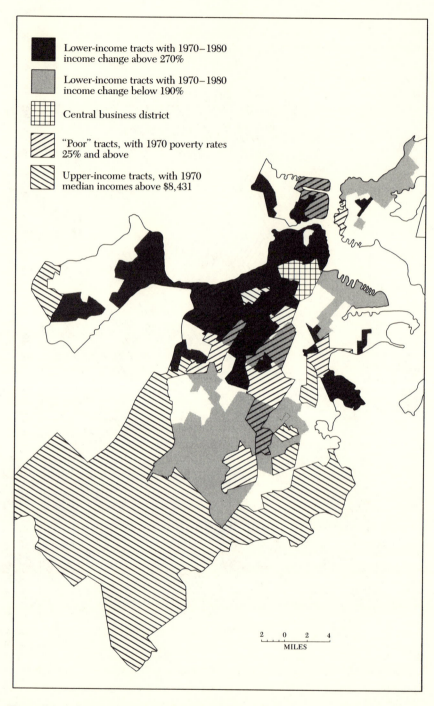

Figure 5.4a. Census Tracts in Boston Classified by Median Income and Poverty Rates in 1970 and by 1970–1980 Change in Median Income.

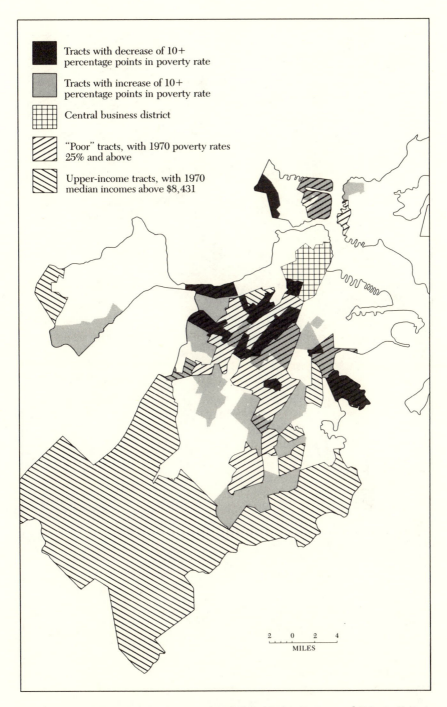

Legend:

Tracts with decrease of 10+ percentage points in poverty rate

Tracts with increase of 10+ percentage points in poverty rate

Central business district

"Poor" tracts, with 1970 poverty rates 25% and above

Upper-income tracts, with 1970 median incomes above $8,431

2 0 2 4
MILES

Figure 5.4b.   Census Tracts in Boston Classified by Median Income and Poverty Rates in 1970 and by 1970–1980 Change in Poverty Rates.

145

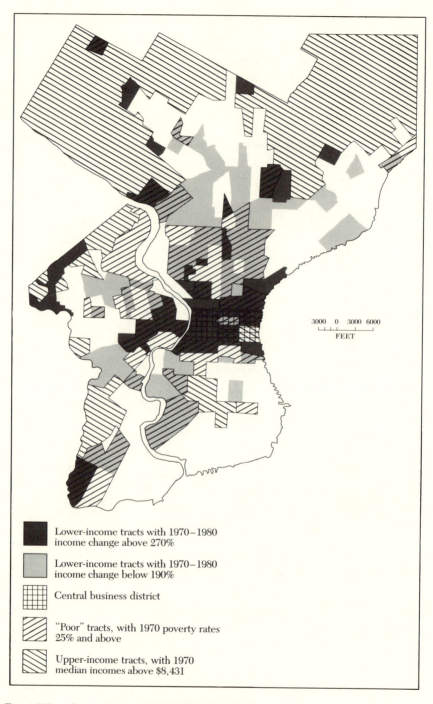

■   Lower-income tracts with 1970–1980
        income change above 270%

     Lower-income tracts with 1970–1980
        income change below 190%

     Central business district

     "Poor" tracts, with 1970 poverty rates
        25% and above

     Upper-income tracts, with 1970
        median incomes above $8,431

Figure 5.5a.   Census Tracts in Philadelphia Classified by Median Income and Poverty Rates in 1970 and by 1970–1980 Change in Median Income.

146

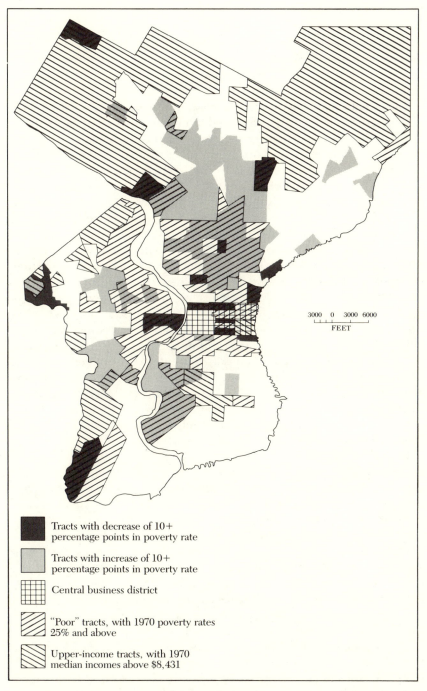

Tracts with decrease of 10+
percentage points in poverty rate

Tracts with increase of 10+
percentage points in poverty rate

Central business district

"Poor" tracts, with 1970 poverty rates
25% and above

Upper-income tracts, with 1970
median incomes above $8,431

Figure 5.5b.   Census Tracts in Philadelphia Classified by Median Income and Poverty
Rates in 1970 and by 1970–1980 Change in Poverty Rates.

147

improvement nearby. The above-average income growth and decreases in poverty to the northeast of the CBD suggest that gentrification was also under way in some of the areas around Howard and Catholic University that have received less publicity.

But in both maps the location of concentrations of tracts with below-average growth in median income and/or poverty increases graphically illustrates the extent of uneven development in Washington. The poor population was markedly shifting into the southeast section of the city across the Anacostia River, where many tracts lagged in income growth and nine tracts had poverty increases of 10 percentage points or more. Increasing poverty rates also spilled over into the middle-class northeast quadrant and several other tracts adjacent to central gentrifying tracts.

In Minneapolis–St. Paul (Fig. 5.3a), gentrification occurred in almost all of the poor tracts that were located near both CBDs, but it was also common in pleasant neighborhoods of single-family housing farther from the centers. Much of the rest of both cities, including the prestigious Lake District in southwest Minneapolis, experienced average and above-average income growth as well. In 1970, the Twin Cities had had one of the lower poverty rates among large cities, and the rates shown in Table 5.3 displayed little relative evidence of displacement. Nevertheless Fig. 5.3b suggests that some geographically concentrated shifts were occurring here as well. Poverty rates decreased sharply in tracts within and around Minneapolis's extensively rebuilt CBD and the University of Minnesota campus, but they increased farther south and around the near-northside concentrations of public housing. St. Paul also had a band of slower income growth and increasing poverty northwest of its CBD.

Boston's gentrification seems firmly tied to downtown redevelopment around the CBD, the waterfront urban renewal project, and the persistent upper-income enclave on Beacon Hill. As Fig. 5.4a shows, gentrification took place in all of the tracts surrounding Beacon Hill, including many that had had high poverty rates in 1970. Gentrification also spread westward through the Back Bay area and the cultural and educational amenities located near the Fenway into the environs of Allston-Brighton across the river from Harvard, extended southward along the South End, and surfaced near Bunker Hill in historic Charlestown. Fig. 5.4b shows that the prevalent above-average income growth in the center of the city was accompanied by sharp drops in poverty rates south of the Charles River and in the South End.

Like Washington, however, Boston saw many tracts more distant from the CBD lag severely in income growth and experience correspondingly sharp increases in poverty rates. This pattern characterized both the old and poor northeast corner of the city and neighborhoods in Roxbury and Dorchester and farther south into Mattapan. Thus in Boston as well, poverty is apparently reconcentrating farther from the CBD.

Philadelphia (Fig. 5.5) may have the most complicated maps because it is the largest city studied, but it also displays striking symptoms of extremely uneven development. Some gentrification occurred: as Fig. 5.5a shows, it was clearly anchored in the core, mainly in the east-west Center City corridor that is not only the city's oldest and most historic section, but also the CBD and the locale of much publicly-funded downtown redevelopment in the past (Weiler 1974). Above-average income growth also spread west across the Schuylkill River and persisted (at some distance from the CBD) in the upper-income northwest Chestnut Hill section and several tracts adjacent to upper-income areas.

As Fig. 5.5b shows, poverty rates dropped correspondingly near Center City and northeast along the Delaware. But many tracts that had below-average income growth and/or sharp increases in poverty rates surround the gentrifying core in three directions—particularly in North Philadelphia. The relative prevalence of extreme values in both income growth and poverty changes within Philadelphia, together with the geographical proximity of some of these extreme values, demonstrate graphically why much of the literature on conflict and clashes between different classes and their values originates from case studies of Philadelphia (Levy 1980; Levy and Cybriwksy 1980; Smith 1979; and Weiler 1980).

Since the remaining cities had few tracts with gentrification, their maps are not included here.[13] Reflecting its hilly topography, Cincinnati's maps juxtapose income growth in several tracts in the vicinity of the CBD against many areas with relative decline. Seven poor central tracts had marked drops in poverty, but poverty rates simultaneously rose sharply in fourteen tracts, particularly in and around a block of already poor tracts along Mill Creek west of the CBD and in a small cluster to the northwest of CBD.

The maps for Providence-Pawtucket-Warwick did demonstrate that the few tracts with above-average income growth were indeed located in Providence and to a lesser degree in Pawtucket, rather than in more prosperous (and "suburban") Warwick. Areas in the northeastern section of Providence around Brown University had the highest income growth, and poverty decreased in some neighboring tracts. Some above-average income growth also occurred along the northwest corridor that had been developed in the late 1800s for higher-status ethnic minorities. Poverty rates rose along the southern fringe of Providence as income lagged there.

Buffalo's maps were interesting in suggesting how geographically concentrated and uneven changes were in a city with very little gentrification overall. Upgrading was concentrated in a band of ten tracts stretching north from the CBD toward the major remaining upper-income area in 1970. This area could provide a beachhead for future revival. But at the

---

13. Copies of computer plots of changes in the other cities are available upon request.

same time, many of the poor tracts became poorer, and poverty concentrations appeared to expand toward the east and north, adjacent to the area with above-average income growth.

Reflecting their summary findings, the remaining two cities had maps swamped by Berry's (1982b) "seas of decline"—with both below-average income growth and increases in poverty. Newark was worst: almost all of its poor tracts became decidedly poorer, and poverty rates rose more than 10 percentage points in much of the rest of the city as well. Cleveland's maps show very low income growth directly east of the CBD, but not many large changes in poverty rates there. Further east, there were a few tracts with above-average income growth, but also scattered sharp increases in poverty. The near West Side had both slower income growth and some poverty increases, while the far West Side, Cleveland's only upper-income area in 1970, remained quite stable, with average income growth and few changes in poverty rates.

Taken together, these maps imply that gentrification has indeed been concentrated in poor tracts near urban cores, probably those with older, and possibly historic, housing. Furthermore, gentrification has tended to displace poor residents differentially farther from city cores; and in several cities other poverty concentrations appear to be forming. San Francisco is the only one of the gentrifying cities to exhibit few drastic shifts in poverty rates or evidence of displacement at summary levels. Such results support its characterization as a (relatively unusual) city in which high private investment has been directed by at least moderate political representation of low-income groups to provide some protection for lower-income neighborhoods and some services and public investment for their residents (Fainstein and Fainstein 1983, ch. 7). But even in San Francisco, the detailed maps show poverty rates rising in several tracts just beyond gentrifying areas. Thus, some displacement seems to be occurring at a low level. And that level of displacement might be low mainly because there are relatively few lower-income residents left to be displaced.

If one assumes with Sternlieb that further gentrification would benefit the poor as well as cities, this examination of the location of gentrification is unsettling on another count. In only two of these cities—Washington and San Francisco—does gentrification appear to extend much beyond "islands of hopeful development" that were mostly publicly funded. In Boston, Minneapolis–St. Paul, and Philadelphia, local experts agreed that many of the "gentrifying" areas were tracts that had received large amounts of publicly funded or subsidized investment.[14]

14. This conclusion is based on discussions with Susan E. Jaster of the Boston Redevelopment Authority, and Michael Munson and Charles Ballantine of the Twin Cities Metropolitan Council.

Summary

By developing estimates of the extent of relative income upgrading at the tract level within ten distressed cities, this chapter has first demonstrated that differences among cities in changes in city selection rates during the 1970s do appear to be related to differences in growth in median income in neighborhoods within distressed cities. Such a correlation supports my hypothesis that monitoring trends in city selection rates for distressed cities between censuses can help indicate progress toward revival or further decline in these cities.

However, both the very small number of cities with upturns in selection—especially among upper-income movers—and the relative scarcity of gentrification mean that my hypothesis cannot be considered proven. In particular, Providence's low level of gentrification over the decade implies that changes in upper-income selection alone are not as dominant an indicator as I had expected. Nor is information about changes in trends sufficient in itself to determine the implications of current migration balances for population and income changes in any city. Monitoring city selection rates does provide a basis for determining directions of change in migration and thus potentially in population and income levels. But other information, such as previous levels of distress and selective outmigration together with levels and rates of net migration for the SMSA as a whole, is desirable to establish the context in which changes in city selection are occurring.

The measures of above-average income growth at the tract level were then used to prepare more comprehensive estimates and comparisons of the extent and location of gentrification within a variety of cities than have previously been available; most previous studies have dealt only with selected neighborhoods within cities or with only one city. Although estimates of the amount of "above-average" income growth necessarily vary with the cutoff chosen as a comparison with the national average growth rate of 250 percent, growth above 270 percent was quite common in Washington, San Francisco, and Minneapolis–St. Paul, occurring in tracts that had housed one-third or more of the 1970 population. In Boston and Cincinnati such rapid growth characterized tracts having about 20 percent of the 1970 population. Above-average growth was much less common in the remaining cities. These estimates showed that in all of these cities, gentrification in lower-income tracts was more common than upgrading in upper-income tracts, although in Washington most upper-income tracts had above-average income growth over the decade.

Comparing changes among different cities is particularly valuable in demonstrating that many of the generalizations that have been made about gentrification actually are atypical or reflect only a few cities or neighborhoods. Examining changes in population and poverty in tracts identified as gentrifying or not, for example, I found that the commonly observed pattern of population losses in gentrifying tracts was not unique to them. Instead, these tracts basically shared in the general population losses experienced by both upper-income and lower-income tracts within these cities. In several instances, gentrifying tracts actually gained population relative to the rest of the city (i.e., lost less rapidly). Above-average population losses were more common in the lower-income tracts that had slower income growth, a differential consistent with claims that abandonment or thinning out produces greater population shifts than does gentrification. The experience of Buffalo, Cleveland, and Newark, the cities with essentially no gentrification, provides a baseline: their poor tracts with low income growth lost one-fourth to one-third of their 1970 population over the decade.

Relocation among the poor population mirrored that of the total population in shifting from the poorest tracts into upper-income tracts. Nevertheless, the location of the poor population shifted more among tracts classified by both 1970 income level and 1970–80 income growth than did the total population. In almost every instance these greater shifts were directed from gentrifying tracts (or occasionally also from upper-income tracts with above-average growth) to the other lower-income tracts with slower income growth. Such differentially greater relocation among the poor was most common in Washington and Boston, with 8–10 percent of the poor affected. This net relocation cannot be directly equated with displacement defined as forced moves, but it does imply that displacement from gentrifying tracts was differentially occurring.

Evidence of displacement was reinforced by maps of the location of census tracts in which these various changes were occurring. In the cities with much gentrification, gentrification was most often located near the CBD and previously upper-income areas near the core. Relatively large drops in poverty rates often accompanied gentrification near the CBD, but poverty rates then rose farther away from the core. The evidence that new, more distant concentrations of poverty were forming was clearest in Washington and Boston; but poverty rates also rose markedly in several rather large concentrations of poor tracts around the Philadelphia CBD and in smaller concentrations in Minneapolis–St. Paul and Cincinnati.

6. Prospects for Future Revival

As Wilbur Thompson noted somewhat ruefully in 1974, for over twenty years we have been waiting for the "new age of services" to "rebuild the cores of our aging metropolises" (1975, 191). During that period, however, the position of older central cities has deteriorated sharply in relation to the rest of the country. Employment has decentralized from central cities and the North, suburbs have skimmed off higher-status residents, cities' fiscal problems have worsened, and demands for public services have mushroomed as concentrations of poor and minority residents increased. Gentrification during the 1970s raised hopes that private preferences for cities and private investment therein might reverse this cycle of decline, and transformation to an advanced services economy does appear to be restructuring employment opportunities and locations in both metropolitan areas and the nation. In response, current urban policies—both federal and local—are premised on encouraging economic development of advanced technologies and services.

Yet the results of this study question whether such development can overcome the unfavorable conditions reinforcing cumulative decline in the most distressed cities. Thorough examination of residential migration trends in the United States since the late 1950s demonstrates that even when demographic and economic conditions were relatively favorable for older cities in the late 1970s, differentially faster net outmigration of higher-status movers continued or even accelerated from many large, distressed cities. Moreover, migration to the suburbs also became more selective in some less distressed cities where selectivity previously had not been a problem. Thus, in most cities, favorable national conditions did not stop or reverse past selective outmigration.

Some improvement occurred. Suburbanization has apparently slowed, and in comparison to the acceleration in flight from central cities between 1960 and 1970, even the few increases in city selection found after 1970 are more impressive. The demographic cushion of the baby boom and its high levels of household formation boosted housing demand in cities; advanced service employment apparently did induce more well-paid young professionals to live in a few "headquarters" cities; and movers—and investors—responded to housing bargains. But through 1981, the extent of the respite seemed mild and the number of distressed cities helped few in relation to the remaining indicators of present and future distress.

Because only residential migration was studied here, this cannot pretend to be the definitive judgment. Changes in attitudes and perceptions accompanying gentrification have given residence in older central-city housing new status, and thus opened up alternatives and possibilities that can be exploited by private development and public policies. These results also confirm the links between residential and employment location, so changes in employment will continue to shape cities. But in light of likely developments in demography, employment, residential preferences and public policy, the chances that most distressed central cities will soon escape the treadmill of further self-reinforcing decline seem slight. The costs of further decline will be most obvious for poor residents with few alternatives, who remain longest in these distressed cities and towns, but the process will drag down metropolitan areas and states, and thus arguably have national costs as well. In a few headquarters cities, revival appears more likely. Even where there are strong demands for downtown space, however, it will be politically difficult to ensure that the poor also benefit. After summarizing the main results of the study, this final chapter pulls together the arguments and thoughts that underlie such dismal conclusions.

Summary of Results

Since the residential decisions of upper-income movers underlie both the present plight and the possible revival of distressed cities, I contend that monitoring patterns of mobility by income over time should provide a basis for evaluating the past extent and future implications of gentrification. Therefore, I have analyzed most of the data on trends in migration since 1955–60 that are available from censuses and national surveys to determine whether central cities in the United States became more attractive to migrants in the late 1970s than previously. Because of the self-reinforcing effect of selectively greater outmigration of higher-income movers on distress in central cities, whether distressed cities became more attractive to higher-status movers was of particular concern. After identifying favorable developments in migration for some distressed cities, I then explored some intracity effects of greater city selection, particularly the extent of gentrification and its impacts on poorer residents in distressed cities. Finally, to better predict the consequences of future migration for distressed cities, I tried to infer from characteristics of both migrants and cities why improvements in migration occurred.

During the 1970s, national and regional data suggest that central cities did become slightly more attractive (or less unattractive) to migrants. Net outmigration from central cities occurred during the 1960s and continued during the 1970s, but the rate of outmigration slowed in the late 1970s. The declines in outmigration occurred among whites rather than blacks, with the reduction most significant among movers in their twenties. Notably, the proportions of young college graduates and professionals migrating to and staying within cities increased, implying that at least some cities attracted higher proportions of higher-status groups. The perception that migration to cities increased after 1970 was supported by trends over a twenty-year period for forty of the largest fifty metropolitan areas (SMSAs). For these areas, the proportion of SMSA movers selecting city residence had generally fallen between 1960 and 1970; but between 1970 and 1980, it increased in more than half of the SMSAs.

But improvement during the 1970s was marginal enough at the national level to imply that few cities markedly benefitted from shifts in migration. Moreover, regionally the greatest improvement was in the South, not in the North, where cities are more often distressed. For the forty SMSAs for which specific trends were studied, increases in city selection rates after 1970 were somewhat more likely in twenty-seven distressed central cities than in less distressed cities. However, such increases were much less common among higher-income movers. Instead, the proportions of higher-income movers selecting city residence decreased sharply in more than half of the distressed cities. Even worse, the few migration improvements that occurred were by 1980 insufficient to increase median income in almost all distressed cities. Thus, rather than attracting more upper-income movers over the decade, most distressed cities saw the flight of upper-income groups continue or accelerate, presaging further declines in city resources and widening of city-suburban disparities, rather than revival. Moreover, four of the thirteen large nondistressed cities studied developed symptoms of self-reinforcing selective outmigration over the decade.

To assess the local implications of increased city selection, changes between 1970 and 1980 were examined at the census-tract level for ten of the seventeen distressed cities that had had at least relative improvements or stability in city selection rates over the decade. As hypothesized, above-average income growth in tracts between 1970 and 1980 was correlated with upturns in city selection. Moreover, such growth occurred more often in lower-income tracts ("gentrification") than in more prosperous tracts. Gentrification was most prevalent in Washington, San Francisco, and Minneapolis–St. Paul, and was also common in Boston and Cincinnati. It was quite unusual, however, in Philadelphia and Providence, and it was practically nonexistent in Buffalo, Cleveland, and Newark, which had had upturns in city selection only among lower-income movers. Generalizing from these findings, I expect that gentrification probably also occurred in some of the other cities with selection upturns, with New York and Los Angeles most likely. However, I expect that gentrification was quite uncommon or nonexistent in the ten distressed cities experiencing marked decreases in city selection rates during the 1970s.

It was unclear, furthermore, that poor residents benefitted from local income growth when it occurred. Instead, in many of the cities, the location of the poor differentially shifted from gentrifying tracts into new pockets of poverty. Mapping these changes shows gentrification to be centered near CBDs or former high-income residential areas in the cities with the most gentrification, while poverty concentrations shifted farther from the CBD. Washington, Boston, and Philadelphia had the most evidence of such displacement, and San Francisco and Minneapolis–St. Paul the least. Such differences suggest that local policies can influence the consequences of gentrification for lower-income residents if there are strong demands for downtown space. But low demand for central access in most distressed cities would imply that the interests of the poor will often be sacrificed to incentives to entice upper-income residential or office development.

Why did city selection increase at all? Determining the relative roles of four major possible explanations in the past "turnaround" (however slight) is desirable because they have rather different implications for continued revival in the future. Most favorable for further, spreading revitalization in older central cities would be a major increase in preferences for urban living and older houses. Development of "advanced" service-based economies in central cities should also encourage residential revival, particularly if their well-educated professional employees desire city amenities such as cultural opportunities, along with better job access than commuting from distant suburbs provides.

Demographic and cost factors have been the other reasons repeatedly advanced during the 1970s as explanations for gentrification, but they would be less likely to provide continuing support for future revival. Although recent compositional shifts in population and households toward groups favoring cities should have increased demand for city housing, if the large size of the young adult cohort was the main factor underlying greater inmigration in the 1970s, housing market bust is likely to follow boom. Similarly, cost advantages of city housing and transportation accessibility hold city futures hostage to housing shortages and to employment opportunities that continue to decentralize. Furthermore, if increased demand for city residence results mainly from cost and income constraints that price more households out of suburban housing, income disparities between cities and their suburbs are likely to widen further, thus fueling rather than damping cumulative decline.

Distinguishing among such explanations is difficult, not only because they are intertwined, but also because of the limitations of statistical techniques when dealing with multicollinearity or with national trends that affect all areas to some degree. The national results provide a partial answer by showing that the slowing in outmigration in the late 1970s resulted more from the aging of the baby boom than from increases in age-specific rates of migration to cities, and that net outmigration increased among household types thought to favor cities. These differences imply that compositional effects, not increased preferences for city life, were mainly responsible for the few migration improvements that did occur. Preferences for future migration support this interpretation, since in 1979 more respondents expected to leave than to enter large cities by 1984. Furthermore, higher-income residents reported themselves more likely than others to leave cities, particularly cities in the northeast and north central regions.

Regression analysis of differences among SMSAs in changes in city selection rates during the 1970s provides more insight into the factors supporting migration improvements. Advanced service economies were the most important determinant of upturns among upper-income movers, with relative housing bargains next most important. Cultural facilities were also positively correlated with upper-income upturn. But cumulative decline appeared in the regressions as a clear threat to revival in the most distressed cities: upturns were significantly deterred by past selective upper-income outmigration. Upturns in city selection among lower-income movers, which were more common in distressed cities, were also more likely for SMSAs with advanced service employment. Interestingly, however, upturns by lower-income movers were significantly deterred by the presence of cultural facilities and negatively correlated with net migration of young adults to the SMSA. These differences by income in determinants of selection changes suggest that lower-income movers are becoming relatively more concentrated in declining cities with fewer cultural facilities.

Thoughts about the Future

Such evidence that demography and advanced service economies, rather than increased preferences for cities, were most responsible for the slight improvements in migration that have occurred, implies that few distressed cities will revive in the near future. The marked shift from past growth to decline that is under way now in the size of the 20–29 age group and that will follow in the 1990s for the 30–39 age group, plus a probable net outmigration from cities of 15 to 20 percent over a five-year period, will sharply deplete the number of households in such age categories in central cities. If interregional migration toward the Sunbelt continues, such declines are likely to be particularly precipitous in northern cities (Newitt 1983).

These results suggest that a continuing transformation to an advanced service economy can aid residential revival in some cities with central concentrations of advanced service employment. Thus, the large expansion in available office space in CBDs during the past decade may encourage revival. But there are at least two reasons for doubting that most distressed cities will be rescued thereby. First, advanced services are organized in a hierarchy, with "an emerging functional dichotomy between places that are well positioned . . . and those which are not" (Noyelle and Stanback 1983). Second, as business services, corporate headquarters, and the rest of the advanced services themselves decentralize and regroup in suburban-office concentrations, even central cities in "well-positioned" SMSAs are not assured of retaining either advanced-service employment or the residences of its work force. The sharp drops in city selection rates that occurred during the 1970s in Chicago, Atlanta, Miami, and Pittsburgh, for example, show that favorable position in the urban hierarchy has not yet assured residential revival in these central cities. On the other hand, the gentrification in Boston and Minneapolis–St. Paul together with New Federalism's devolution of responsibilities to states leads me to speculate that distressed state capitals may be more likely to revive.

In such a context, urban policies that encourage economic growth while reducing revenue sharing and other domestic programs are unlikely to benefit the most distressed cities or their residents (see Glickman 1984). If evolution to an economy based on advanced services and high technology increases the hierarchical nature of the urban system, it is unlikely that each downtown can become an advanced services/convention center. Trying to do so within constrained budgets not only is counterproductive, but encourages competition among cities. As cities compete to offer incentives for economic development, the interests of the poor are likely to suffer. Fewer resources will be available for human services, and even when central redevelopment is successful, the poor are likely to be displaced farther from the city center, with poorer access to services and employment. Pressures on city budgets will also make the spiral of selective outmigration more likely to continue, as pioneering gentrifiers and other residents age and become discouraged by poor city services.

Although this assessment is pessimistic, creative public policies for retaining, involving, and training present residents and maintaining housing and neighborhoods could help retain and attract movers of different income levels and thus help cities, if the political will and necessary funding become available (Bradbury, Downs, and Small 1982). Improving schools and reducing crime should be high priorities, both to improve living conditions in general and to retain as much as possible of the baby boom generation now living in cities. Reducing crime would also make cities more livable for the elderly group that will increase quickly over the next several decades. Policies that encourage maintenance, reuse, and rehabilitation of existing buildings and other capital also will be important.

By comprehensively examining recent changes in migration for the nation and forty major SMSAs, this study has shown that a basic determinant of changes in population and income levels within cities has improved for some distressed cities over the past two decades. It has also, however, documented the diversity of migration patterns among major cities and the evidence that basic problems of selectively greater outmigration by higher-income groups remain, unsolved by the slight improvements in national migration patterns. By demonstrating that changes in city selection rates anticipate changes in city population and income, it has further provided a basis for monitoring and understanding future developments in both distressed and less distressed cities as the 1980s and 1990s unfold.

Bibliography

Index

Bibliography

Abler, Ronald, John S. Adams, and John R. Borchert. 1976. *The Twin Cities of St. Paul and Minneapolis.* Cambridge, Mass.: Ballinger.

Abravenal, Martin, and Paul Mancini. 1980. "Attitudinal and Demographic Constraints." Pp. 27–48 in Rosenthal 1980.

ACIR. *See* Advisory Commission on Intergovernmental Relations.

Adams, John S., ed. 1976a. *Contemporary Metropolitan America: Twenty Geographic Vignettes.* Comparative Metropolitan Analysis Project, vol. 1. Cambridge, Mass.: Ballinger.

———, ed. 1976b. *Urban Policy-Making and Metropolitan Dynamics: A Comparative Geographical Analysis.* Comparative Metropolitan Analysis Project, vol. 2. Cambridge, Mass.: Ballinger.

———, ed. 1976c. *A Comparative Atlas of America's Great Cities: Twenty Metropolitan Regions.* Comparative Metropolitan Analysis Project, vol. 3. Minneapolis: University of Minnesota Press.

Advance Mortgage Corporation. 1980. "Revitalization/Gentrification Trend Brings Overlooked Values to Light in City Markets." *U.S. Housing Markets,* April 25.

Advisory Commission on Intergovernmental Relations. 1965. *Metropolitan Social and Economic Disparities: Implications for Intergovernmental Relations in Central Cities and Suburbs.* Washington, D.C.: U.S. Government Printing Office.

———. 1967. *Fiscal Balance in the Federal System.* Washington, D.C.: U.S. Government Printing Office.

———. 1973. *City Financial Emergencies: The Intergovernmental Dimension.* Washington, D.C.: U.S. Government Printing Office.

———. 1977. *Trends in Metropolitan America.* Report M-108. Washington, D.C.: U.S. Government Printing Office.

———. 1980a. *Regional Growth: Historic Perspective.* Report A-74. Washington, D.C.: U.S. Government Printing Office.

———. 1980b. *Central City–Suburban Fiscal Disparities and City Distress, 1977.* Report M-119. Washington, D.C.: U.S. Government Printing Office.

Ahlbrandt, Roger S. 1984. "Ideology and the Reagan Administration's First National Urban Policy Report." *Journal of the American Planning Association* 50:479–84.

Ahlbrandt, Roger S., and Paul C. Brophy. 1975. *Neighborhood Revitalization: Theory and Practice.* Boston: D.C. Heath.

Albin, P. S. 1971. "Unbalanced Growth and the Intensification of the Urban Crisis." *Urban Studies* 8:139–46.

Alcaly, Roger, and David Mermelstein. 1977. *The Fiscal Crisis of American Cities.* New York: Random House.

Allen, Irving. 1980. "The Ideology of Dense Neighborhood Redevelopment." *Urban Affairs Quarterly* 15:409–29.

Allman, T. D. 1978. "The Urban Crisis Leaves Town (and Moves to the Suburbs)." *Harper's,* Dec., 41–56.

Alonso, William. 1964. *Location and Land Use.* Cambridge: Harvard University Press.

———. 1972. "Location Theory." Pp. 16–37 in Edel and Rothenberg 1972.

———. 1980. "The Demographic Factor." Pp. 32–51 in Solomon 1980b.

Althaus, Paul G., and Joseph Schachter. 1983. "Interstate Migration and the New Federalism." *Social Science Quarterly* 64:35–45.

Ashton, Patrick J. 1978. "The Political Economy of Suburban Development." Pp. 64–89 in W. Tabb and L. Sawyers, eds. *Marxism and the Metropolis.* New York: Oxford University Press.

Auger, Deborah A. 1979. "The Politics of Revitalization in Gentrifying Neighborhoods: The Case of Boston's South End." *Journal of the American Planning Association* 45:515–22.

Baker, Donald P. 1984. "Is Baltimore Truly Back? New Showcase City Faces Old Problems." *Washington Post,* Nov. 24, 1.

Baldassare, Mark. 1984. "Evidence for Neighborhood Revitalization." Pp. 90–102 in Palen and London 1984.

Bartelt, David W. 1985. "Economic Change, Systems of Cities, and the 'Life Cycle' of Housing" (mimeo). Report to the U.S. Department of Housing and Urban Development. Temple University.

Baumol, William J. 1967. "The Macroeconomics of Unbalanced Growth." *American Economic Review* 57:415–26.

Berry, Brian J. L. 1968. *Theories of Urban Location.* Resource Paper no. 1. Association of American Geographers.

———. 1972. *City Classification Handbook: Methods and Applications.* New York: Wiley-Interscience.

———. 1982a. "Inner-City Futures: An American Dilemma Revisited. Pp. 187–220 in Stave 1982.

———. 1982b. "Islands of Renewal—Seas of Decay: The Evidence of Inner-City Gentrification" (mimeo). Prepared for the Urban Policy Conference, Chicago, Ill., June 18–19.

Berry, Brian J. L., and Lester Silverman, eds. 1980. *Population Redistribution and Public Policy.* Washington, D.C.: National Academy of Sciences.

Birch, David. 1970. *The Economic Future of City and Suburb.* New York: Committee for Economic Development.

———. 1971. "Towards a Stage Theory of Urban Growth." *Journal of the American Institute of Planners* 37:78–87.

Black, J. Thomas. 1975. "Private-Market Housing Renovation in Central Cities," *Urban Land* 34 (November):3–9.

Bluestone, Barry, and Bennett Harrison. 1982. *Capital and Communities: The Causes and Consequences of Private Disinvestment.* Washington, D.C.: The Progressive Alliance.

Bogue, Donald J. 1953. *Population Growth in Standard Metropolitan Areas, 1900–1950, with an Explanatory Analysis of Urbanized Areas.* Washington, D.C.: U.S. Government Printing Office.

Borchert, J. R. 1978. "Major Control Points in American Economic Geography." *Annals of the American Association of Geographers* 68:214–32.

Boyer, Richard, and David Savageau. 1981. *Places Rated Almanac.* New York: Rand McNally.

Bradbury, Katherine. 1982. "Fiscal Distress in Large U.S. Cities." *New England Economic Review,* Winter, 33–44.

Bradbury, Katherine, Anthony Downs, and Kenneth Small, 1980. "Some Dynamics of Central City–Suburban Interactions." *American Economic Review* 70:410–14.

———, 1981. *Futures for a Declining City: Simulations for the Cleveland Area.* New York: Academic Press.

———. 1982. *Urban Decline and the Future of American Cities.* Washington, D.C.: Brookings.

Bradford, C. P., and L. S. Rubinowitz. 1975. "The Urban-Suburban Investment-Disinvestment Process: Consequences for Older Neighborhoods." *Annals of the American Academy of Political and Social Sciences* 422:77–86.

Bradford, D. F., and H. H. Kelejian. 1973. "An Econometric Model of the Flight to the Suburbs." *Journal of Political Economy* 81:566–89.

Brunn, Stanley D., and James O. Wheeler, eds. 1980. *The American Metropolitan System: Present and Future.* New York: V. H. Winston.

Bryce, Herrington J. 1979. *Revitalizing Cities.* Lexington, Mass.: Lexington Books.

Bunce, Harold L., and Robert L. Goldberg. 1979. *City Need and Community Development Funding.* HUD-PDR-406. Washington, D.C.: U.S. Government Printing Office.

Bunce, Harold L., and Sue G. Neal. 1983. "Are Distressed Cities Becoming Worse Off?" (mimeo). Washington, D.C.: U.S. Department of Housing and Urban Development.

Burchell, Robert W., James H. Carr, Richard L. Florida, and James Nemeth. 1984. *The New Reality of Municipal Finance: The Rise and Fall of the Intergovernmental City.* New Brunswick: Center for Urban Policy Research.

Burchell, Robert W., and David Listokin, eds. 1981. *Cities under Stress: The Fiscal Crises of Urban America.* New Brunswick: Center for Urban Policy Research.

Burchell, Robert W., David Listokin, George Sternlieb, James W. Hughes, and Stephen C. Casey. 1981. "Measuring Urban Distress: A Summary of the Major Urban Hardship Indices and Resource Allocation Systems." Pp. 159–229 in Burchell and Listokin 1981.

Carter, Harold. 1983. *An Introduction to Urban Historical Geography.* Baltimore: Edward Arnold.

Chall, Daniel. 1983–84. "Neighborhood Changes in New York City during the 1970s: Are the 'Gentry' Returning?" *Federal Reserve Bank of New York Quarterly Review,* Winter, 38–48.

Clark, Terry Nichols, ed. 1981. *Urban Policy Analysis.* Beverly Hills: Sage Publications.

Clay, Phillip L. 1979. *Neighborhood Renewal: Middle-Class Resettlement and Incumbent Upgrading in American Neighborhoods.* Lexington, Mass.: Lexington Books.

————. 1984. "Demographic Change and Urban Finance: The Outlook for the 1980s." Pp. 51–66 in Ebel 1984.

Clotfelter, Charles. 1979. "School Desegregation as Urban Public Policy." Pp. 359–88 in Mieskowski and Straszheim 1979.

Cohen, Robert B. 1981. "The New International Division of Labor: Multinational Corporations and Urban Hierarchy." Pp. 287–318 in Dear and Scott 1981.

Coleman, James. 1978. "Social Process and Social Policy in the Stable Metropolis." Pp. 43–62 in Leven 1978.

Congressional Research Service. 1984. *The President's National Urban Policy Report: A Critique.* Report no. 84-119 S. Washington, D.C.: Library of Congress.

Cybriwksy, Roman A. 1980. "Revitalization Trends in Downtown-Area Neighborhoods." Pp. 21–36 in Brunn and Wheeler 1980.

Daugherty, Ann, and Robert Van Order. 1982. "Inflation, Housing Costs, and the Consumer Price Index." *American Economic Review* 72: 154–64.

Davis, Albert J., and Nonna A. Noto. 1984. "Changing Federal-Local Relations in a Period of Fiscal Austerity." Pp. 147–66 in Ebel 1984.

Davis, J. T. 1965. "Middle-Class Housing in the Central City." *Economic Geography* 41:238–51.

Dear, Michael, and Allen J. Scott, eds. 1981. *Urbanization and Urban Planning in Capitalist Society.* New York: Methuen.

Diamond, Douglas, 1980a. "Income and Residential Location: Muth Revisited." *Urban Studies* 17:1–12.

————. 1980b. "Taxes, Inflation, Speculation, and the Cost of Homeownership." *Journal of the American Real Estate and Urban Economics Association* 8:281–98.

Dolbeare, Cushing N. 1978. *Involuntary Displacement: A Major Issue for People and Neighborhoods.* Report prepared for the National Commission on Neighborhoods, Washington, D.C.

Downs, Anthony. 1973. *Opening Up the Suburbs: An Urban Strategy for America.* New Haven: Yale University Press.

————. 1976. "Investing in Housing Rehabilitation Can Be Successful." *Real Estate Review* 6:66–73.

————. 1979. "Key Relationships between Urban Development and Neighborhood Change." *Journal of the American Planning Association* 45: 462–72.

———. 1981. *Neighborhoods and Urban Development*. Washington, D.C.: Brookings.

Droettboom, Theodore, Jr.; Ronald J. McAllister; Edward J. Kaiser; and Edgar W. Butler. 1971. "Urban Violence and Residential Mobility." *Journal of the American Institute of Planners* 36:319–25.

Ebel, Robert D., ed. 1984. *Changing Economic and Fiscal Conditions*. Research in Urban Economics, vol. 4. Greenwich, Conn.: JAI Press.

Edel, Matthew. 1972a. "Development vs. Dispersal: Approaches to Ghetto Poverty." Pp. 307–25 in Edel and Rothenberg 1972.

———. 1972b. "Planning, Market, or Warfare? Recent Land Use Conflict in American Cities." Pp. 134–50 in Edel and Rothenberg 1972.

———. 1981. "Capitalism, Accumulation, and the Explanation of Urban Phenomena." Pp. 19–44 in Dear and Scott 1981.

Edel, Matthew, and Jerome Rothenberg, eds. 1972. *Readings in Urban Economics*. New York: Macmillan.

Ellickson, Bryan. 1977. "The Politics and Economics of Decentralization." *Journal of Urban Economics* 4:135–49.

———. 1981. "An Alternative Text of the Hedonic Theory of Housing Markets." *Journal of Urban Economics* 9:56–79.

Embry, Robert. 1977. "Urban Reinvestment and the Effects of Displacement of Low- and Moderate-Income Persons." Testimony before the Senate Committee on Banking, Housing, and Urban Affairs, July 7.

Fainstein, Norman I., and Susan S. Fainstein. 1982. "Restructuring the American City: A Comparative Perspective." Pp. 161–89 in Fainstein and Fainstein, eds., *Urban Policy under Capitalism*. Beverly Hills: Sage Publications.

———. 1983. "Regime Strategies, Communal Resistance, and Economic Forces." Pp. 245–81 in Fainstein et al. 1983.

Fainstein, Susan S., Norman I. Fainstein, Richard Child Hill, Dennis Judd, and Michael Peter Smith. 1983. *Restructuring the City: The Political Economy of Urban Redevelopment*. New York: Longman.

Federal National Mortgage Association. 1973. *Forum One: Mobilization of Private Initiative for Inner-City Residential Development*. Washington, D.C.: Federal National Mortgage Association.

———. 1975. *Forum Two: The Changing Market for Inner-City Housing*. Washington, D.C.: Federal National Mortgage Association.

Fichter, R. 1977. *Young Professionals and City Neighborhoods*. Boston: Parkman Center for Urban Affairs.

Fleetwood, Blake. 1979. "The New Elite and an Urban Renaissance." *New York Times Magazine*, Jan 14, 16–22.

Fleischmann, Arnold. 1977. "Sunbelt Boosterism: The Politics of Postwar Growth and Annexation in San Antonio." Pp. 151–68 in Perry and Watkins 1977.

Follain, James, and Dixie Blackley. 1984. "The Standard Urban Economics Model: Are Rumors of Its Death Exaggerated?" Report presented to the Department of Housing and Urban Development, Syracuse University.

Follain, James, and Malpezzi, Stephen. 1981. "The Flight to the Suburbs: Insights Gained from an Analysis of Central City vs. Suburban Housing Costs." *Journal of Urban Economics* 9:381–98.

Fossett, James W., and Richard P. Nathan. 1981. "The Prospects for Urban Revival." Pp. 63–104 in Roy Bahl, ed., *Urban Government Finance*. Beverly Hills: Sage Publications.

Frey, William. 1978. "Population Movement and City-Suburb Redistribution: An Analytic Framework." *Demography* 15:571–88.

———. 1979a. "Central-City White Flight; Racial and Nonracial Causes." *American Sociological Review* 44:425–48.

———. 1979b. "White Flight and Central-City Loss: Application of an Analytic Migration Framework." *Environment and Planning* 11:129–47.

———. 1980. "Status-Selective White Flight and Central-City Population Change." *Journal of Regional Science* 20:71–89.

———. 1983. "A Multiregional Population-Projection Framework that Incorporates Both Migration and Residential Mobility Streams: Application to Metropolitan City-Suburb Redistribution." *Environment and Planning* 15:1613–32.

Frey, William, and Frances Kobrin. 1982. "Changing Families and Changing Mobility: Their Impact on the Central City." *Demography* 19:261–78.

Frieden, Bernard. 1964. *The Future of Old Neighborhoods*. Cambridge: MIT Press.

Frieden, Bernard, and Marshall Kaplan. 1975. *The Politics of Neglect*. Cambridge: MIT Press.

Friedland, Roger. 1983. *Power and Crisis in the City*. New York: Schocken Books.

Friedland, Roger, and William T. Bielby. 1981. "The Power of Business in the City." Pp. 133–52 in Clark 1981.

Gale, Dennis E. 1976. "The Back-to-the-City Movement . . . Or Is It? A Survey of Recent Homeowners in the Mount Pleasant Neighborhood of Washington, D.C." (mimeo). Department of Urban and Regional Planning, George Washington University.

———. 1979. "Middle-Class Resettlement in Older Urban Neighborhoods: The Evidence and the Implications." *Journal of the American Planning Association* 45:293–304.

———. 1980. Review of *Neighborhood Renewal* by Phillip Clay. *Journal of the American Planning Association*. 46:928–29.

———. 1984. *Neighborhood Revitalization and the Postindustrial City: A Multinational Perspective*. Lexington, Mass.: Lexington Books.

Gans, Herbert J., John Kasarda, and Harvey Molotch. 1982. Contributors to "Symposium: The State of the Nation's Cities." *Urban Affairs Quarterly* 18:163–86.

Glaab, Charles N., and A. Theodore Brown. 1967. *A History of Urban America*. New York: Macmillan.

Glickman, Norman J. 1984. "Economic Policy and the Cities: In Search of Reagan's Real Urban Policy." *Journal of the American Planning Association* 50:471–78.

Goetze, Rolf. 1976. *Building Neighborhood Confidence: A Humanistic Strategy for Urban Housing*. Cambridge, Mass.: Ballinger.

―――. 1979. *Understanding Neighborhood Change*. Cambridge, Mass.: Ballinger.

Goetze, Rolf, and Kent Colton. 1980. "The Dynamics of Neighborhoods: A Fresh Approach to Understanding Housing and Neighborhood Change." *Journal of the American Planning Association* 46:184–96.

Goldfield, David R. 1976a. "Historic Planning and Redevelopment in Minneapolis." *Journal of the American Planning Association* 42:76–87.

―――. 1976b. "The Limits of Suburban Growth: The Washington, D.C., SMSA." *Urban Affairs Quarterly* 12:83–102.

―――. 1980. "Private Neighborhood Redevelopment and Displacement: The Case of Washington, D.C." *Urban Affairs Quarterly* 15:453–68.

Goldman, Mark. 1983. *High Hopes: The Rise and Decline of Buffalo, New York*. Albany: State University of New York Press.

Goldstein, B., and R. Davis, eds. 1977. *Neighborhoods in the Urban Economy: The Dynamics of Decline and Revitalization*. Lexington, Mass.: Lexington Books.

Goldstein, Gerald S., and Leon Moses. 1973. "A Survey of Urban Economics." *Journal of Economic Literature* 11:471–515.

Goldstein, Sidney, and Kurt Mayer. 1965. "The Impact of Migration on the Socioeconomic Structure of Cities and Suburbs." *Sociology and Social Research* 50:5–23.

Goodman, John L. 1978. *Housing-Market Determinants of Movers' City/Suburban Choice*. Working Paper 1014-1. Washington, D.C.: Urban Institute Press.

―――. 1979. "Reasons for Moves out of and into Large Cities." *Journal of the American Planning Association* 45:407–16.

―――. 1980. "People of the City." *American Demographics* 2:14–17.

Gordon, David. 1977a. "Capitalism and the Roots of Urban Crisis." Pp. 82–112 in Alcaly and Mermelstein 1977.

―――. 1977b. "Class Struggle and the Stages of American Urban Development." Pp. 55–82 in Perry and Watkins 1977.

Gorham, William, and Nathan Glazer, eds. 1976. *The Urban Predicament*. Washington, D.C.: Urban Institute Press.

Gottdiener, M. 1983. "Understanding Metropolitan Deconcentration: A Clash of Paradigms." *Social Science Quarterly* 64:227–47.

Greenwood, Michael J. 1980. "Metropolitan Growth and the Intrametropolitan Location of Employment, Housing, and Labor Force." *Review of Economics and Statistics* 62:491–501.

————. 1981. *Migration and Economic Growth in the United States: National, Regional, and Metropolitan Perspectives.* New York: Academic Press.

————. 1984. *A Descriptive and Interpretative Study of Housing, Employment, and Population Patterns for Regions, Metropolitan Areas, and Central Cities and Suburbs.* Report to U.S. Department of Housing and Urban Development.

Grier, George, and Eunice Grier. 1976. *Movers to the City: New Data on the Housing Market for Washington, D.C.* Washington, D.C.: Washington Center for Metropolitan Studies.

————. 1978. *Urban Displacement: A Reconnaissance.* Report prepared for U.S. Department of Housing and Urban Development.

Grigsby, William. 1963. *Housing Markets and Public Policy.* Philadelphia: University of Pennsylvania Press.

Grodzins, Morton. 1958. *The Metropolitan Area as a Racial Problem.* Pittsburgh: University of Pittsburgh Press.

Grubb, W. Norton. 1982. "The Flight to the Suburbs of Population and Employment, 1960–70." *Journal of Urban Economics* 11:348–67.

Guest, Avery M. 1972. "Population Densities and Higher-Status Residential Location." *Economic Geography* 48:375–87.

Guterbock, Thomas M. 1980. "The Political Economy of Urban Revitalization: Competing Theories." *Urban Affairs Quarterly* 15:429–38.

Hamnett, Christopher, and Peter R. Williams. 1980. "Social Change in London: A Study of Gentrification." *Urban Affairs Quarterly* 15:469–85.

Hanson, Royce. 1982. *The Evolution of National Urban Policy, 1970–80: Lessons from the Past.* Washington, D.C.: National Academy Press.

————, ed. 1983. *Rethinking Urban Policy: Urban Development in an Advanced Economy.* Washington, D.C.: National Academy Press.

Hanten, Edward W., et al. 1979. *New Directions for the Mature Metropolis.* Cambridge: Schenkman Publishing Co.

Harrison, Bennett. 1974. *Urban Economic Development.* Washington, D.C.: Urban Institute Press.

Harrison, David, and John F. Kain. 1975. "Cumulative Urban Growth and Urban Density Functions." Pp. 233–60 in Kain 1975.

Hartman, Chester. 1979a. "Comment on 'Neighborhood Revitalization and Displacement: A Review of the Evidence' [Sumka 1979]" *Journal of the American Planning Association* 45:488–90.

————. 1979b. "Displacement: A Not-So-New Problem." *Social Policy* 10:22–27.

Harvey, David. 1973. *Social Justice and the City.* Baltimore: Johns Hopkins University Press.

————. 1981. "The Urban Process under Capitalism: A Framework for Analysis." Pp. 91–122 in Dear and Scott 1981.

————. 1982. "Government Policies, Financial Institutions, and Neighborhood Change in United States Cities." Pp. 123–40 in M. Harloe, ed., *Captive Cities.* New York: John Wiley & Sons.

Heilbrun, James. 1972. "Poverty and Public Finance in the Older Central Cities." Pp. 523–45 in Edel and Rothenberg 1972.

Hirschman, Albert O. 1970. *Exit, Voice, and Loyalty*. Cambridge, Mass.: Harvard University Press.

Hoover, Edgar, and Raymond Vernon. 1959. *Anatomy of a Metropolis*. Garden City, N.Y.: Doubleday.

Houston, Lawrence O., and Feather O'Connor. 1980. "Neighborhood Change, Displacement, and City Policy." Pp. 299–301 in Laska and Spain 1980.

Hoyt, Homer. 1939. *The Structure and Growth of Residential Neighborhoods in American Cities*. Washington, D.C.: Federal Housing Administration.

———. 1941. "Forces of Urban Centralization and Decentralization." *American Journal of Sociology* 66:843–52.

———. 1966. *Where the Rich and the Poor Live*. Technical Bulletin no. 55. Washington, D.C.: Urban Land Institute.

HUD. *See* United States Department of Housing and Urban Development.

Hudson, James R. 1980. "Revitalization of Inner-City Neighborhoods: An Ecological Approach." *Urban Affairs Quarterly* 15:397–408.

Huth, Mary Jo. 1980. "New Hope for Revival of America's Central Cities." *Annals of the American Academy of Political and Social Sciences* 451:118–29.

Ingram, Gregory K. 1979. "Simulation and Econometric Approaches to Modeling Urban Areas." Pp. 130–64 in Mieskowski and Straszheim 1979.

James, Franklin J. 1977a. *Back to the City: An Appraisal of Housing Reinvestment and Population Change in Urban America*. Report 0241-03. Washington, D.C.: Urban Institute Press.

———. 1977b. "Private Reinvestment in Older Housing and Older Neighborhoods: Recent Trends and Forces." Statement before the Senate Committee on Banking, Housing, and Urban Affairs, July 10.

———. 1980. "The Revitalization of Older Urban Housing and Neighborhoods." Pp. 130–60 in Solomon 1980b.

James, Franklin J., and John P. Blair. 1984. "The Role of Labor Mobility in a National Urban Policy." *Journal of the American Planning Association* 50:307–15.

Johnston, Ronald J. 1971. *Urban Residential Patterns*. New York: Praeger Publishers.

Kain, John F. 1975. *Essays on Urban Spatial Structure*. Cambridge, Mass.: Ballinger.

———. 1979. "Race and Poverty: Keys to Central-City Revitalization." Pp. 105–28 in Bryce 1979.

Kasarda, John D. 1980. "The Implication of Contemporary Distribution Trends for National Urban Policy." *Social Science Quarterly* 61:373–400.

———. 1982. "Symposium: The State of the Nation's Cities." *Urban Affairs Quarterly* 18:163–86.

———. 1983a. *Urban Industrial Transformation and Minority Opportunity*. Report to U.S. Department of Housing and Urban Development.

————. 1983b. "Entry-Level Jobs, Mobility, and Minority Unemployment." *Urban Affairs Quarterly* 19:21–40.

Kern, Clifford. 1981. "Upper-Income Renaissance in the City: Its Source and Implications for the City's Future." *Journal of Urban Economics* 9:106–24.

————. 1984. "Upper-Income Residential Revival in the City: Some Lessons from the 1960s and 1970s for the 1980s." Pp. 79–96 in Ebel 1984.

Keys, Langley C. 1969. *The Rehabilitation Game: A Study in the Diversity of Neighborhoods*. Cambridge, Mass.: MIT Press.

Kotler, M. 1977. "Dislocation of Long-Time Residents Caused by the Growing Pace of Neighborhood Revitalization in Many of Our Older Cities." Testimony before the Senate Committee on Banking, Housing, and Urban Affairs, July 8.

Lachman, M. Leanne, and Anthony Downs. 1978. "The Role of Neighborhoods in the Mature Metropolis." Pp. 207–24 in Leven 1978.

Lang, Michael H. 1982. *Gentrification amid Urban Decline: Strategies for America's Older Cities*. Cambridge, Mass.: Ballinger.

Laska, Shirley B., and Daphne Spain. 1979. "Urban Policy and Planning in the Wake of Gentrification: Anticipating Renovators' Demands." *Journal of the American Planning Association* 45:523–31.

————, eds. 1980. *Back to the City: Issues in Neighborhood Renovation*. Elmsford, New York: Pergamon Press.

Lee, Everett S., James Bresee, Kathryn P. Nelson, and David A. Patterson. 1971. *An Introduction to Urban Decentralization Research*. ORNL-HUD-3. Oak Ridge, Tenn.: Oak Ridge National Laboratory.

Leven, Charles L., ed. 1978. *The Mature Metropolis*. Lexington, Mass.: Lexington Books.

Levy, Paul R. 1978. *Queen Village: The Eclipse of Community*. Philadelphia: Institute for the Study of Civic Values.

————. 1980. "Neighborhoods in a Race with Time: Local Strategies for Countering Displacement." Pp. 302–17 in Laska and Spain 1980.

Levy, Paul R., and Roman A. Cybrinsky. 1980. "The Hidden Dimensions of Culture and Class: Philadelphia." Pp. 138–55 in Laska and Spain 1980.

Levy, Paul R., and Dennis McGrath. 1979. "Saving Cities for Whom?" *Social Policy* 10:20–28.

Lewis, Pierce. 1975. "To Revive Urban Downtowns, Show Respect for the Spirit of the Place." *Smithsonian* 6:32–41.

Ley, David. 1983. *A Social Geography of the City*. New York: Harper & Row.

Lipton, S. Gregory. 1977. "Evidence of Central-City Revival." *Journal of the American Institute of Planners* 43:136–47.

————. 1980. "The Future Central City: Gentrified or Abandoned?" *Journal of Urban Affairs* 2:1–15.

————. 1984. "An Analysis of Neighborhood Condition and Change in Metropolitan Areas" (mimeo). Report submitted to U.S. Department of Housing and Urban Development.

Little, James T. 1976. "Residential Preferences, Neighborhood Filtering, and Neighborhood Change." *Journal of Urban Economics* 3:68–81.

Loewenstein, L. K. 1965. *The Location of Residences and Work Places in Urban Areas*. New York: Scarecrow Press.

Logan, John R., and Mark Schneider. 1981. "The Stratification of Metropolitan Suburbs, 1960–70." *American Sociological Review* 46:175–86.

London, Bruce. 1980. "Gentrification as Urban Reinvasion: Some Preliminary Definitional and Theoretical Considerations." Pp. 77–92 in Laska and Spain 1980.

London, Bruce, Donald Bradley, and James R. Hudson, eds. 1980. *The Revitalization of Inner-City Neighborhoods*. Vol. 15 of *Urban Affairs Quarterly*.

London, Bruce, and John Palen. 1984. "Introduction." Pp. 1–26 in Palen and London 1984.

Long, John F. 1981. *Population Deconcentration in the United States*. CDS-81-5. Washington, D.C.: U.S. Government Printing Office.

Long, Larry H. 1972. "The Influence of Number and Ages of Children on Residential Mobility." *Demography* 9:371–82.

———. 1975. "How the Racial Composition of Cities Changes." *Land Economics* 51:258–67.

———. 1980a. "Back to the Countryside and Back to the City in the Same Decade." Pp. 61–76 in Laska and Spain 1980.

———. 1980b. "What the Census Will Tell Us about Gentrification." *American Demographics* 2:18–22.

———. 1982. "Residential Preferences: Some Clues to U.S. Migration between 1979 and 1984." U.S. Bureau of the Census, Center for Demographic Studies (mimeo).

Long, Larry H., and Donald Dahmann. 1980. *The City-Suburb Income Gap: Is It Being Narrowed by a Back-to-the-City Movement?* CDS-80-1. Washington, D.C.: U.S. Government Printing Office.

Long, Larry H., and Daphne Spain. 1978. "Racial Succession in Individual Housing Units." *Current Population Reports*, P-23, no. 71. Washington, D.C.: U.S. Government Printing Office.

Lowry, Ira S. 1972. "Seven Models of Urban Development: A Structural Comparison." Pp. 151–74 in Edel and Rothenberg 1972.

———. 1980. "The Dismal Future of Central Cities." Pp. 161–203 in Solomon 1980b.

McGuire, Chester C. 1979. "Maintenance and Renewal of Central Cities." Pp. 469–98 in F. So, I. Stollman, F. Beal, and D. Arnold, eds. *The Practice of Local Government Planning*. Washington, D.C.: International City Management Association.

Malpezzi, Stephen, Larry Ozanne, and Thomas Thibodeau. 1980. *Characteristic Prices of Housing in Fifty-nine Metropolitan Areas*. CR 1367-1. Washington, D.C.: Urban Institute Press.

Markusen, Ann R., Annalee Saxenian, and Marc Weiss. 1981. "Who Benefits from Intergovernmental Transfers?" Pp. 617–64 in Burchell and Listokin 1981.

Marshall, Harvey. 1979. "White Movement to the Suburbs: A Comparison of Explanations." *American Sociological Review* 44:975–94.

Marshall, Harvey, and Bonnie L. Lewis. 1982. "Back to the City: An Analysis of Trends in the Sixties and Seventies." *Journal of Urban Affairs* 4:19–32.

Masotti, Louis, and Jeffrey Masotti, eds. 1973. *The Urbanization of the Suburbs*. Beverly Hills: Sage Publications.

May, Peter J. 1982. "Expectations and Urban Revitalization." *Social Science Quarterly* 63:225–35.

Meadows, George R., and Steven T. Call. 1978. "Combining Housing-Market Trends and Resident Attitudes in Planning Urban Revitalization." *Journal of the American Planning Association* 45:297–305.

Mieskowski, Peter, and Mahlon Straszheim. 1979. *Current Issues in Urban Economics*. Baltimore: Johns Hopkins University Press.

Mills, Edwin S. 1972a. *Urban Economics*. Glenview, Ill.: Scott, Foresman.

———. 1972b. *Studies in the Structure of the Urban Economy*. Baltimore: Johns Hopkins University Press.

Mills, Edwin S., and Richard Price. 1984. "Metropolitan Suburbanization and Central-City Problems." *Journal of Urban Economics* 15:1–17.

Mollenkopf, John H. 1981a. "Paths toward the Post-Industrial Service City: The Northeast and the Southwest." Pp. 77–112 in Burchell and Listokin 1981.

———. 1981b. "Community and Accumulation." Pp. 319–38 in Dear and Scott 1981.

Molotch, Harvey, 1976. "The City as a Growth Machine: Toward a Political Economy of Place." *American Journal of Sociology* 82:309–32.

Morgan, David. 1978. *Patterns of Population Distribution: A Residential Preference Model and Its Dynamic*. Chicago: University of Chicago, Department of Geography.

Muller, Thomas. 1975. "The Declining and Growing Metropolis: A Fiscal Comparison." Pp. 197–220 in Sternlieb and Hughes 1975.

———. 1980. *The Urban Household in the 1980s*. HUD-CPD-631. Washington, D.C.: Urban Institute.

Mumford, Lewis. 1963. *The Highway and the City*. New York: Harcourt, Brace, and World.

Muth, Richard F. 1969. *Cities and Housing: The Spatial Pattern of Urban Residential Land Use*. Chicago: University of Chicago Press.

———. 1984. "Energy Prices and Urban Decentralization." Pp. 85–110 in Anthony Downs and Katherine Bradbury, eds., *Energy Costs, Urban Development, and Housing*. Washington, D.C.: Brookings.

Nathan, Richard P., and Charles Adams. 1976. "Understanding Central-City Hardship." *Political Science Quarterly* 91:47–62.

Nathan, Richard P., and James W. Fossett. 1978. "Urban Conditions: The Future of the Federal Role." Paper presented at the National Tax Association, Philadelphia, Nov. 13.

National Advisory Commission on Civil Disorders. 1968. *Report.* New York: Bantam Books.

National Research Council. 1982. *Critical Issues for National Urban Policy: A Reconnaissance and Agenda for Further Study.* Washington, D.C.: National Academy of Sciences.

National Urban Coalition. 1978. *Displacement: City Neighborhoods in Transition.* Washington, D.C.: National Urban Coalition.

National Urban Policy Advisory Committee. 1984. "Urban America 1984: A Report Card" (mimeo).

Nelson, Kathryn P. 1980. "Recent Suburbanization of Blacks: How Much, Who, and Where." *Journal of the American Planning Association* 46: 287–300.

———. 1981. *Back to the City? Recent Trends in White Intrametropolitan Migration.* HUD-Annual Housing Survey no. 8. Washington, D.C.: U.S. Department of Housing and Urban Development.

———. 1984. "Urban Economic and Demographic Change: Recent Shifts and Future Prospects." Pp. 25–49 in Ebel 1984.

Newitt, Jane. 1983. "Behind the Big-City Blues." *American Demographics*, June, 26–39.

Newsweek. 1979. "A City Revival." Jan. 15, 28–35.

Noll, Roger. 1970. "Metropolitan Employment and Population Distribution and the Conditions of the Urban Poor." Pp. 481–509 in John P. Crecine, ed., *Financing the Metropolis.* Beverly Hills: Sage Publications.

Norton, R. D. 1979. *City Life-Cycles and American Urban Policy.* New York: Academic Press.

Noyelle, Thierry. 1983. "The Rise of Advanced Services: Some Implications for Economic Development in U.S. Cities." *Journal of the American Planning Association* 49:280–90.

Noyelle, Thierry, and Thomas H. Stanback, Jr. 1983. *The Economic Transformation of American Cities.* Totowa, N.J.; Allanheld, Osmun.

Oakland, William H. 1979. "Central Cities: Fiscal Plight and Prospects for Reform." Pp. 322–58 in Mieskowski and Straszheim 1979.

Olsen, R. A., and A. M. Guest. 1977. "Migration and City-Suburb Status Differences." *Urban Affairs Quarterly* 12:523–32.

Palen, John, and Bruce London, eds. 1984. *Gentrification, Displacement, and Neighborhood Revitalization.* Albany: State University of New York Press.

Perry, David C., and Alfred J. Watkins, eds. 1977. *The Rise of the Sunbelt Cities.* Beverly Hills: Sage Publications.

Peterson, George E. 1976. "Finance." Pp. 35–118 in Gorham and Glazer 1976.

Phillips, Phillip D., and Stanley D. Brunn. 1980. "New Dynamics of Growth in the American Metropolitan System." Pp. 1–20 in Stanley D. Wheeler and James O. Wheeler, eds. *The American Metropolitan System: Present and Future*. New York: V. H. Winston & Sons.

Phillips, Robyn S., and Avis C. Vidal. 1983. "The Growth and Restructuring of Metropolitan Economies: The Context for Economic Development Policy." *Journal of the American Planning Association* 49:291–306.

Pierce, Neil. 1977. "Cities Make a Comeback." *Washington Post*, July 7.

———. 1983. "Tacoma, Oakland Closing the Gap with Richer Neighbors." *Washington Post*, Oct. 8, E8.

Pinkerton, James R. 1968. "City-Suburban Residential Patterns by Social Class: A Review of the Literature." *Urban Affairs Quarterly* 4:499–519.

Plattner, Robert H. 1982. "Will People Move Back to the City?" *Appraisal Journal* 50:187–94.

Porter, Paul R. 1976. *The Recovery of American Cities*. New York: Sun River Press.

———. 1979. "The Neighborhood Interest in a City's Recovery." *Journal of the American Planning Association* 45:473–79.

Puryear, David L., and John P. Ross. 1984. "Urban Government Expenditures in the 1980s." Pp. 243–56 in Ebel 1984.

Quayle, Vincent P., and Jean Crolius. 1978. "Is Preservation Bad for the Poor?" *Preservation News* 18:12.

Rapkin, Chester, and William Grigsby. 1960. *Residential Renewal in the Urban Core*. Philadelphia: University of Pennsylvania Press.

Renaud, Bertrand. 1984. "Structural Changes in Advanced Economies and Their Impact on Cities." Pp. 1–24 in Ebel 1984.

Richardson, H. W. 1977. *The New Urban Economics and Alternatives*. London: Pion.

Rosenthal, Donald B., ed. 1980. *Urban Revitalization*. Beverly Hills: Sage Publications.

Rothenberg, Jerome. 1972. "The Nature of Redevelopment Benefits." Pp. 215–26 in Edel and Rothenberg 1972.

Russell, Louise B. 1982. *The Baby Boom and the Economy*. Washington, D.C.: Brookings.

Rust, Edgar. 1975. *No Growth: Impacts on Metropolitan Areas*. Lexington, Mass.: Lexington Books.

Salins, Peter D. 1983. "New York in the Year 2000 Revisited." *New York Affairs* 7:4–19.

Savas, E. S. 1983. "A Positive Urban Policy for the Future." *Urban Affairs Quarterly* 18:447–53.

Savitch, H. V. 1979. *Urban Policy and the Exterior City: Federal, State, and Corporate Impacts upon Major Cities*. New York: Pergamon Press.

Sawyers, Larry. 1975. "Urban Form and the Mode of Production." *Review of Radical Political Economics* 7:52–68.

Schaffer, Richard, and Neil Smith. 1984. "The Gentrification of Harlem."

Paper presented at annual meeting of American Association for the Advancement of Science, New York City, May.

Schneider, Mark, and John R. Logan, 1982. "The Effects of Local Government Finances on Community Growth Rates." *Urban Affairs Quarterly* 18:91–104.

Schnore, Leo. 1965. *The Urban Scene: Human Ecology and Demography.* New York: Free Press.

——. 1972. *Class and Race in Cities and Suburbs.* Chicago: Markam.

——. 1973. "Social Class in Cities and Suburbs." Pp. 189–235 in Amos Hawley and Vincent Rock, eds. *Segregation in Residential Areas.* Washington, D.C.: National Academy of Sciences.

Schnore, Leo, and Joy Jones. 1968. "The Evolution of City-Suburban Types in the Course of a Decade." *Urban Affairs Quarterly* 4:421–42.

Schur, R. 1977. "Dislocation of Long-Time Residents Caused by Neighborhood Revitalization." Testimony before the U.S. Senate Committee on Banking, Housing, and Urban Affairs, July 7.

Smith, Neil. 1979. "Toward a Theory of Gentrification: A Back-to-the-City Movement by Capital, Not People." *Journal of the American Planning Association* 45:538–48.

Smith, Neil, and Michele LeFaivre. 1984. "A Class Analysis of Gentrification." Pp. 43–63 in Palen and London 1984.

Solomon, Arthur. 1980a. "The Emerging Metropolis." Pp. 1–17 in Solomon 1980b.

——, ed. 1980b. *The Prospective City.* Cambridge: MIT Press.

Spain, Daphne. 1980. "Black-to-White Successions in Central-City Housing: Limited Evidence of Urban Revitalization." *Urban Affairs Quarterly* 15: 381–98.

——. 1981. "A Gentrification Scorecard." *American Demographics* 3: 14–20.

Speare, Alden, and Larry H. Long, 1985. "Neighborhood Satisfaction and Residential Mobility in Cities and Suburbs." Paper presented at the annual meeting of the Population Association of America, Boston.

Stanback, Thomas M., Jr., and Thierry J. Noyelle. 1982. *Cities in Transition.* Totowa, N.J.: Allanheld, Osmun.

Stave, Bruce M., ed. 1982. *Modern Industrial Cities: History, Policy, and Survival.* Beverly Hills: Sage Publications.

Stegman, Michael A., ed. 1979. "Symposium on Neighborhood Revitalization." *Journal of the American Planning Association* 45:460–558.

Steinnes, Donald N. 1977. "Causality and Intraurban Location." *Journal of Urban Economics* 4:69–79.

Stephens, John D., and Brian P. Holly. 1980. "The Changing Patterns of Industrial Corporate Control in the Metropolitan United States." Pp. 161–79 in Brunn and Wheeler 1980.

Sternlieb, George, and Kristina Ford. 1979. "The Future of the Return-to-the-City Movement." Pp. 77–104 in Bryce 1979.

Sternlieb, George, and James W. Hughes, eds. 1975. *Post-Industrial America: Metropolitan Decline and Interregional Job Shifts*. New Brunswick: Center for Urban Policy Research.

———. 1981. "New Dimensions of the Urban Crisis." Pp. 51–75 in Burchell and Listokin 1981.

———. 1983. "The Uncertain Future of the Central City." *Urban Affairs Quarterly* 18:455–72.

Sternlieb, George; James W. Hughes; and Connie O. Hughes. 1982. *Demographic Trends and Economic Realities*. New Brunswick: Center for Urban Policy Research.

Sumka, Howard J. 1979. "Neighborhood Revitalization and Displacement: A Review of the Evidence." *Journal of the American Planning Association* 45:480–87.

———. 1980. "Federal Antidisplacement Policy in a Context of Urban Decline." Pp. 269–87 in Laska and Spain 1980.

Taeuber, Irene B. 1972. "The Changing Distribution of the Population in the United States in the Twentieth Century." Pp. 29–107 in Sara M. Mazie, ed., *U.S. Commission on Population and the American Future, Research Report 5: Population Distribution and Policy*. Washington, D.C.: U.S. Government Printing Office.

Taeuber, Karl E., and Alma F. Taeuber. 1964. "White Migration and Socioeconomic Differences between Cities and Suburbs." *American Sociological Review* 29:718–29.

Timms, Duncan. 1971. *The Urban Mosaic: Towards a Theory of Residential Differentiation*. Cambridge: Cambridge University Press.

Tucker, C. J. 1984. "City-Suburban Population Redistribution: What Data from the 1970s Reveal." *Urban Affairs Quarterly* 19:539–49.

Thompson, Wilbur. 1975. "Economic Processes and Employment Problems in Declining Metropolitan Areas." Pp. 187–96 in Sternlieb and Hughes, 1975.

United States Bureau of the Census. 1962. *County and City Data Book*. Washington, D.C.: U.S. Government Printing Office.

———. 1963. Census of Population, 1960. *Mobility for Metropolitan Areas*, PC(2)-2C. Washington, D.C.: U.S. Government Printing Office.

———. 1971. Census of Population, 1970. *General Demographic Trends for Metropolitan Areas, 1960 to 1970*. Washington, D.C.: U.S. Government Printing Office.

———. 1972a. *City-County Data Book*. Washington, D.C.: U.S. Government Printing Office.

———. 1972b. Census of Population, 1970. *Mobility for Metropolitan Areas*. PC(2)-2C. Washington, D.C.: U.S. Government Printing Office.

———. 1975. "Mobility of the Population of the United States: March 1970 to

March 1975." *Current Population Reports*, P-20, no. 285. Washington, D.C.: U.S. Government Printing Office.

————. 1976. "Population Profile of the United States: 1975." *Current Population Reports*, P-20, no. 292.

————. 1978, 1979, 1980, 1981a. "Annual Housing Survey: Housing Characteristics for Selected Metropolitan Areas." *Current Housing Reports*, Series H-170-. Washington, D.C.: U.S. Government Printing Office.

————. 1981b. "Population Profile of the United States: 1980." *Current Population Reports*, P-20, no. 363.

————. 1981c. "Geographic Mobility: March 1975–80." *Current Population Reports*, P-20, no. 368.

United States Department of Housing and Urban Development. 1979. "Whither or Whether Urban Distress." Working Paper, Office of Community Planning and Development.

————. 1980a. *The President's National Urban Policy Report*. HUD-583-1-CPD. Washington, D.C.: U.S. Government Printing Office.

————. 1980b. *1980 National Housing Production Report*. HUD-PDR-642. Washington, D.C.: U.S. Department of Housing and Urban Development.

————. 1981. *Residential Displacement: An Update*. Washington, D.C.: U.S. Government Printing Office.

————. 1982a. *The President's National Urban Policy Report*. Washington, D.C.: U.S. Government Printing Office.

————. 1982b. *1982 National Housing Production Report*. Washington, D.C.: U.S. Department of Housing and Urban Development.

————. 1984. *The President's National Urban Policy Report*. Washington, D.C.: U.S. Government Printing Office.

Urban Land Institute. 1976. *New Opportunities for Residential Development in Central Cities*. Report 25. Washington, D.C.: Urban Land Institute.

————. 1977. *Reinvestment in the City*. Report 36. Washington, D.C.: Urban Land Institute.

Vaughn, Roger J. 1980. "The Impact of Federal Policies on Urban Economic Development." Pp. 348–98 in Solomon 1980.

Vaughn, Roger, and Mary E. Vogel. 1979. *The Urban Impacts of Federal Policies*, vol. 4: *Population and Residential Location*. R-2205-KF/HEW. Santa Monica: Rand.

Walker, Richard A. 1981. "A Theory of Suburbanization: Capitalism and the Construction of Urban Space in the United States." Pp. 383–430 in Dear and Scott 1981.

Warner, Sam Bass. 1962. *Steetcar Suburbs: The Process of Growth in Boston, 1870–1900*. New York: Atheneum.

————. 1968. *The Private City: Philadelphia in Three Periods of Its Growth*. Philadelphia: University of Pennsylvania Press.

Wasylenko, Michael J. 1984. "Disamenities, Local Taxation, and the Intrametropolitan Location of Households and Firms." Pp. 97–116 in Ebel 1984.

Watkins, Alfred. 1980. *The Practice of Urban Economics*. Beverly Hills: Sage
    Publications.
Watkins, Alfred, and David C. Perry. 1977. "Regional Change and the Impact
    of Uneven Urban Development." Pp. 19–54 in Perry and Watkins 1977.
Weiler, Conrad. 1974. *Philadelphia: Neighborhood, Authority, and the Urban
    Crisis*. New York: Praeger.
———. 1980. "The Neighborhood's Role in Optimizing Reinvestment: Phila-
    delphia." Pp. 220–37 in Laska and Spain 1980.
Wheaton, William C. 1979. "Monocentric Models of Urban Land Use: Contri-
    butions and Criticisms." Pp. 107–29 in Mieskowski and Straszheim 1979.
White, Michael J. 1980. *Urban Renewal and the Changing Residential Struc-
    ture of the City*. Chicago: University of Chicago Press.
Williams, Peter. 1984. "Gentrification in Britain and Europe." Pp. 205–35 in
    Palen and London 1984.

Index

DESIGNED BY OMEGA CLAY
COMPOSED BY G&S TYPESETTERS, INC., AUSTIN, TEXAS
MANUFACTURED BY BRAUN-BRUMFIELD, INC., ANN ARBOR, MICHIGAN
TEXT AND DISPLAY LINES ARE SET IN CALEDONIA

Library of Congress Cataloging-in-Publication Data
Nelson, Kathryn P.
Gentrification and distressed cities.
(Social demography)
Bibliography: pp. 163–180.
Includes index.
1. Urban renewal—United States. 2. Gentrification—
United States. 3. Residential mobility—United States.
4. Metropolitan areas—United States. 5. Urban
policy—United States. I. Title. II. Series.
HT175.N398   1987   307.2   87-40370
ISBN 0-299-11160-1
ISBN 0-299-11164-4 (pbk.)